ERALD

FINAL 6.30

, 1924.   PRICE ONE PENNY.

on Abolished

OR

in a

ate of

THE GAS STRIKE

No Sign of Ending Dispute So Far

MEETING TO-NIGHT

Union Members, Including Executive, Summoned

A settlement of the strike of the Dublin gas workers appears to be as remote as on the first day of the stoppage, an "Evening Herald" representative was informed on inquiry at the head office of the company this afternoon.

The efforts to arrive at an accommodation have been seriously impeded by the dissensions in the Transport Union, and until the strikers and their union are able to agree on a common basis no progress can be made towards a solution of the deadlock.

A notice issued this afternoon by the Strike Committee announces that

A GENERAL MEETING

of the members of the Union, including the Executive, has been summoned for the Mansion House to-night to consider the position.

It is hoped as a result of this meeting the Union will be in a position to reopen negotiations with the Ministry of the Ministry and Commerce and the Gas Company.

HOUSEBREAKING CHARGE

Constable's Early Morning Find in Drumcondra Shop

RUN OVER BY MOTOR

Verdict of Cause of Death in Clon Motor Tragedy

CRIME DENOUNCED

"Cowardly and Brutal in the Extreme"

The adjourned inquest into the circumstances surrounding the death of Miss Winifred Sweeney, who died from injuries received by being knocked down by a motor car between Inchicore and Clondalkin on the 25th April, was resumed to-day at the City Morgue by Dr. O. J. Murphy, Deputy Coroner.

Inspector Reynolds represented the Civic Guards, and Mr. H. Hughes, B.L. (instructed by Messrs. Boxwell and Erskine), appeared for the next of kin.

VICTIM'S EVIDENCE

Said he Noticed Nothing till they Were Hit

VINDICATING DUBLIN

The story behind the
controversial dissolution of
Dublin Corporation in 1924

Aodh Quinlivan

Comhairle Cathrach
Bhaile Átha Cliath
Dublin City Council

Comhairle Cathrach
Bhaile Átha Cliath
Dublin City Council

First published in 2021 by
Dublin City Council
c/o Dublin City Library & Archive
138-144 Pearse Street
Dublin 2

© Aodh Quinlivan 2021

A catalogue record is available for this book
from the British Library.

ISBN 978-0-9505488-3-8

Designed by Source Design
Printed by Impress Printing Works

Distributed by Four Courts Press
7 Malpas St, The Liberties, Dublin 8, D08 YD81

Dedicated to

Emmanuelle, Adam, Lucie, Alice and Théo – my wonderful,
loving and supportive family.

Councillor Richard O'Carroll – A principled public representative
who died on 5 May 1916 from injuries sustained in the Easter Rising.

Contents

Part 3: The Commissionership Years

Acknowledgements

'The virtuous felt themselves obliged to take away from the local councils powers that might be wielded by unsuitable people ... consequently, they created the most centralised democratic state in Europe.'

Tom Garvin, County and Town: One Hundred Years of Local Government in Ireland (2001)

The title of this book refers to a document called 'A Vindication of the Municipal Council of the City of Dublin' written by Seán T. O'Kelly and ten of his former Dublin Corporation colleagues in August 1924, following the dissolution of Ireland's oldest public body. I share their view that the dissolution of Dublin Corporation was unwarranted, but why did it happen? I believe there were two primary reasons. First, in the aftermath of the Civil War there was a jostling for political power in the capital and central Government was increasingly agitated by the Corporation which continued to engage itself in issues such as the treatment of prisoners. Better than anybody else, William T. Cosgrave, a former member of the Corporation, knew how local councils had been used to subvert British rule. He did not want them to subvert Irish rule in the same manner. Secondly, the Government wished to proceed with the reorganisation of governance structures in Dublin. Attempting to do this while an awkward, politically-driven Corporation with eighty members was in place, would have been very difficult. An easier option was to push the elected members to one side and proceed with the reorganisation, safe in the knowledge that the three appointed Commissioners were reliable, professional, politically neutral, and popular with the citizens.

There will always be a mystery about the circumstances which led to the dissolution, partly because it appears that the official report by Nicholas O'Dwyer was never published, even though the newspapers carried a summary. The National Archives of Ireland has in its catalogue a file listed as 'D/E Dublin files, Box 167 – Dissolution of Dublin Corporation'; this file, presumably containing a copy of Nicholas O'Dwyer's report, is missing. So too, there is no copy of the report in the Custom House, headquarters of what is now called the Department of Housing, Local Government and Heritage. Did O'Dwyer recommend the dissolution of Dublin Corporation or was the inquiry a charade because the decision had already been made politically?

I greatly enjoyed writing this book, which would not have come to fruition without the help of very many people. My family offered me great support, especially my beautiful wife, Emmanuelle. My four fantastic children – Adam (13), Lucie (10), Alice (8) and Théo (15 months) – all made sacrifices in their own way and I thank them from the bottom of my heart. This book follows on from the publication of *Dissolved* in 2017 which investigated the dissolution of Cork Corporation. When I approached Dublin City Council, I received an enthusiastic response and, from the first minute to the last, the recently retired City Archivist, Dr Mary Clark has been terrific. Thank you Mary, I hope you are happy with the final product. My introduction to Mary was made by the redoubtable Councillor Dermot Lacey whose passion for local government and local democracy is greater even than my own! *Vindicating Dublin* would not have happened without Dermot's help – I hope he is happy with how it turned out and I know he will recognise many of the themes which are explored in the following two hundred pages! Equally, it is an honour for me that this book is being launched during the Mayoralty of Councillor Hazel Chu; I thank her for her support and her generous foreword.

I am grateful to all of the fine people who helped me from a variety of public organisations – Dublin City Library and Archive, National Library of Ireland, and National Archives of Ireland, to name but three. The staff in the National Archives spent hours looking for the 'missing file' and could not have been more helpful; they were as frustrated as me to come up empty-handed! I received great support, for which I am grateful, from my colleagues in University College Cork and especially those in the Department of Government and Politics.

In the last six months of the project when we were putting the book together, Anne-Marie McInerney (librarian in Dublin City Library and Archive) was a tremendous help and, in turn, she received great support from her colleague, Tara Doyle. Barry McLaughlin in *Source Design* created a beautiful finished product and I am thankful to Four Courts Press for their support in distributing the book.

Finally, it is my sincere wish that you enjoy *Vindicating Dublin* and that it sheds some light on the development of local government in our capital city and beyond. For any errors or omissions, I take full responsibility.

Aodh Quinlivan
June 2021

Foreword

As Lord Mayor of this historic city, it gives me great pleasure to provide this foreword for Aodh's book, *Vindicating Dublin: The story behind the controversial dissolution of Dublin Corporation in 1924*. As someone who is passionate about local democracy, I welcome this detailed and fascinating study of a major episode in the history of the civic administration of Dublin. The dissolution of Dublin Corporation, and what followed, was part of a wave of reform in local government in the early years of the State which led ultimately to the system of local government that we have today.

Local government in Dublin in the 1920s faced many challenges, among them the need to provide social housing and maintain and improve the city for its growing population. These are challenges not dissimilar to those faced in the city today.

The importance of local representation was at the heart of discourse around local government in the 1920s, as were efficiency, effectiveness, and value for money. These are themes which remain central.

We live in an exciting time for local democracy and local government reform in Ireland but, in looking to the future of local government, we must not forget its history. With that in mind, I believe that Aodh's book, with its account and discussion of the 1924 dissolution of Dublin Corporation, will prove a useful resource for historians and practitioners of local government in Ireland generally and in Dublin in particular. Aodh has done us a great service and *Vindicating Dublin* is a valuable addition to the existing works on the rich history of local government in this city, especially in the tumultuous period around the foundation of the State.

Hazel Chu
Lord Mayor of Dublin

Abbreviations

ESB	Electricity Supply Board
GAA	Gaelic Athletic Association
IPP	Irish Parliamentary Party
IRA	Irish Republican Army
IRB	Irish Republican Brotherhood
LGB	Local Government Board
MP	Member of Parliament (House of Commons)
PR-STV	Proportional Representation [by the] Single Transferable Vote
RIC	Royal Irish Constabulary
TD	Teachta Dála (Deputy of Dáil Éireann)

Main Cast of Characters

Séamus Burke was the Minister for Local Government and Public Health who ordered the inquiry into Dublin Corporation and signed the subsequent order of dissolution.

Alfie Byrne was elected Lord Mayor of Dublin after the Corporation was reinstated in 1930. Known as the 'Shaking Hand of Dublin', he held the role until 1939.

The Commissioners, i.e. Séamus Murphy, Dr William C. Dwyer, and Patrick J. Hernon served from 1924 to 1930 and held one hundred and fifty-nine meetings in that time.

William T. Cosgrave had been a member of Dublin Corporation but – at the time of the inquiry and dissolution – he was President of the Executive Council of the Irish Free State.

The Legal Teams were prominent at the inquiry. The case for dissolving the Corporation was made by Norman Keough (Dublin Citizens' Association) and W. J. Larkin (Dublin Tenant's Association). The Corporation's impressive legal team was led by two senior barristers, Patrick Lynch and James Carrige Rushe Lardner.

Edward (E. P.) McCarron was the controversial Secretary in the Department of Local Government and Public Health who was ultimately dismissed by the Government in November 1936.

Nicholas O'Dwyer was Chair of the inquiry and Chief Engineering Inspector in the Department of Local Government and Public Health. A mystery remains about the content of his report and his recommendation, if any. He later chaired the inquiry which led to the dissolution of Cork Corporation.

Seán T. O'Kelly, as a member of Dublin Corporation, was the main contributor to 'A Vindication of the Municipal Council of the City of Dublin' in August 1924, following the dissolution of Ireland's oldest public body. Later, he joined Éamon de Valera's newly founded Fianna Fáil party and was appointed Minister for Local Government. He went on to serve two terms as President of Ireland.

Laurence O'Neill was Lord Mayor of Dublin from 1917 to 1924 (albeit Tom Kelly was elected Lord Mayor in January 1920 but was unable to take on the role due to a combination of imprisonment and ill-health). O'Neill staunchly defended Dublin Corporation at the inquiry, but to no avail.

Gerald Sherlock, former Town Clerk, was appointed as Dublin's first City Manager after the passing of the Local Government (Dublin) Act 1930.

Part 1: Dublin in Rare Old Times, 1914–1923

Chapter 1
Dublin and the Corporation in 1914 and 1915

Representative local government in Ireland, following the passing of the Local Government (Ireland) Act, 1898 had a difficult birth as the new councils struggled to gain legitimacy while wider political objectives dominated. Basil Chubb (1982) describes Ireland's local authorities in the early years of the twentieth century as centres of nationalism and it is the true that the ground-breaking act of 1898 effectively gave Ireland a weapon to advance its claim for independence (1). One such centre of nationalism was Dublin Corporation. At the time of the local elections in March 1914, membership of the Corporation was eighty (seventy-nine seats were filled and one was left vacant). The biggest party by far was the Irish Parliamentary Party (IPP) which claimed fifty-six seats. Led by John Redmond, the party was seen as moderate and its primary aim was the achievement of Home Rule in Ireland. The Irish Parliamentary Party dominated the City Hall, with the remaining members of the Corporation drawn from the Labour Party, the Irish Unionist Party, Sinn Féin and Independents. Unsurprisingly, the Corporation was a male-dominated environment. Women had not been eligible to stand for local elections until the passing of the Local Government (Ireland) Votes for Women Act 1911. The first woman to be elected to Dublin Corporation was Sarah Cecilia Harrison in 1912 (her self-portrait hangs in Dublin City Gallery, the Hugh Lane) and she was followed by Martha J. Williams in 1915 (2).

Dublin Corporation was not a popular institution and it had many critics. The most fervent and consistent was *The Irish Times* which delighted in the catchphrase, 'Dublin has the worst municipal government in the world' (3). The following extract from an editorial in *The Irish Times* in January 1913 gives a flavour of the newspaper's attitude towards the local authority (4).

> *Municipal business has no natural association with politics ... so long as our Corporation continues to be dominated by politics, it will continue to neglect and mismanage the ratepayers' interests. When men are not elected to business bodies solely on their merits*

as business men, everything is bound to go wrong. Taken as a whole, the personnel of the Dublin Corporation is today thoroughly unsatisfactory. The most competent administrators in the city do not offer themselves for election because they dislike and despise the squalid atmosphere of jobbery and intrigue which envelopes the City Hall.

In particular, the newspaper complained of what it described as 'the political bigotry of the nationalist majority in the Corporation' (5). Aside from *The Irish Times*, Dublin Corporation regularly received criticism from a variety of pressure groups and organisations. One such influential body was the Dublin Citizens' Association which highlighted fiscal irresponsibility and high rates (6).

The politics of City Hall was very much to the fore in the Corporation meeting on 10 August 1914, the first since the assassination of Archduke Franz Ferdinand triggered the start of the Great War (First World War). While there was scarcely a mention of potentially momentous world events, the elected members, under the Chairmanship of Lord Mayor, Councillor Lorcan Sherlock, agreed to grant a request from the Irish Volunteers for the use of a room in City Hall for their meetings. The Irish Volunteers was a military organisation set up the previous year with the aim 'to secure and maintain the rights and liberties common to the whole people of Ireland' (7). While this phrase is open to interpretation, the manifesto adopted by the organisation stated that the duties of the Volunteers would be 'defensive and protective' and that 'either aggression or domination' would not be contemplated (8). Many members of Dublin Corporation were present at the founding meeting of the Volunteers in the Rotunda in 1913, including the influential Sinn Féin trio of councillors, William T. Cosgrave, Tom Kelly and Seán T. O'Kelly.

A motion was also passed at the Corporation meeting of 10 August, condemning the shooting dead of three citizens – Mary Duffy, Patrick Quinn, and James Brennan – by British forces at Bachelor's Quay on 26 July. There were calls for the dismissal of officials in Dublin Castle, the seat of British rule in Ireland, and one member of the Corporation, Alderman Dr James McWalter, argued that the officers and soldiers involved should be charged with murder (9).

THE IRISH VOLUNTEERS,
HEADQUARTERS: 206 GREAT BRUNSWICK STREET,
DUBLIN, 17*th July*, 1914.

The Town Clerk,
City Hall, Dublin.

DEAR SIR,

I am directed by the Provisional Committee of the Irish Volunteers to apply for the use of the Members' Room, City Hall, for the meetings of the Provisional Committee. Owing to the re-constructions of the Provisional Committee we require larger premises for meetings, and I would be glad if you would bring this application before the proper quarter.

Trusting you will see your way to accede to our request.

Yours sincerely,
LIAM MELLONS,
Assistant Secretary,
Headquarters Staff.

Letter from the Irish Volunteers, dated 17 July 1914, asking Dublin Corporation for the use of the Members' Room in City Hall. The elected members agreed to the request.

Minutes of the Municipal Council of the City of Dublin, 10 August 1914, Dublin City Library and Archive.

On the fateful day of 26 July, members of the King's Own Scottish Borderers were walking through the city, following an operation where they had seized guns from the Irish Volunteers, when they were met by a hostile crowd hurling abuse and missiles. The soldiers opened fire, resulting in the deaths of three Dubliners with more than thirty others suffering injury.

Pádraig Yeates (2011) asserts that Dublin was plunged into mourning after the Bachelor's Walk shootings and that the city was still in the process of recovering from the upheaval of the previous year's Great Lock-Out (10). The Lock-Out was the most significant industrial conflict in Ireland and lasted from August 1913 to February 1914. It centred on a prolonged struggle between the Irish Transport and General Workers' Union (ITGWU), led by James ('Big Jim') Larkin, and the Dublin Employers' Federation, led by William Martin Murphy. Along the way it developed into a social and political conflict and 'memories of the Lock-Out and the ferocious police baton charges that accompanied it were still fresh in the public memory when more civilian blood was shed on Bachelor's Walk in July 1914' (11).

In September, there was much rejoicing amongst the nationalist majority in Dublin Corporation with the passing of the Government of Ireland Act 1914, which legislated for Home Rule. The operation of the legislation, however, was initially suspended for twelve months and then until the end of the First World War (ultimately, it never came into effect).

Dublin Corporation had an unsettling and sad start to 1915. On Saturday 23 January, at the statutory annual general meeting, the experienced councillor, Alderman John Clancy, was elected as Lord Mayor. In his acceptance speech, Alderman Clancy, declared: 'I will make no promises, so that I break none' (12). He called on his fellow councillors to assist him and the Corporation in the necessary work that lay ahead, especially the building of houses for the working classes in the city.

Tragically, the new Lord Mayor died within the week after a short illness. It is reputed that he was caught in a downpour of rain while walking home from a Corporation meeting and developed pneumonia, which proved fatal. *The Irish Times* observed that, in his roles as councillor and as Sheriff of the city, Clancy had discharged his duties fairly and had exercised his powers with a kindness and consideration for those in difficulty (13). Dublin Corporation held a regular meeting the following Monday, 1 February, but the business of the meeting was adjourned. Instead, the members paid tribute to their deceased colleague and passed the following motion (14):

> *That this council desires to express its extreme regret at the death of Alderman John Clancy, one of the oldest and most respected members of the Dublin Corporation; that it tenders to his widow and the other members of his family its sincere sympathy with them in the loss which they, in common with the citizens of Dublin generally, have sustained by his demise; and that the Council do now adjourn for a week as a mark of respect to the deceased Alderman.*

There was controversy at the Corporation meeting which followed one week later. With Councillor Lorcan Sherlock chairing the meeting, a motion in the name of Alderman David Quaid was discussed. Alderman Quaid wanted the name of Kuno Meyer expunged from the list of honorary freemen of Dublin due to the pro-German speeches he had made in America. German-born Meyer was a close associate of the Gaelic League founder, Douglas Hyde, and was the co-founder of the School of Irish Learning in Dublin. His translations from old Irish poetry and saga inspired William Butler Yeats and other figures in the revival of their literary work (15).

Councillor Sherlock ruled that the motion would not proceed at that time but could be revisited when a new Lord Mayor was elected. A disappointed Alderman Quaid took to the letter page of *The Irish Times* to express his frustration (16):

> *Sir,*
>
> *The Lord Mayor of Dublin, though of a contrary opinion up to the last moment, has this day, in the teeth of the opinion of the city's Law Agent and Town Clerk, ruled out of order my motion to remove the name of Kuno Meyer from the freeman roll of this city, thus allowing it to be stigmatised as having the name of a dangerous alien enemy on its roll of honorary freemen. I am prepared to successfully invoke the Courts, if I am indemnified by a patriotic public from costs, as, while I shall subscribe myself, I do not think I should litigate this matter at my own expense. Let, if necessary, a committee be formed. What is legal in Cork under the Municipal Privileges Act, 1876, is apparently not legal in Dublin.*
>
> *Yours, etc.*
> *David A. Quaid, Alderman*

Alderman Quaid's reference to Cork related to the fact that the Corporation there had expunged the name of Kuno Meyer from their list of freemen on 8 January (he was posthumously re-elected as a freeman of Cork on 14 May 1920).

Councillor Sherlock had pushed the Meyer controversy onto the desk of the next Lord Mayor of Dublin. That honour fell to the Independent councillor, James Gallagher, who was elected as the city's first citizen at a special meeting on 23 February. In his acceptance speech, Councillor Gallagher drew attention to the large proportion of people in Dublin suffering from the effects of unemployment and chronic poverty. In predicting increases in the price of food and coal, he warned his fellow councillors that they would have to be exceedingly careful in their spending of rates in the year ahead (17).

Little did Gallagher know that a hugely turbulent period for the city lay ahead during his Mayoralty. First up was a fractious meeting of the Corporation on 15 March to debate whether the Celtic scholar, Kuno Myer, should remain on the roll of freemen of Dublin. In proposing the motion, Alderman David Quaid read from reports of speeches that Meyer had delivered in America. Meyer had 'justified Germany's position on the war, was avowedly anti-British, and had contacts with the revolutionary Clan na Gael in New York' (18). William T. Cosgrave was amongst those who spoke against the motion, saying that the proposal was made 'at a time when passions and prejudice cloud the better qualities of the human mind'. He urged his council colleagues 'not to degrade a scholar who loved our country and served her soul' (19). The respected Councillor Laurence O'Neill put forward a counter-motion, seconded by Councillor Seán T. O'Kelly, 'that a further consideration of Alderman Quaid's motion be postponed until after the war, and that the council begs to place on record its strong condemnation of Alderman Quaid's action in bringing forward a contentious matter of a political nature at this crisis of our history' (20). Despite the best efforts of Cosgrave, O'Neill and O'Kelly, anti-German sentiment won the day and, by a vote of thirty to sixteen, it was agreed to expunge the name of Kuno Meyer from the roll of freemen. Marie O'Neill (1994) describes the decision as a sad example of 'the false judgements made in the heat of war-time fervour' (21).

Housing was a priority for the new Lord Mayor. The report from the 1913 Dublin Housing Inquiry, held in City Hall, painted a damning picture of slum conditions in the city with chronic over-crowding contributing to a range of public health problems. The inquiry itself had been established following strong public criticism after seven people had been killed with the collapse of two tenements in Church Street in September 1913. The horrific details in the report received much press attention and the Chief Secretary to Ireland, Augustine Birrell, commented: 'This report cannot be allowed to rest, as so many other reports have done, in the pigeon holes of offices' (22). Birrell was also the President of the Local Government Board, set up in 1872 and based in the Custom House, to oversee the Irish local authorities.

One measure which was meant to ease the housing pressures in Dublin was the extension of the Housing (No. 2) Act to Ireland. This legislation had been passed in Westminster in August 1914 and it provided for £4 million to be made available to British local authorities for slum clearance. However, Dublin Corporation was not given details of the scheme until early 1915, at which point much of the funding had already been allocated. The Corporation did prepare requests for funding under the scheme but the secretary of the Local Government Board did not forward them to the Treasury (23). Corporation members were outraged and, at a special meeting, they passed a motion of no confidence in the Local Government Board. Corporation officials, such as the City Architect, Charles McCarthy, and the City Treasurer, Edmund Eyre, were equally irate and they informed a meeting of the Housing Committee that the extension of the Housing Act to Ireland was little more than a make believe and a sham (24).

The remainder of 1915 proved to be relatively quiet for Dublin Corporation, although political differences emerged from time to time. For example, when the Corporation extended a welcome to the new Viceroy and Lord Lieutenant of Ireland, Lord Wimborne, and assured him of its 'loyalty to the throne and person of his Majesty the King', an animated debate followed before the motion was carried by twenty votes to thirteen (25).

When reports broke during the summer of conscription possibly being imposed in Ireland, the members of Dublin Corporation reacted swiftly and organised a conference, after which Alderman Tom Kelly wrote a warning letter to many organisations in Dublin, stating: 'There is no use in shutting our eyes … We are faced with the attempt to exterminate the remnant of our young and vigorous manhood, and we must resist it' (26).

By the end of 1915, Dublin Corporation was in an interesting place and found itself facing many challenges and uncertainties. The council chamber itself was a highly political environment and the Corporation as a body was deeply unpopular with *The Irish Times*, citizens and business people due to high rates, poverty and a housing crisis. Relations with the Local Government Board were fractured and, nationally, there was an uneasy peace as the Home Rule legislation was on hold. In the background, the First World War added to the insecurity and anti-German sentiment was rising. Nobody could predict, with any certainty, what the year 1916 would bring.

Chapter 2
The Easter Rising

The statutory annual general meeting of Dublin Corporation was held on 24 January 1916, in front of a packed public gallery. Councillor James Gallagher was re-elected as Lord Mayor, defeating Alderman Laurence O'Neill by 44 votes to 29. As he had done the previous year, Gallagher stressed the need for more and better quality housing in the city. He expressed confidence that the 'untiring and unselfish members of parliament' would succeed in getting extra money for the Corporation to build housing schemes (1). The following month, Lord Mayor Gallagher presided over a major recruiting conference for Irish soldiers in the Mansion House. He urged young Irishmen to take up arms to help the allied forces. Amongst the other speakers were the Lord Lieutenant of Ireland, Lord Wimborne, and the leader of the Irish Parliamentary Party, John Redmond. Redmond asserted that Irish farmers were now 'free, independent and prosperous' and he concluded: 'I venture to say there is not a single part of the British Empire that Germany would more greedily seize upon than the fertile fields of Ireland' (2).

In the early months of 1916, the Irish Volunteers and the Irish Citizen Army were visibly active with public marches and manoeuvres. Despite this, the insurrection against the British which took place in April was a surprise to many people. The Easter Rising of 1916 which 'became the mythical foundation point for modern armed Republicanism' (3) was an almost entirely Dublin-based affair. The Rising resulted in over three thousand casualties, with four hundred and fifty deaths. In its aftermath, hundreds of people were arrested, many of whom had no involvement in the insurrection. This included members of Dublin Corporation, even though 'the council, as a body, played no role in the Rising' (4).

As noted by Pádraig Yeates (2016), 'the vast majority of council members approached Easter 1916 blissfully unaware of what was impending. However, in the week prior to the outbreak of the Rising they found themselves playing an unsuspecting role in seeking to justify armed insurrection' (5). On Wednesday 19 April, just a few days before the Rising was planned to take place, a member of Dublin Corporation, Alderman Tom Kelly, rose to speak at a special Corporation meeting chaired by William T. Cosgrave. He read aloud what became known as the Castle Document, which had supposedly been smuggled out of Dublin Caste – the administrative centre of British rule in Ireland – in cipher form. The Castle Document outlined a plan from the British undersecretary, Sir Matthew Nathan, 'to intern all known nationalists prior to Easter Week and to suppress all nationalist organisations as well as ordering the disarming of the Irish Volunteers' (6). Alderman Kelly's speech and the contents of the Castle Document caused quite a stir: 'The following day's newspapers electrified the political atmosphere in Dublin and stimulated a war fever at Volunteer Headquarters' (7).

According to historian, James Stephens (1965), who was the Registrar of the National Gallery in 1916 (8):

> One remembers today the paper which Alderman Kelly read to the Dublin Corporation, and which purported to be state instructions, that the military and police should raid the Volunteers, and seize their arms and leaders. The Volunteers had sworn they would not permit their arms to be taken from them. The press, by instruction apparently, repudiated the document, but the Volunteers, with most of the public, believed it to be true, and it is more than likely that the rebellion took place in order to forestall the Government. This is also an explanation of the rebellion and is just as good as any other.

The authenticity of the Castle Document is debated to this day. Unsurprisingly, Sir Matthew Nathan subsequently described it as an imaginary document which had never been in existence in the files of Dublin Castle or elsewhere (9). At the Corporation meeting itself on 19 April, there too were doubters. Sir Patrick Shortall objected to the council being used for political propaganda and he warned, 'Alderman Kelly's words will do nothing but stir up the worst passions of Irishmen' (10). Michael Foy (2014), a biographer of Tom Clarke, asserts that the Castle Document was concocted by Joseph Plunkett and was approved by the military council of the Irish Republican Brotherhood (IRB) as 'an exercise in disinformation' (11).

In later life, Alderman Kelly reminisced: 'As to the genuineness of the document, I have grave doubts. I think myself it was part of a move in the military plan – justifiable in war; and it did have the desired effect. But I think it was forged' (12). There is no doubt that Alderman Kelly, a respected councillor with pacifist views, suffered as a result of his exposure of the Castle Document. Following the Rising,

Bachelor's Walk in Dublin, 1916 Easter Rising.

Dublin City Library and Archive, Birth of the Republic collection.

his home was ransacked and he was imprisoned in Kilmainham Jail (13).

As noted previously, Dublin Corporation, as a body, played no role in the Rising of Easter 1916 – 'its predominantly Redmonite members were largely detached from the burgeoning revolution on the streets of the capital' (14). However, individual councillors – and, indeed, Corporation staff – were heavily involved. Only two councillors were members of the Irish Volunteers, Richard O'Carroll and William T. Cosgrave. In addition, William Partridge was a member of the Irish Citizen Army and Seán T. O'Kelly was in the Irish Republican Brotherhood (15).

The insurrection commenced on Easter Monday, 24 April 1916 and Dublin was placed under martial law once the fighting started. Over the days which followed, Councillor Richard O'Carroll – secretary of the Bricklayers' Union – was a central figure, serving under the command of Thomas MacDonagh and Major John MacBride. On 26 April he was captured and, according to accounts, was held at gunpoint with his hands raised, by the Irish-born officer, Captain John Bowen-Colthurst. Bowen-Colthurst asked O'Carroll if he was a Sinn Féiner and received the reply: 'From the backbone out'. At this point, Bowen-Colthurst shot O'Carroll with his revolver, and he died from his injuries nine days later, on 5 May in Portobello Military Hospital (16)[1]. O'Carroll's widow, Annie, gave birth to their seventh child two weeks later.

---

1   On 29 April 2016, it was reported in *The Irish Times* that relatives of the victims of the notorious Captain John Bowen-Colthurst were seeking an apology from the British government for his actions during Easter Week 1916. Bowen-Colthurst, a British officer commanding the Third Royal Irish Rifles 100 years ago, was responsible for the deaths of at least five people during the Easter Rising, including the pacifist Francis Sheehy-Skeffington, who was executed on his orders. Bowen-Colthurst was declared guilty but insane, and lived out the rest of his life in Canada. He also ordered the execution of two journalists, Thomas Dickson and Patrick McIntyre, who had nothing to do with the Rising.

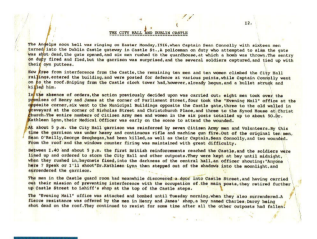

THE CITY HALL AND DUBLIN CASTLE

The Angelus noon bell was ringing on Easter Monday,1916,when Captain Sean Connolly with sixteen men turned into the Dublin Castle gateway in Castle St..A policeman on duty who attempted to slam the gate was shot dead,the gate opened,and six men rushed to the guardhouse,at which a bomb was thrown.The sentry on duty fired and fled,but the garrison was surprised,and the several soldiers captured,and tied up with their own puttees.

Now free from interference from the Castle,the remaining ten men and ten women climbed the City Hall railings,entered the building,and were posted for defence at various points,while Captain Connolly went on to the roof.Sniping from the Castle clock tower had,however,already begun,and a bullet struck and killed him.

In the absence of orders,the action previously decided upon was carried out: eight men took over the premises of Henry and James at the corner of Parliament Street,four took the "Evening Mail" office at the opposite corner,six went to the Municipal Buildings opposite the Castle gate,three to the old walled in graveyard at the corner of Nicholas Street and Christchurch Place,and three to the Synod House at Christ Church.The entire numbers of Citizen Army men and women in the six posts totalled up to about 50.Dr. Kathleen Lynn,their Medical Officer was early on the scene to attend the wounded.

At about 5 p.m. the City Hall garrison was reinforced by seven Citizen Army men and Volunteers.By this time the garrison was under heavy and continuous rifle and machine gun fire.Out of the original ten men, Sean O'Reilly,George Geoghegan,had been killed,as well as their Captain,Sean Connolly,and two wounded. From the roof and the windows counter firing was maintained with great difficulty.

Between 1.40 and about 5 p.m. the first British reinforcements reached the Castle,and the soldiers were lined up and ordered to storm the City Hall and other outposts.They were kept at bay until midnight, when they rushed in,bayonets fixed,into the darkness of the central hall,an officer shouting:"Anyone here ? Speak or I'll shoot"Dr.Kathleen Lynn then stepped out of the shadows into the moonlight,and surrendered the garrison.

The men in the Castle guard room had meanwhile discovered a door into Castle Street,and having carried out their mission of preventing interference with the occupation of the main posts,they retired further up Castle Street to Lahiff's shop at the top of the Castle steps.

The "Evening Mail" office was attacked and bombed until Tuesday morning,when they also surrendered.A fierce resistance was offered by the men in Henry and James' shop,a boy named Charles.Darcy being shot dead on the roof.They continued to resist for some time after all the other outposts had fallen.

Pamphlet describing the fighting in City Hall and Dublin Castle.

Dublin City Library and Archive, Birth of the Republic collection.

Dublin City Hall, home of Dublin Corporation, was one of 'the most prestigious buildings seized by the rebels during Easter Week' (17) and became a garrison for the Irish Citizen Army. Though it was the first garrison to be completely overwhelmed by the military during the insurrection, City Hall – where the body of Jeremiah O'Donovan Rossa was laid out before his funeral in August 1915 – had a symbolic value (18). Conor McNamara (2016) asserts that the occupation of City Hall was a hopeless mission and it was the scene of a high number of casualties. This included the two commanding officers, Seán Connolly and Seán (John) O'Reilly who were shot on the roof of the City Hall (19).

Some staff members of Dublin Corporation were also heavily involved in the Rising, most notably Éamonn Ceannt who worked in the Rates Department. Ceannt was a leading member of the Irish Volunteers executive who sat on both the supreme council and military council of the IRB; with Joseph Plunkett he developed the plan for the Rising (20). He was also one of the seven signatories on the 1916 Proclamation of an Irish Republic which essentially was 'a manifesto, a declaration of war, and, above all, an assertion of sovereignty' (21). The text of the Proclamation, and with it the establishment of a Provisional Government, had been approved at a meeting of the IRB military council on 18 April. On Easter Monday 1916, having secured occupancy of the General Post Office (GPO), the Proclamation was read aloud by Patrick Pearse and hundreds of copies were distributed to people in Dublin city centre.

IRISH REBELLION, MAY, 1916.

RICHARD O'CARROLL, T.C. (Dublin).
Shot in Action.

Councillor Richard O'Carroll died on 5 May 1916, from injuries sustained in the Easter Rising on 26 April, having been shot by Captain John Bowen-Colthurst.

National Library of Ireland.

POBLACHT NA H EIREANN.
THE PROVISIONAL GOVERNMENT
OF THE
IRISH REPUBLIC
TO THE PEOPLE OF IRELAND.

IRISHMEN AND IRISHWOMEN: In the name of God and of the dead generations from which she receives her old tradition of nationhood, Ireland, through us, summons her children to her flag and strikes for her freedom.

Having organised and trained her manhood through her secret revolutionary organisation, the Irish Republican Brotherhood, and through her open military organisations, the Irish Volunteers and the Irish Citizen Army, having patiently perfected her discipline, having resolutely waited for the right moment to reveal itself, she now seizes that moment, and, supported by her exiled children in America and by gallant allies in Europe, but relying in the first on her own strength, she strikes in full confidence of victory.

We declare the right of the people of Ireland to the ownership of Ireland, and to the unfettered control of Irish destinies, to be sovereign and indefeasible. The long usurpation of that right by a foreign people and government has not extinguished the right, nor can it ever be extinguished except by the destruction of the Irish people. In every generation the Irish people have asserted their right to national freedom and sovereignty: six times during the past three hundred years they have asserted it in arms. Standing on that fundamental right and again asserting it in arms in the face of the world, we hereby proclaim the Irish Republic as a Sovereign Independent State, and we pledge our lives and the lives of our comrades-in-arms to the cause of its freedom, of its welfare, and of its exaltation among the nations.

The Irish Republic is entitled to, and hereby claims, the allegiance of every Irishman and Irishwoman. The Republic guarantees religious and civil liberty, equal rights and equal opportunities to all its citizens, and declares its resolve to pursue the happiness and prosperity of the whole nation and of all its parts, cherishing all the children of the nation equally, and oblivious of the differences carefully fostered by an alien government, which have divided a minority from the majority in the past.

Until our arms have brought the opportune moment for the establishment of a permanent National Government, representative of the whole people of Ireland and elected by the suffrages of all her men and women, the Provisional Government, hereby constituted, will administer the civil and military affairs of the Republic in trust for the people.

We place the cause of the Irish Republic under the protection of the Most High God, Whose blessing we invoke upon our arms, and we pray that no one who serves that cause will dishonour it by cowardice, inhumanity, or rapine. In this supreme hour the Irish nation must, by its valour and discipline and by the readiness of its children to sacrifice themselves for the common good, prove itself worthy of the august destiny to which it is called.

Signed on Behalf of the Provisional Government,

THOMAS J. CLARKE.

SEAN Mac DIARMADA,   THOMAS MacDONAGH,
P. H. PEARSE,   EAMONN CEANNT,
JAMES CONNOLLY.   JOSEPH PLUNKETT.

The 1916 Proclamation of an Irish Republic, signed by Éamonn Ceannt who worked in the Rates Department of Dublin Corporation; he also featured in a poster with members of the Provisional Government of the Irish Republic 1916.

Dublin City Library and Archive, Birth of the Republic collection.

Members of the Provisional Government
of the Irish Republic 1916.

Dublin City Library and Archive,
Birth of the Republic collection.

During the rebellion, Ceannt was in charge of operations at the South Dublin Union workhouse where fighting was fierce (22). Following the surrender, with which he did not agree, Ceannt was arrested on 30 April and was tried by court-martial in Richmond Barracks. At the court-martial he sought to rebut the evidence of the only witness called by the prosecution, Major J. A. Armstrong, whom he cross-examined aggressively (23). William Wylie, the prosecuting counsel described Ceannt as a 'brave man [who] showed no sign whatsoever of nervousness before the court. I would say, in fact, that he was the most dignified of any of the accused' (24). Having been found guilty and sentenced to death, Éamonn Ceannt was shot at dawn on 8 May 1916 (25). The night before, in his final statement, Ceannt denounced the decision to surrender, rather than fight to the finish: 'I see nothing gained but grave disaster caused by the surrender which has marked the end of the Irish Insurrection of 1916' (26).

Another Dublin Corporation employee who was executed after the Rising was John MacBride. MacBride, who had been married to Maud Gonne, was shot by British troops in Kilmainham Jail on 5 May (27).

The Lord Mayor of Dublin, Councillor James Gallagher, distinguished himself during the Rising in helping to prevent looting in Grafton

EAMONN CEANNT
(Executed in Kilmainham Prison, 8th May, 1916).

Éamonn Ceannt, an employee of Dublin Corporation, was executed on 8 May 1916.

Dublin City Library and Archive,
Birth of the Republic collection.

Street and he was later knighted (28). Some members of the Corporation were arrested in the aftermath of the insurrection, most notably Patrick T. Daly, Laurence O'Neill, Tom Kelly, Seán T. O'Kelly, William Partridge and William T. Cosgrave.

Laurence O'Neill and Seán T. O'Kelly were amongst those imprisoned in Richmond Barracks and they spent some of their time taking part in a theatrical trial of fellow prisoner, Éamon de Valera, who was charged with high treason (29). O'Neill was one of the lucky ones in that he was released after twelve days, due to the intercession of his son, William, who was a serving captain in the British army's medical corps (30). O' Neill's biographer, Thomas Morrissey (2014), notes that the time spent in prison was a 'badge of distinction' for O'Neill and it helped his political career (31).

William T. Cosgrave was not as fortunate as O'Neill and did not benefit from an early release. He was tried on 4 May and accused of taking part 'in an armed rebellion and in the waging of war against his Majesty the King ...... with the intention and for the purpose of assisting the enemy' (32). Cosgrave entered a plea of 'not guilty' and character witnesses were provided by Lord Mayor James Gallagher and former Lord Mayor Lorcan Sherlock. Despite the interventions of Gallagher and Sherlock, the verdict – after a trial of less than fifteen minutes – was 'Guilty: Death by being shot' (33). However, after the trial, General Maxwell, the British commander-in-chief, reduced Cosgrave's sentence to penal servitude for life. As it transpired, Cosgrave was released in June 1917, after thirteen months in prison, mainly spent in jails in Dorset and Essex (34).

With some members and employees in prison, and with City Hall having suffered damage, the first full regular meeting of Dublin Corporation after the Rising did not take place until 5 June. However, prior to that, on 10 May, a special meeting took place to discuss financial relief of distress consequent on the recent disturbances in the city (referred to in a letter by the Local Government Board as 'the Sinn Féin Rebellion') (35).

Lord Mayor, James Gallagher, commenced the meeting with the following words (36):

We are called together today for a special purpose, under exceedingly gloomy circumstances. I will not speak about the events that have recently occurred for I think the time has not yet arrived for me to say anything on the subject. In my opinion, the council should confine itself to the business for which it has specially been called together. The other matters can be discussed at the ordinary meetings of the council.

Somewhat bizarrely, the councillors then proceeded to deliberate on the distress visited on citizens in Dublin as a result of the rebellion, without discussing the event itself. They approved a motion to apply to the Local Government Board for permission for the Poor Law Guardians to administer relief under Section 13 of the Local Government (Ireland) Act, 1898 (37).

At the subsequent full meeting of the Corporation on 5 June, Pádraig Yeates (2011) records: 'It was necessary to tread carefully, as the first item on the agenda was the potentially inflammatory series of votes of sympathies for deceased members and their relations' (38). In the event, the votes passed off without controversy. The first was for the unionist councillor, John Thornton, who had died of natural causes. This was followed by a vote of sympathy for Councillor Richard O'Carroll who had been killed by Captain John Bowen-Colthurst. There was also an overall vote of sympathy to the relatives of the citizens who had lost their lives during the rebellion (39). Though the votes of sympathy went through without incident, the Rising provided the backdrop for the remainder of the meeting, with frequent references to members who were absent from the proceedings due to imprisonment. Lord Mayor, James Gallagher, referred to the calamity of the rebellion which had hit the city like a thunderbolt and he bemoaned the extensive damage to buildings which would create a financial burden for the Corporation (40). He announced an immediate recruitment embargo. In a lengthy and impassioned contribution, the Lord Mayor referred to the 'catastrophe' which had befallen Dublin and said that the city today 'presented as sad and heart-rending a spectacle as could be found on the continent of Europe' (41). He stressed that the Government had blown down the centre and most beautiful part of the city and it now was the duty of the Government to restore and beautify it. His closing words drew applause from his fellow councillors and from the public gallery: 'I hope that out of the darkness and calamity that has come upon us will emerge a condition of things which will be a guarantee for all-time of peace and good feeling amongst all Irishmen' (42).

While the Corporation meeting on 5 June was largely a calm affair with little or no acrimony, it was clear that by the time of the next meeting a fortnight later there had been a change in mood and political climate. One of the first pieces of business for the meeting was to fill the seats left vacant by the deaths of John Thornton and Richard O'Carroll. Going against the tradition of supporting the nominee of the party of the deceased, Labour and Sinn Féin councillors voted for Michael Maher to replace Thornton. The unionists, whose nominee was defeated, were now finding themselves isolated in the Corporation (43). Nationalist councillors also came together to co-opt John Long as the replacement for O'Carroll. At the meeting, councillors expressed outrage at the discovery of the bodies of fifteen civilians in the ruins of North King Street.

At the next full meeting on 3 July, members protested at 'the hundreds of citizens, men, women and boys' who had been arrested on suspicion of an involvement in the Rising and who were being held in detention camps (44). Lord Mayor Gallagher spoke strongly and warned the Government: 'Only the promptest action … in restoring to their homes people against whom there was not serious evidence, could allay the public resentment which has been occasioned' (45).

As an aside, at the same meeting, the Lord Mayor read a letter from one of the Corporation's Aldermen, Dr James McWalter. McWalter was the only member of the council to join the British Army and his letter outlined that as he had received instructions from the War Office to take up duty in the Mediterranean, he would not be able to attend council meetings 'for some time' (46). McWalter went on to serve in the Royal Army Medical Corps until the end of the war. Over the coming months, members of Dublin Corporation became increasingly vocal in calling for the release of those who had been interned without trial and an amnesty for those who had been sentenced to prison. Members also set in train the holding of an all-Ireland conference to establish a Political Prisoners' Amnesty Association (47).

At the Corporation meeting on Monday 2 October, Lord Mayor Gallagher read a lengthy statement in response to a recent editorial from its harshest critic, *The Irish Times*. The editorial had once again referred to Dublin as having the worst municipal government in the world. The Lord Mayor presented a detailed summary of the financial status of the city and refuted the claim that English cities enjoyed much lower rates than Dublin. He also attacked *The Irish Times* for what he called its dishonest journalism: 'The Irish Times is with us in Dublin, but it is not of us. Its spiritual home is north of the Boyne. Its controversial methods belong to the last century. Its attitude towards Dublin Corporation is like that of an Orangeman of the old school towards the Pope' (48). Unsurprisingly, *The Irish Times* hit back the next day with another stinging editorial which described the Lord Mayor's statement as 'feeble and futile' (49). It repeated its claims that Dublin Corporation was over-staffed and that the city was administered extravagantly and badly (50):

> *We are asked to believe that all the inefficiency and extravagance of the Dublin Corporation are due to 'historical and economic causes' which are beyond its control. The Lord Mayor explains the superior prosperity and high civic spirit of Belfast on the grounds that a long time ago British legislators helped Belfast and discouraged Dublin. We confess that this sort of talk sickens us, and we hope that it has the same effect on a steadily increasing body of Irish people. For at least thirty years, the Nationalist Corporation of Dublin has had complete control of the municipal administration of Dublin. It has enjoyed during that time all the opportunities which Belfast has enjoyed. It has received exactly the same treatment as Belfast – in some respects very generous treatment – from the State. The resources of the Imperial Treasury have been as open to it as to Belfast or any English city. The blame for our filthy slums and for our heavy rates can be diverted from our own heads by no casuistry or mis-reading of history.*

By the end of 1916 – as exemplified by the spat with *The Irish Times* – Dublin Corporation had, to a large extent, 'reverted to type' and both the Easter Rising and the First World War were background music as local matters and controversies dominated. However, as noted by Pádraig Yeates (2011) one trend was apparent at Corporation meetings: 'An ever increasing resentment towards the British authorities' (51).

Chapter 3
Municipal problems, the Irish Convention and the conscription crisis

In January 1917, Independent councillor, Alderman Laurence O'Neill was elected as Dublin's new Lord Mayor. During his acceptance speech, he referred to his imprisonment after the Rising, stating: 'One day a political convict, the next placed in the highest position of trust which his fellow citizens can bestow upon him; thus carrying out the old maxim that the lower the degradation by English methods, the higher the elevation in the esteem of the Irish people' (1). In a very long and bombastic address, O'Neill stated (2):

> *My dream today – it may be utopian – is that I may be allowed to represent Dublin as I represented Ireland in the past, irrespective of creed, politics, or class. To represent Dublin and its people as a whole, is the aim and ambition of my life … Dublin, where I was born, where I was reared, where I mitched from school, where I have my being, and which, with one exception, I hold everything that in my life is most dear to me! Dublin, where I hope to husband out life's taper to the close! Dublin, my own, my all! I love you!*

That same month, the members of Dublin Corporation unanimously co-opted three councillors who remained in prison – Seán T. O'Kelly, William T. Cosgrave and William Partridge – 'thus making good the vacancies created by their enforced absence' (3). The increasing politicisation of the Corporation became even more apparent the following month. A parliamentary by-election in North Roscommon led to a stunning Sinn Féin success for George Noble Plunkett, father of Joseph Plunkett, one of the executed leaders of the Easter 1916 Rising. A full meeting of Dublin Corporation was being held when the result from Roscommon was announced. It was greeted with 'wild excitement and much cheering and waving of hats by councillors and the crowd in the gallery' (4). Nationalist sentiment and support for Sinn Féin were steadily increasing, boosted by events like the release of rebel prisoners, such as William T. Cosgrave and Éamon de Valera in June.

Prior to these releases however, the elected members of Dublin Corporation expressed their protest at the re-arrest in April of Councillor Seán T. O'Kelly. A motion was passed saying that O'Kelly should be brought to trial or released immediately. William Partridge remained in jail and a letter from him was read out at a Corporation meeting. He concluded his letter with a defiant statement that he did not want any compromise which would 'retard or reduce the original demand of our people' (5). Members of Dublin Corporation continued to express their concern about the welfare of prisoners in internment. A special meeting was held in City Hall on 2 April at which Lord Mayor O'Neill referred to the first Russian revolution of 1917. He noted the 'general political amnesty' that had been declared by the Provisional Government of Russia and he put forward a motion as follows (6):

> It is hereby resolved that this meeting of the Dublin Corporation, representing all shades of political opinion ... demands that the British Government shall adopt a similar policy to that upon which they have congratulated the Provisional Government of Russia, and declare a general amnesty of Irish political prisoners, and a revocation of the recent order of deportation upon other Irishmen. And that a copy of this resolution be forwarded to the Prime Minister and Mr. John Redmond, M.P.; to his Holiness the Pope; the Presidents of the United States and the French Republic; the Russian Duma; the Premiers of the Colonial Governments, and also (with a request for its endorsement) to the public in Ireland.

The minutes of this special meeting of Dublin Corporation record that the motion was passed unanimously. However, this does not tell the full story of the meeting. Alderman David Quaid argued that the motion was poorly worded and noted: 'The majority of the people of Ireland are overwhelmingly in favour of the British Empire in this crisis. To say, as the motion does, that this council represents all shades of political opinion is inconsistent with fact' (7). He added: 'If there was a little broadmindedness amongst Nationalists in the council, the Unionists would be just as patriotic as they are' (8). At this point, amidst much heckling, Alderman Quaid left the council chamber along with the other Unionist members of the Corporation. While thanking the remaining elected members for supporting the motion, Lord Mayor O'Neill expressed his regret at the direction the discussion had taken – he said it was not edifying, gracious or patriotic (9). The Lord Mayor was a somewhat polarising figure in the city, partly due to the fact that he allowed political meetings to take place in his residence, the Mansion House. One such meeting was held on Monday 21 May with regard to the treatment of Irish prisoners in English jails. Amongst the speakers were George Plunkett, Cathal Brugha and Arthur Griffith and they called for those interned to be treated as prisoners of war rather than criminals. The meeting had a chaotic end, with *The Irish Times* reporting: 'A man, who was said to be a detective, was jeered and hustled; and several others were shown that their presence was unwelcome. After a little excitement, a body of uniformed police entered the Mansion House and the people then went away' (10). The Lord Mayor received criticism for hosting the meeting but he continued to make the Mansion House available for political gatherings. He also made his feelings known to the authorities in Dublin Castle that it was injudicious to send police into public meetings in the Mansion House (11).

On the same day as the controversial Mansion House meeting, 21 May 1917, the British Prime Minister, Lloyd George, announced a Convention of representative Irishmen in Ireland to submit to the British government a constitution for the future government of Ireland within the Empire. He expressed the view that all previous efforts to secure a settlement in Ireland had failed because the proposals had emanated from British governments (12). Speaking in the House of Commons, John Redmond welcomed the proposal and stressed that the Convention should be an open representative assembly: 'Every man must go into it free to put forward his own views, no section must be shut out, and no proposal put forward by any man must be ruled out' (13). In advance of the Convention there was renewed focus on the release of prisoners in British custody. After much negotiating and the determined involvement of the Lord Mayor, Lloyd George announced the release of the prisoners, as a conciliatory gesture. However, according to Pádraig Yeates (2011): 'The hope that the prisoners' release would create an atmosphere of goodwill in which the spirit of compromise could flourish, proved ill-founded' (14). In the early morning of Monday 18 June, the releases took place and, on their return to Dublin, the prisoners 'were cheered loudly as they were led past the ruins of the GPO and on to Fleming's Hotel in Gardiner Place for a celebratory luncheon' (15). Later on, Lord Mayor Laurence O'Neill hosted a reception for the released prisoners in the Mansion House. He noted that many of them had never travelled beyond the confines of their own parish or county before their internments and they had now returned as bearded men (16).

The Lord Mayor was emerging as a very prominent figure and it came as no surprise that he was invited to be a member of the Irish Convention. The opening meeting of the Convention took place in Trinity College, Dublin, on Wednesday 25 July. There were over ninety members of the Convention which was opened by the Chief Secretary to Ireland, Henry Duke. Sir Horace Plunkett, a former Unionist member of parliament for South Dublin and supporter of Home Rule, was elected Chairman. The Convention would sit for nine months until April 1918 and it received 'generous press coverage' during this period (17). Whether the Irish Convention was a sincere attempt by Lloyd George to find a negotiated solution to the question of Home Rule in Ireland, is open to debate. Ronan Fanning (2017) asserts that it was 'a stalling device to allow the Irish question to be put on the long finger while Britain focused on the war' (18).

With the Convention ongoing, the death of Thomas Ashe in September 1917 generated even more support for Sinn Féin and the policy of self-determination. Ashe, President of the Irish Republican Brotherhood, had taken part in the Easter Rising. Following arrest and release after a term in prison, he was subsequently re-arrested on a charge of sedition. He went on hunger strike in Mountjoy Prison and died due to forced feeding (19). Ashe's funeral was a massive affair, used by Michael Collins as a show of strength for the Irish Volunteers and Sinn Féin. Dublin Corporation was at the heart of it all, as the City Hall was used for Ashe to lie in state. The English *Daily Express* newspaper noted that the funeral had made '100,000 Sinn Féiners out of 100,000 constitutional nationalists' (20). The *Irish Independent* claimed that the death of Ashe had driven the country to the verge of desperation and it became clear that the tide was turning against the Irish Party and John Redmond (21):

> [Ashe's death has] embittered thousands of Irish Nationalists who had no real sympathy with the policy of Sinn Féin. The Irish Party … is now fighting for its life and … hates the Sinn Féiners more than it does the Unionists, and longs for their complete extermination.

Lord Mayor, Laurence O'Neill, had withstood enormous pressure from authorities in Dublin Castle who wanted him to refuse the request for Ashe to lie in state in the City Hall, and in October he hosted a significant Sinn Féin convention, at which Éamon de Valera was elected president. The Lord Mayor had put himself at the heart of local and national politics and he lobbied strongly, with some success, for prisoners on hunger strike to be released. O'Neill had visited Ashe the day before he died and he was in constant contact with the Chief Secretary to Ireland, Henry Duke, to try and negotiate concessions for those prisoners who had not been released in June. In particular, they wished to be classed as prisoners of war and not as criminals. Subsequently, the prisoners thanked the Lord Mayor by presenting him with an inscribed scroll which now hangs on display in Kilmainham Jail Museum (22):

> *Our sincere thanks for your efforts on behalf of our gallant*
> *comrade, Thomas Ashe, …. and on our own behalf during*
> *that trying period and subsequently when you spared no*
> *efforts to have the concessions which we won – to be treated*
> *as political prisoners – carried out.*

Aside from these ongoing political challenges, Lord Mayor O'Neill and the members of Dublin Corporation were faced with a series of municipal problems during 1917. Poverty was rife in the city, unemployment levels were high, there were regular disputes between employers and employees, and there was a food shortage. Housing was a constant agenda item at Dublin Corporation meetings and the Lord Mayor – acting on the recommendation of the Archbishop of Dublin, Dr William Walsh – agreed to convene a housing conference. As explained by Thomas Morrissey (2014) however: 'As with all attempts to solve the housing problem, it was clear that the cost and work involved would require considerable government funding. Circumstances were to dictate that the hoped for government assistance would not be forthcoming' (23).

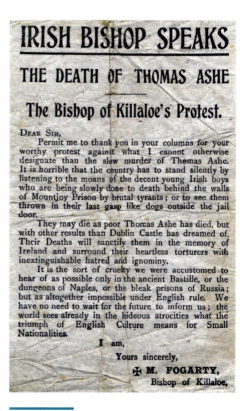

Dublin City Library and Archive,
Birth of the Republic Collection.

In the final months of the year, the food shortage in the city was dominating the thoughts of the Lord Mayor and the elected members of Dublin Corporation. At a council meeting on 3 December, the Lord Mayor expressed the view that there was plenty of food in the country if it were properly guarded and distributed. He referred to the potato crop being the largest in the last thirty years but, through mismanagement and profiteering, there was a shortage of potatoes for the middle classes and poor of Dublin, a situation he described as 'utterly ridiculous' (24). It was agreed that a committee of six members would be appointed to consider food supply in the city. Furthermore, the committee was empowered 'to convene an All-Ireland Conference to consider the whole question of Irish food supplies' (25).

The election of Lord Mayor was on the agenda for the Corporation meeting of Monday 23 January 1918. At the start of the meeting, the Town Clerk read a letter from Alderman James McWalter in which he apologised for his absence due to ongoing military duties abroad. He called on his fellow councillors to unanimously re-elect Laurence O'Neill who had done so much in the past twelve months to uphold the honour of the Mayoralty and to promote the advantage of the citizens (26). Many councillors spoke in tribute to O'Neill, with one predictable exception. Alderman David Quaid contradicted the view that the Lord Mayor represented the entire body of Dublin citizens. He said that the council had repeatedly failed to take into consideration the claims of the minority with regard to representation and the occupancy of the Mayoral chair. He added his criticism of the Lord Mayor for his use of the Mansion House for political and labour-related meetings. Quaid, however, was the sole dissenting voice and Laurence O'Neill was re-elected as Lord Mayor of Dublin for 1918. In thanking his fellow councillors for the honour they had again bestowed upon him, O'Neill expressed his fear that the food problems in the city would get worse. On the broader political issue, he hoped that a settlement could be reached through the work of the Irish Convention or otherwise. In response to the one dissenting voice at the meeting, he urged the councillors to 'treat with contempt the foul things which came from Alderman Quaid' (27).

Five days later, the Lord Mayor chaired the All-Ireland Conference on food supplies. He warned that in many parts of Ireland they 'were coming nearer to a dreaded famine' and he criticised the government 'who rule our destinies in London' (28). Meanwhile, the Irish Convention continued to meet but hopes were receding that an agreement would be reached. With little progress being made, the chair of the Convention, Sir Horace Plunkett, sought a meeting with the British

Prime Minister, Lloyd George. The meeting took place in 10 Downing Street in London on 13 February and Lord Mayor O'Neill was part of the deputation which accompanied Plunkett. The Lord Mayor was left dispirited by the encounter with Lloyd George, later recalling: 'I don't know what my colleagues' feelings were, but after our interview, I felt the Convention must soon end, and that Lloyd George was not honest about Ireland' (29).

On 6 March, the leader of the Irish Parliamentary Party, John Redmond, died after heart failure. Following a Requiem Mass in Westminster Cathedral, attended by Lloyd George, Redmond's body was taken back to Ireland where he was buried in Wexford. With Sinn Féin support on the rise at the expense of the Irish Parliamentary Party, Redmond's death represented the end of an era (which was borne out in December in the General Election). Dublin Corporation met on 11 March and the Lord Mayor led tributes to Redmond, stating (30):

> This is not the time to raise contentious matters by referring to the policy of Mr. Redmond, either in his early career or at the time of his death; but as to his motives, none, not even his most bitter enemy, can say with the slightest degree of truth, that the motives of John Redmond were anything but pure, and that his efforts – sometimes mistaken, some people may consider – were not directed according to his ideas, solely in the interests of his country.

As a mark of respect, the Corporation adjourned for a period of two weeks, but its daily work continued. A lively estimates and rates Corporation meeting later in March led to the following headline in the *Freeman's Journal*: 'City's Burden of Rates: Citizens' Deputation Indicts the Corporation' (31). The Chairman of the Dublin Citizens' Association severely criticised the running of the local authority and claimed that rates were at the highest level in the history of the Corporation. The Lord Mayor was fire-fighting on many issues at this time and he was soon to the fore as another major political row erupted.

In response to a major German offensive through Allied lines, the British war cabinet raised the age limit for compulsory military service in Britain to fifty-one and extended conscription to Ireland (32). Dublin Corporation reacted swiftly, with Alderman Alfie Byrne submitting the following motion for discussion on 8 April (33):

> *That this council, representing all sections of the city of Dublin, hereby warns the Government against the disastrous results of any attempt to enforce conscription in Ireland, and we earnestly request them not to be driven by a hostile anti-Irish press campaign against considering any such insane proposal which, if put into operation, would be resisted violently in every town and village in the country, ending in a great loss of life and the establishing of a battle front in Ireland that would not be of any advantage to the Allies or the cause which they are fighting for.*

Alderman Byrne's motion was comfortably passed, along with an addendum from Alderman Lorcan Sherlock that the Lord Mayor should organise a conference to arrange a united Irish opposition to conscription. The conscription crisis effectively coincided with the breakdown of the Irish Convention. Sir Horace Plunkett submitted his report from the Convention to the British Government on 8 April but it was signed by less than half of its members (34). According to Dorothy Macardle (1968): 'Whether he [Lloyd George] read it [the report] remains in doubt. When the House of Commons reassembled on the following day he announced the terms of the new Manpower Bill by which conscription could be applied to Ireland ... at any time' (35).

The all-party conference against conscription, agreed to by Dublin Corporation on 8 April, started in the Lord Mayor's Mansion House on 18 April. It was essentially a national cabinet meeting. The Irish Party was represented by Joseph Devlin and John Dillon, Sinn Féin by Éamon de Valera and Arthur Griffith, the All-for-Ireland League by William O'Brien, and Labour by William X. O'Brien, Michael Egan and Thomas Johnson (36). The threat of conscription had generated a lot of fear and panic and huge crowds gathered outside the Mansion House on 18 April. The *Irish Independent* reported that there were 'young and old, rich and poor, with ... a considerable sprinkling of the Unionist element' (37). Attendees at the conference passed a declaration asserting Ireland's separate and distinct nationhood, claiming that the British government had no authority to impose compulsory service in Ireland against the expressed will of the Irish people (38). De Valera argued that the passing of the Conscription Bill in the House of Commons should be regarded as 'a declaration of war on the Irish nation' (39).

On the second day of the conference, 19 April, it was agreed that a statement of Ireland's case should be circulated across the world and Lord Mayor O'Neill was asked to go to Washington to present the statement in person to the United States of America (40). The Lord Mayor of Dublin now had a growing local, national and international status and, in an interview with the *Daily Express* in early May, he outlined the position in which he found himself (41):

> *Consider the paradox; I am serving my second year as Lord Mayor of Dublin by the unanimous selection of the council. I am Chairman of the Mansion House Conference opposed to conscription. During the Easter Rebellion of two years ago, I was imprisoned for ten days. Now I expect to go to America on what some would describe as an errand of disloyalty, and yet, I have a son in the British army.*

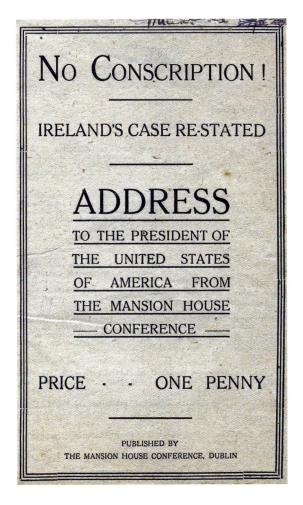

On 20 April, a conference of labour against conscription drew a crowd of over one and-a-half thousand people and a massive general strike across the country took place on 23 April. Dublin Corporation gave permission to Alice Stopford Green to use the City Hall on 9 June for a Women's Day of Protest (42). Thousands of women across Dublin marched to City Hall and signed their own anti-conscription pledge which read (43):

Dublin City Library and Archive, Birth of the republic Collection.

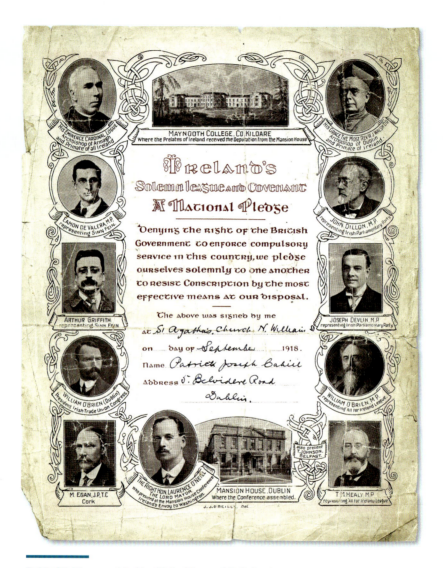

Dublin City Library and Archive, Birth of the republic Collection.

Because the enforcement of conscription on any people without their consent is tyranny, we are resolved to resist the conscription of Irishmen. We will not fill the places of men deprived of their work through refusing enforced military service. We will do all in our power to help the families of men who suffer through refusing enforced military service.

Ultimately, the British Government backed down on the issue of conscription but Pauric Travers (2017) describes the crisis as a landmark one which impacted negatively on Anglo-Irish relations: 'The affair was significant in developing British-Government policy towards Ireland, changing the balance of political power and hastening the advent of guerrilla war' (44). The balance of political power shift was in favour of Sinn Féin and the Volunteers (both now led by Éamon de Valera) with the Irish Parliamentary Party – still reeling from the death of John Redmond – suffering.

ARTHUR GRIFFITH and EAMONN DE VALERA.
A SNAPSHOT RECENTLY TAKEN WHEN LEAVING THE MANSION HOUSE ANTI-CONSCRIPTION CONFERENCE.

Arthur Griffith and Éamon de Valera leaving the Mansion House after the Anti-Conscription Conference.

Cumann na mBan Conlon Collection, Cork Public Museum.

The misguided Conscription Act was not the only piece of legislation introduced by the British Government in April 1918. An amendment to the Defence of the Realm Act stated that any person acting in a manner deemed prejudicial to public safety or the defence of the realm count be arrested and interned in England. This legislation paved the way for what became known as the 'German Plot' – essentially an implausible retaliatory measure by the British Government due to the fierce opposition to conscription. Acting on highly dubious information, supplied by Sir Edward Carson (the Irish Unionist Alliance M.P. for Trinity College Dublin and leader of the Irish Unionist Council in Belfast), arrest orders were made against Sinn Féin leaders on the basis that they were colluding with Germany (45). Over

> 412. It was moved by Councillor John T. O'Kelly ; and, seconded by Alderman O'Beirne :—" We hereby enter our emphatic protest against the cowardly and unwarranted action of the British Government in recently arresting and deporting eighty-eight of our fellow-countrymen and women, who are now imprisoned in various gaols in England :
>
> " We protest against the cruel and inhuman treatment they have been subjected to in being refused permission to communicate in any way with their families, relatives or friends, many of whom are—though more than two weeks have elapsed—still in ignorance of even the whereabouts of the prisoners.
>
> " We call the attention of all lovers of liberty to the methods adopted by English Ministers, whose declared aims in this present war are the liberation of small nations, to try to suppress and abolish by brute force the rights and liberties of the people of Ireland : " The motion was put and carried unanimously.

Minutes of the Municipal Council of the city of Dublin, 3 June 1918.

Dublin City Library and Archive.

seventy senior members of the Sinn Féin and Irish Volunteers leadership were arrested including Éamon de Valera, Arthur Griffith, George Noble Plunkett, Constance Markievicz, Maud Gonne MacBride, and William T. Cosgrave. Interestingly, Michael Collins evaded capture having received advance warning of the planned arrests. Pádraig Yeates (2011) notes: 'It was ironic that the decision to carry out the arrests led to the most militant and committed separatists taking control of the radical Nationalist movement – most notably [Michael] Collins' (46). At its meeting on Monday 3 June, Dublin Corporation passed a resolution protesting against the arrests and imprisonment of the anti-conscription leaders and the fact that the prisoners were not allowed to communicate with their families. There was only one dissenting voice, the ever-consistent Alderman David Quaid, but even he ultimately supported the motion. Taken together, it can be argued that the conscription crisis and the 'German Plot' arrests did more to unite the Irish than compel them to fight for England in the war (47).

Other factors also contributed to rising anti-British sentiment and led to votes of protest in City Hall. Captain John Bowen-Colthurst, who had been found guilty of the murder of Francis Sheehy-Skeffington during the 1916 Easter Rising, was released from prison having been declared insane at the time. He was never charged with the murder of Councillor Richard O'Carroll (48). By this point, Lord John French had been appointed the Lord Lieutenant in Ireland and the Military Viceroy and he proved to be a divisive figure. French had no sympathy for the cause of Irish independence and was a central figure in the 'German Plot' arrests. When Hanna Sheehy-Skeffington, the widow of Francis Sheehy-Skeffington, was arrested on her return from America on the pretext that she had breached 'passport rules', Lord Mayor Laurence O'Neill immediately went to Lord French to protest. The Lord Mayor left the meeting 'with the tacit understanding that she would be released at once. To his surprise, he subsequently learned that she had been transported to prison in England' (49).

Further flames were added to the fire in September when almost one hundred people 'likely to influence opinion or given leadership were cast into prison without charge' (50). Lord Mayor Laurence O'Neill summoned the councillors to a special meeting in City Hall on 23 September and he delivered a hard-hitting speech in which he said that the British Government were enemies not only of Ireland but their own country also (51):

> *Their action in arresting, deporting, and interning in English jails so many of our countrymen and women, without any trial, without even any charge being professed against them, constitutes one of the greatest breaches towards the liberty of the subject which any Government could be guilty of.*

With so many political distractions, the Lord Mayor and his fellow councillors struggled to address the numerous municipal problems facing the Corporation during 1918. Housing remained the single largest challenge. In August, P. C. Cowan, Chief Engineering Officer with the Local Government Board, presented a damning report on the housing situation in Dublin. It was acknowledged however that Dublin Corporation, though not blameless, was not responsible for the disgraceful conditions of the poor in Dublin: 'It is doubtful if any fault can be found with the Corporation. Their powers are limited, their resources are limited, and the difficulties in their way have accumulated through long years of neglect into an almost hopelessly immoveable mess' (52). Cowan proposed an ambitious plan to deliver at least 16,500 additional dwellings for workers at a cost of £8,640,000 (53).

Of course, implementation was always going to be the crux of the Cowan proposals and resourcing the housing plan through the British Government became more difficult, if not impossible, after the General Election of December 1918. By any standards, the election was an extraordinary one. It was the first election held in eight years and the passing of the Representation of the People

Act 1918 had extended the franchise to virtually all men over the age of twenty-one and women over thirty who were householders (54). The Irish electorate rose from seven-hundred thousand to almost two million voters. The odds were stacked against Sinn Féin in that 'most of its leaders and workers were in jail, much of the country was under martial law, and Republican papers were suppressed and censored' (55). On the other hand, the tide had been with Sinn Féin during 1918 and both its popularity and membership had increased steadily due to issues such as the conscription crisis and the 'German Plot'. As Pauric Travers (2017) points out, the party was young and populist, in stark contrast to the Irish Parliamentary Party which was ageing and middle-class and struggling for relevance after the death of John Redmond. The election results, which were announced on 28 December, 'shook the United Kingdom to its foundations and may be said to have signalled the threat to the British empire that was to materialise over the next three years' (56). Sinn Féin claimed a staggering seventy-three seats from the one hundred and five on offer; in fact, the party secured a seat for every one of its seventy-three candidates. Many seats were won by candidates still incarcerated, including Dublin Corporation's William T. Cosgrave who was returned as a Member of Parliament for North Kilkenny. The vote of the Irish Parliamentary Party, under the leadership of John Dillion, collapsed and the formerly dominant party fell from sixty-eight seats to a mere six. In Dublin, out of nine contested seats, Sinn Féin won eight and took around forty per cent of the vote (57).

It was clear that Ireland and Dublin were changing. According to Pádraig Yeates (2011): 'Dublin was a divided city in 1914. It was divided by nationality, religion, class, culture and conflicting loyalties. All those divisions had deepened by 1918 and resulted in significant realignments' (58). The political realignment was massive – the Sinn Féin election manifesto summoned the electorate to the flag of the Irish Republic and promised to boycott the Westminster parliament while establishing its own assembly. The manifesto also vowed that Sinn Féin would use 'any and all means available to render impotent the power of England to hold Ireland in subjection by military force or otherwise' (59). It is little wonder that, in the aftermath of the election results, Edward Shortt, Chief Secretary to Ireland under Lord French, predicted: 'The Irish question will be settled peacefully or bloodily within six months' (60).

Chapter 4
The War of Independence

The Lord Mayor's Mansion House was the venue for the historic first meeting of Dáil Éireann on the afternoon of Tuesday 21 January 1919. Having kept its promise not to take seats in Westminster but to establish its own parliament, the twenty-seven Sinn Féin members present confidently declared Irish independence. The low turnout reflected the fact that more than thirty members of the new parliament were still in prison; additionally, four of the Sinn Féin deputies were duplicates – in other words, they had been elected for two seats in different constituencies. Despite the low numbers, *The Irish Times* reported (1):

> *There have been many remarkable assemblies in the spacious Round Room of the Dublin Mansion House from time to time, but that which opened its proceedings yesterday afternoon at three-thirty possessed many characteristics which rendered it unique. It was the first meeting of the Constituent Assembly summoned by the Sinn Féin Party.*

Cathal Brugha chaired the meeting and, speaking in Irish, he declared that the members had much work ahead of them, 'the most important, perhaps, that has been undertaken for Ireland since the Gaels first landed on our shores' (2). The meeting lasted just under two hours and was a productive one, in front of approximately one hundred journalists, many of them from overseas. The members, or Teachtaí Dála (TDs), 'approved a short, provisional constitution, appointed three delegates to the post-war peace conference in Paris, and issued a Declaration of Independence, a message to the Free Nations of the World, and a Democratic Programme, setting out core principles to inform socio-economic policy' (3).

Earlier in the day, the Mansion House was used to host a reception for soldiers of the Royal Dublin Fusiliers who had been prisoners of war in Germany. One correspondent for *The Irish Times* noted the 'mingled portents' of the display of Union Jacks and Sinn Féin colours at the Mansion House. He wrote that the Mansion House, and possibly the Lord Mayor, were playing two parts: 'Thoroughly loyal in the morning and exceedingly disloyal in the afternoon' (4).

Tuesday 21 January 1919 is known however for more than the first meeting of the Dáil. The same day, members of the Irish Volunteers – or the Irish Republican Army (IRA) as it began to call itself – killed two policemen in Tipperary. As noted by John Dorney (2017): 'Together the events, though unconnected, signalled the beginning of a new insurrection against British Rule in Ireland' (5).

Two days later, on 23 January, Laurence O'Neill was once again elected Lord Mayor of Dublin for the coming year. The vote was unanimous and, in his words of acceptance, O'Neill stated: 'It is a great tax upon the generosity of the council to elect me for a third year. For the past two years, the position of Lord Mayor has been an arduous one, but it is one that is looked up to, not only be the citizens, but the vast majority of the people of the country, as a position of dignity and responsibility' (6). Meanwhile, dramatic events were unfolding. On 3 February, after two failed attempts, Éamon de Valera escaped from Lincoln Jail with Seán Milroy and Seán McGarry. By 20 February, disguised as a priest, de Valera was back in Dublin. His much-celebrated escape was a major propaganda coup for Sinn Féin. The Lord Mayor became embroiled in the escape of the prisoners when, in early March, Seán McGarry attended the Robert Emmet commemoration at the Mansion House. The *Freeman's Journal* noted: 'Mr. McGarry, who wore the uniform of the Irish Volunteers, received a tremendous ovation when he entered the Round Room, accompanied by the Lord Mayor of Dublin, wearing his chain of office' (7). McGarry had already left the Mansion House by the time a large number of policemen arrived on the scene. A fortnight later – on the instructions of Michael Collins – Harry Boland called to the Lord Mayor to ask would he publicly receive Éamon de Valera for a reception in the Mansion House. The Lord Mayor answered in the affirmative and arrangements were put in place, much to the consternation of the new Chief Secretary to Ireland, Ian MacPherson (he had replaced Edward Shortt who was appointed Home Secretary). MacPherson, who had a frosty relationship with the Lord Mayor, ordered the Commander-in-Chief, Sir Frederick Shaw, to issue a proclamation under the Defence of the Realm Act forbidding the reception for de Valera. The proclamation was sent to the Lord Mayor and was printed in the *Irish Independent* and *The Irish Times* (8). Lord Mayor O'Neill refused to back down and announced his intention to proceed with the original plan the following Wednesday; he would receive de Valera at the 'gate of the city' and accompany him by procession to the Mansion House for a reception. The Lord Mayor had large posters printed about the event which were placed in various locations in Dublin. Aware of heightened tensions, the Lord Mayor pleaded with citizens to avoid provocative action. MacPherson promptly ordered police to remove the posters.

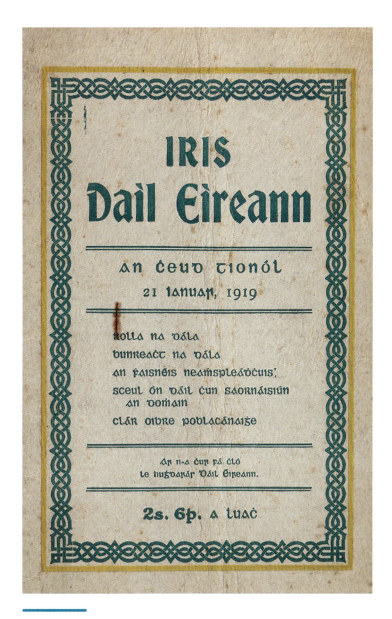

Report from the meeting of Dáil Éireann on 21 January 1919.

Cork Public Museum.

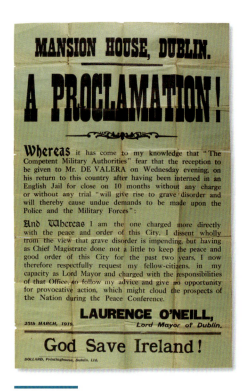

An example of the poster issued by the Lord Mayor in defiance of British attempts to restrict the welcome for Éamon de Valera; the new Chief Secretary to Ireland, Ian MacPherson, ordered the removal of the posters.

National Library of Ireland.

A few days later, in what Thomas Morrissey (2014) calls a 'judicious decision', de Valera opted to cancel the reception, due to fears of public disorder and violence (9). Remarkably however, on Friday 28 March, Éamon de Valera walked undetected through Dublin and called to the Lord Mayor in the Mansion House. They had a private meeting and photographs were taken which appeared the following day in the *Daily Sketch*.

The Lord Mayor subsequently engaged in a furious exchange of letters with Chief Secretary MacPherson in which he asked on what basis his posters had been torn down by police. Unsurprisingly, MacPherson pointed out that de Valera was claiming unlawfully to be president of an Irish Republic. The Lord Mayor retorted: 'I am afraid, Chief Secretary, that it will take you a long time to learn, or to understand, the Irish temperament, or what is bred in the Irish bone, namely, our hatred of oppression and injustice' (10). Never shy of publicity, the Lord Mayor sent all of his letters, and the replies from MacPherson, to *The Irish Times*, which printed them on 17 April.

During this time, the Dáil and Dublin Corporation were keen to curry favour with America, with mixed results. In March, the U.S. Congress, by a strong majority, passed the following resolution: 'That it is the earnest hope of the Congress of the United States of America that the Peace Conference now sitting in Paris will favourably consider the claims of Ireland to self-determination' (11). The Peace Conference, after the end of the First World War, ultimately resulted in the signing of the Treaty of Versailles and the three delegates nominated to attend by the Dáil were Éamon de Valera, Arthur Griffith and George Noble Plunkett. By now, de Valera was in an immensely strong position in Ireland. After his escape from

Lincoln Jail and return to Ireland, he had been voted President of the Dáil. Of course he was also President of Sinn Féin and of the Irish Volunteers (or IRA). Despite intense lobbying, the Irish delegation never received an audience before the Peace Conference, whose Committee of Four (United States of America, France, Britain, and Italy) decided that no small nation should appear before it without the unanimous support of the whole committee. Britain rejected Ireland's application (12). To help the Irish cause, the members of Dublin Corporation had gone as far as offering the Freedom of Dublin to the American President, Woodrow Wilson. Alas, via a statement handed into the Mansion House by the United States Consul, the offer was refused (13).

Éamon de Valera and Lord Mayor Laurence O'Neill outside the Mansion House on Friday 28 March 1919. This picture appeared in the *Daily Sketch* on 29 March and is reproduced by Thomas Morrissey (2014) in his biography of O'Neill.

National Library of Ireland.

My Lord Mayor,

I have the honour to appear before you, acting under instructions from the Right Honourable Robert Lansing, Secretary of State, said instructions being sent to me from the Offices of the American Commission to Negotiate Peace, and dated Paris, March 21st, 1919.

The President desires me to acknowledge to your Lordship, with his appreciation, the invitation received by him from your Lordship to visit Dublin and receive the freedom of the city; to apologise for the delay in replying hereto, and to express the President's regrets that it will not be possible for him to visit Dublin because of the constant pressure of his engagements, which he is confident your Lordship will recognise.

I have the honour, therefore, to present his reply most respectfully to your Lordship.

Heading into the summer of 1919, British administration over Ireland was falling apart. The Dáil had approved the appointment of William T. Cosgrave as Minister for Local Government in direct 'competition' with the Local Government Board which was based in the Custom House. There were now two central authorities overseeing local government in Ireland. Guerrilla warfare was developing in Dublin with the formation of the shooting 'Squad' by Michael Collins to eliminate detectives of the Dublin Metropolitan Police (14). *The Freeman's Journal* of 10 June described Dublin in the following way (15):

> *Soldiers with fixed bayonets, wearing trench-helmets, paraded the streets; a machine-gun post commanded Liberty Hall; military cordons with armoured lorries surrounded whole districts of Dublin while military and police carried out raids … Dublin's quays are jammed with tanks, armoured cars, guns and motor lorries, and thousands of troops, as if the port was the base of a formidable expeditionary force.*

Minutes from Dublin Corporation meetings during this period show that the elected members were keen to advance the daily business of the city in areas such as housing, slum clearances, public health, and the funding of local services. Their efforts were hampered not only by political events and violence but by a severe outbreak of influenza which was rampant across Europe. For much of 1919, Dublin was declared an infectious disease area. At its meeting of 11 August, the councillors passed a motion submitted by Alderman David Quaid condemning recent killings which had taken place in the city and elsewhere in the country. His motion ended with the call that 'all right-minded citizens will do everything in their power to prevent a reoccurrence in future of such crimes' (16).

On 10 August, the Dáil passed a resolution that all TDs, Volunteers, officers and clerks of the parliament should swear allegiance to the Irish Republic and Dáil Éireann. The proposal came from Cathal Brugha, who held the position of Secretary for Defence in the rebel cabinet. Though illegal, meetings of the Dáil had taken place unhindered since the start of the year. That changed after 10 September when the British Government declared that the Dáil was a dangerous association which would now be prohibited. Eoin Neeson (1998) argues that 'the suppression of the Dáil was seen as a declaration of war by England. It was followed by an acceleration of military aggression against the civil population' (17). Perhaps distracted by outside events, the meeting of Dublin Corporation on Monday 20 October, only attracted an attendance of the Lord Mayor and eighteen other elected members. As twenty members were required to constitute a quorum and a legal meeting, the Lord Mayor was left with no choice but to cancel the session. In the background, prominent business people in the city were determined to shake-up the membership of the Corporation, with municipal elections scheduled to take place in three months, in January 1920. Significantly, these elections were to be contested using a new electoral system. The Local Government (Ireland) Act, 1919, made proportional representation the voting mechanism in Irish local elections. As events transpired, this was to be the final piece of British legislation on local administration in Ireland. Sensing that the new electoral model could offer opportunities, the Dublin Chamber of Commerce, the Mercantile Association, the Citizens' Association and the Rotary Club held a meeting in the Mansion House on 27 October at which they agreed to run candidates under the banner of 'Municipal Reform' at the next elections in order 'to ensure professional and business representation on the municipal council' (18).

Lord Mayor O'Neill had always been consistently generous in opening the rooms of the Mansion House for meetings, lectures, fairs and dances but that now became more difficult. Earlier in October, he had been informed by Police Commissioner Johnstone that the British Government had issued an order prohibiting him from allowing Sinn Féin, Sinn Féin clubs, the Irish Volunteers, Cumann na mBan, and the Gaelic League from using the Mansion House. Things came to a head when the Lord Mayor was told in early December that the Mansion House could not be used for the annual Aonach na Nollag, a Christmas Fair. The fair had been running since 1906 and was an occasion for the sale and exhibition of Irish goods. More than one hundred and fifty police and five hundred soldiers turned up at the Mansion House to enforce the ban. The Lord Mayor was left with little choice but to announce the closure of the Mansion House for public events until further notice, stating: 'It is no longer safe to hold even a children's fancy dress there under the present Government' (19). Writing to Michael Collins on 17 December, the Lord Mayor explained that he felt compelled to make the decision: 'As I do not desire to have any conflict between the citizens and the soldiers which might end in bloodshed' (20). Bloodshed was on the cards that very night when a failed assassination attempt was carried out on the Lord Lieutenant to Ireland, John French. The following week, the Lord Mayor supported a motion at a meeting of the Port and Docks Board which expressed thankfulness that the assassination attempt had been unsuccessful. Later that night, he had two unwelcome visitors at the Mansion House who warned him that if he was not more careful with his language in future, they would 'plug' him (21).

December 1919 was a tough month for the Lord Mayor who was horrified when one of his closest friends on the council, Sinn Féin's Alderman Tom Kelly, was taken from his bed by the military on the morning of 11 December before being deported and imprisoned in London's Wormwood Scrubs (22). At a special meeting of the Corporation on 15 December, the Lord Mayor expressed his outrage at Kelly's treatment (23):

> *The treatment of Alderman Kelly is only a sample of what is going on throughout the country. Men, on the flimsiest of evidence, are being sentenced to long terms of imprisonment; men, for merely walking the roads at night, are sent to prison for periods extending from three to twelve months and, very often, an attempt is made to treat them as criminals. And these actions, to my mind – I say with some experience and advisedly – are the main cause of most of the disturbances which have taken place throughout the country for some time past.*

Councillor John McGarry argued that Kelly was not 'an apostle of violence'; in fact, there was no more peacefully disposed man in the council than the Alderman. As a protest against the arrest of one of their colleagues, he tabled a motion that the meeting be adjourned (24). This was carried, despite the protestations of Alderman David Quaid who asserted that the ordinary business of the Corporation should continue. He criticised councillors who were sympathising with the 'insane policy of establishing an Irish Republic' (25).

Local elections took place in Dublin on Thursday 15 January 1920. These were the first elections since 1914 and, as mentioned previously, proportional representation was the new electoral system used. The results were another triumph for Sinn Féin who took forty-two of the eighty seats – the party was now 'in a position to consolidate its grip on municipal power in the capital and to purge the old Corporation regime' (26). Lord Mayor, Laurence O'Neill, received the highest vote in the city, a demonstration of his popularity as an Independent Nationalist who was broadly acceptable to all. The Minister for Local Government in the new Dáil, William T. Cosgrave, was returned with a large vote, as was Tom Kelly who remained in jail in Wormwood Scrubs. The newly formed Municipal Reform Association claimed a creditable nine seats; included in their number were the former Lord Mayor, James Gallagher, and the long-time councillor, Dr

James McWalter. Five women were elected to the Corporation – Kathleen Clarke (widow of Tom Clarke, executed in 1916), Margaret McGarry, Anne Ashton, Jennie Wyse-Power and Hanna Sheehy-Skeffington. David Quaid, the bête noir of the Lord Mayor, failed to retain his seat. He was a victim of the new electoral system, unable to win a seat despite finishing fifth in first preference votes in an electoral ward where eight places were on offer. He was passed on transfers by three Sinn Féin candidates and one from the Municipal Reform Association.

One of the first duties of the new council was to elect a Lord Mayor at its meeting on Friday 30 January. Sinn Féin had led a campaign to elect the imprisoned Tom Kelly. Thomas Morrissey (2014) contends: 'Sinn Féin saw his election as Lord Mayor as an embarrassment for the Government and as a possible means of securing his release' (27). The meeting drew an enormous crowd to City Hall and the Tricolour was raised over the historic building. Outgoing Lord Mayor, Laurence O'Neill, chaired the meeting and delivered a highly-charged opening speech (28):

> *The Lord Mayor of Dublin is in an independent position if he maintains it; he signs no pledge, he takes no oath, he owes no allegiance to any power or authority except the people who returned him, and to the members who elected him to the position. Consequently, it is a position the most fastidious might occupy without his conscience being annoyed, without his morals being corrupted or his principles being interfered with in any way. Therefore, to fill such a position we are called together today, and it is my privilege to propose the name of Alderman Thomas Kelly.*

Councillor Tom Kelly was unanimously elected as Lord Mayor for the year ahead and he even enjoyed the support of the Corporation's sole Unionist representative, Councillor William McCarthy. When the date of inauguration arrived, 23 February, Kelly was still in prison and 'it appeared that he had not signed the declaration of acceptance of the Mayoralty' (29). It was agreed that Laurence O'Neill would remain in office until his successor could be properly installed. Following his eventual release from prison, Kelly returned to Dublin on 28 April but – in poor health and having suffered a severe mental breakdown – he was not able to assume the position of Lord Mayor. Thus, Laurence O'Neill stayed in the role.

By now, Ireland was in a state of war and the struggle for independence 'escalated in a guerrilla campaign of raids and ambushes' (30). On the night that the inauguration meeting for the Lord Mayor was taking place, 23 February, a military curfew was enforced on Dublin city for the first time since 1916. Former British servicemen – who became known as the Black and Tans – were deployed to Ireland, 'after which open warfare and terror became the norm' (31). British rule in Ireland was now disintegrating and the Dublin Castle administration effectively ground to a halt during 1920 (32).

In 1939 Kathleen Clarke became the first woman to be elected Lord Mayor of Dublin. Dublin City Library and Archive.

Laurence O'Neill was shaken to his core on Saturday 20 March when he was told that his counterpart in Cork, Lord Mayor Tomás MacCurtain, had been murdered in his home by Royal Irish Constabulary (RIC) officers in front of his wife and children. The murder caused outrage and near universal condemnation at home and abroad. *The Cork Examiner* of 20 March 1920 predicted that MacCurtain's death would create a profound sensation throughout the country and would likely lead to a rallying of public opinion behind Sinn Féin. The subsequent coroner's inquest passed a verdict of wilful murder against Lloyd George and certain RIC officers (33).

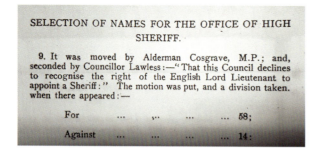

SELECTION OF NAMES FOR THE OFFICE OF HIGH SHERIFF.

9. It was moved by Alderman Cosgrave, M.P.; and, seconded by Councillor Lawless:—"That this Council declines to recognise the right of the English Lord Lieutenant to appoint a Sheriff:" The motion was put, and a division taken. when there appeared:—

| For | ... | ... | ... | ... | 58; |
| Against | ... | ... | ... | ... | 14: |

With British rule in Ireland falling apart, the elected members of Dublin Corporation passed a resolution not to recognise the power of the Lord Lieutenant

Minutes of the Municipal Council of the City of Dublin, 30 January 1920, Dublin City Library and Archive.

Dublin Corporation adjourned for a week as a mark of respect after MacCurtain's death and Lord Mayor O'Neill travelled to Cork for the funeral, accompanied by Councillor Jennie Wyse-Power. The funeral was a massive affair, as described by *The Irish Times*: 'A striking feature was the presence of about 8,000 Sinn Féin Volunteers,

Funeral procession of Lord Mayor of Cork, Tomás MacCurtain. The Lord Mayor of Dublin, Laurence O'Neill, attended the funeral and he was accompanied by Councillor Jennie Wyse-Power.

Cork Public Museum.

a good portion of whom wore their uniforms, attended by pipers' bands in in old Gaelic costumes, all walking four abreast' (34). According to Micheál Martin (2009): 'Cork virtually closed down. Thousands of young men and women wore the tricolour crossed with black, some houses draped their windows, the theatres and places of amusement closed, and concerts, lectures and other fixtures were cancelled' (35).

As noted by F. S. L. Lyons (2010): 'The pattern of assassination and counter-assassination, once embarked on, has an ugly tendency to repeat itself almost indefinitely. As the year 1920 progressed, such incidents multiplied and each side could claim both to have suffered and to have inflicted atrocities' (36). Against this background, Dublin Corporation struggled to conduct its daily business and it was disrupted further by the arrests and imprisonments of three council

Aldermen, William O'Brien, William T. Cosgrave, and Joseph MacDonagh. On the day of MacDonagh's arrest, the retired magistrate, Alan Bell, who was leading an inquiry into Sinn Féin and Dáil Éireann funds, was shot dead on the orders of Michael Collins. On foot of this, the Lord Mayor received a death threat on Dublin Castle notepaper (37):

> *O'Neill*
> *Your time has come*
> *Your life for Alan Bells*
> *Avenger*

It was accompanied by 'a drawing of a dagger dripping with red ink, and a coffin, drawn in black, with his name of the breastplate' (38).

At its meeting on Monday 3 May – in common with many local authorities across the country – Dublin Corporation pledged allegiance to the underground parliament, Dáil Éireann. The motion was tabled by the Sinn Féin councillor, Michael Dowling (39):

> *That this council of the elected representatives of Dublin hereby acknowledges the authority of Dáil Éireann as the duly elected Government of the Irish people, and undertakes to give effect to all decrees promulgated by the said Dáil Éireann in so far as affects this council. That copies of this resolution be transmitted to the Governments of Europe, and to the President and Chairman of the Senate and the House of Representatives of the U. S. A.*

The Lord Mayor read aloud the opinion of the council's Law Agent that the motion was out of order as the Dáil itself was illegal. In reply, the Lord Mayor said: 'I am not going to rule the motion out of order, and neither am I going to entirely rule it in order, but I am going to allow Councillor Dowling to propose the motion' (40). Dr James McWalter spoke against the motion, arguing that the financial implications would be dire for the Corporation and no citizens would pay rates, as they would not know if they should obey the orders of the British Government or Dáil Éireann. The Corporation was at risk of losing £1.1 million in rates. When the division was called, the resolution was passed by thirty-eight votes to five, with the Lord Mayor declining to vote. The five councillors who voted against were Alderman Hubbard Clark, and Councillors Moran, Stritch, Maxwell-Lemon, and McWalter – all of the Municipal Reform Association.

There was some reasoning behind Dr McWalter's arguments against pledging allegiance to the Dáil, as the local councils, already cash-strapped, were soon plunged into a deepening financial crisis. First, the British Government announced that damage caused by the IRA, the British Army, and the Black and Tans could be charged to the rates. Second, it was decided that British grants-in-aid, which were paid to local authorities to augment their income, would be withheld if the councils did not accept the authority of the British Government and submit their financial records to the Local Government Board. In effect, 'the British Government became tired of subsidising a shooting war aimed at dislodging it from power in Ireland' (41). Faced with severe financial difficulties, one of the measures undertaken by Dublin Corporation was to sell off pictures and paraphernalia associated with British kings (42). The members of the Corporation were also very concerned with the threat to food supplies as the War of Independence escalated and the Lord Mayor convened a Food Emergency Committee, one of the aims of which was to recommend shopkeepers to stock up on non-perishable foods, such as condensed milk.

With local authorities struggling to stay afloat, Dáil Éireann established a 'Commission of experts to enquire into the possibility of carrying on local administration without financial aid from the English Government'. In the absence of the imprisoned William T. Cosgrave, Kevin O'Higgins was appointed Chairman of the Commission and, speaking in the Dáil, he argued against a break with the Local Government Board. He was supported by Terence MacSwiney, the new Lord Mayor of Cork, but was opposed by Michael Collins (43). The Commission approached its work very efficiently, producing an interim report on 6 August and a final report on 17 September. The final report recommended a clear break with British administration and the Local Government Board – even though O'Higgins had previously opposed this position. Following the acceptance of the report, William T. Cosgrave, having been released from jail, issued a circular to all of the local authorities in which he stated 'the fate of the country hangs in the balance' and that 'a favourable outcome partly depends on the energy and integrity of those who have been elected to control the internal administration of the country' (44). Heeding Cosgrave's plea, the local councils played a valuable part in resisting the British Government. This came at a cost however and Dublin Corporation was virtually bankrupt by August 1920. The withdrawal of grants by the British Government left it with an overdraft of £100,000 and a need to find £160,000 to fund three major contracts (45). As both the Minister for Local Government and a prominent member of Dublin Corporation, Cosgrave could not allow the council to declare bankruptcy and he managed to persuade the banks to buy Corporation stock at a fifty per cent discount (46).

729. It was moved by the Right Hon. the Lord Mayor; and, seconded by Councillor Forrestal:—"Cúir bróin dúinne Luct Comáiple Catrac Baile Áta Cliat bár Toirbéalaig Mic Suibne, T.O., Árd-Méire Corcaige a béag i gcarcair gall ar ron a tíre, agur cuirimíd roin i n-umál bá muintir agur do Luct Catrac Corcaige: act fairir rin cúir bróid bá muintir ir do Gaedlaib a fearamuide a fulang ré bár ar ron na h-Éireann. Cé gur tráoc na gall é, mairfid a cuimne go buan cun cine Gaedeal a rciurad ar bealac na Saoirre:" The motion was put and carried.

The vote of condolence proposed by Lord Mayor, Councillor Laurence O'Neill, and seconded by Councillor John Forrestal, following the death of the Lord Mayor of Cork, Councillor Terence MacSwiney.

Minutes of the Municipal Council of the City of Dublin, 27 October 1920, Dublin City Library and Archive.

While Dublin Corporation was battling to keep its head above water, dramatic events were unfolding in Cork. On 12 August, Lord Mayor Terence MacSwiney was arrested by British forces on charges of possession of a cipher code machine. MacSwiney was wearing the Lord Mayor's chain of office at the time of his arrest and he refused to part with it, declaring he would rather die first (47). Tragically, this is what happened as MacSwiney died after a seventy-four-day hunger strike in Brixton Prison, London, on 25 October 1920.

Lord Mayor Laurence O'Neill attended the Requiem Mass in St. George's Cathedral, Southwark, before MacSwiney's body was returned home to Ireland. Other members of Dublin Corporation who attended the Mass in Southwark were the Sinn Féin duo of William T. Cosgrave and Joseph MacDonagh. MacSwiney's coffin notably contained an inscription on the lid, written in Irish (48):

[As translated]

> *Murdered by the Foreigner*
> *in*
> *Brixton Prison*
> *on*

October 25th, 1920
The fourth year of the Republic
Aged 40 years
God have mercy on his soul

The Irish contingent to Southwark was led by George Noble Plunkett, who gave an interview to the Press Association, stating: 'It is generally recognised among the Irish people, and will probably be recognised too late by the English people, that in the death of the Lord Mayor of Cork, Ireland has not been defeated, but has won the greatest victory which self-sacrifice can achieve' (49).

Surprisingly, on his return to Ireland, Lord Mayor O'Neill was not part of the large Dublin Corporation delegation which attended the funeral of Terence MacSwiney in Cork. Rather, he was embroiled in a battle to save the life of eighteen year-old, Kevin Barry, a first year medical student at University College Dublin.

Funeral of

The Late Lord Mayor of Cork.

Thursday, October 28th., 1920.

Admit Bearer to

St. George's Cathedral

at 1.30 p.m. for the

Funeral Procession

to Euston.

Signed _____

The Lord Mayor of Dublin was accompanied by William T. Cosgrave and Joseph MacDonagh to London for the funeral Mass of Terence MacSwiney.

Cork Public Museum.

Barry had been condemned to death for the murder of a British soldier, 'even though the evidence that he fired the fatal shot was doubtful' (50). The Lord Mayor wrote a personal appeal to the British Prime Minister, Lloyd George, against the death sentence. Dissatisfied with the reply he received, O'Neill set off for Downing Street. Thomas Morrissey (2014) describes the almost farcical pursuit of the Prime Minister which followed (51). When the Lord Mayor arrived in London, he was informed that Lloyd George was in Caernarvon; he made his way there only to be told that the Prime Minister was in Swansea. After two days, a determined Lord Mayor finally tracked down Lloyd George at Chequers and pleaded Barry's case. The Lord Mayor departed Chequers confident that the sentence might be commuted but this is not how it transpired. Instead, Kevin Barry was hanged on 1 November, the first execution since the aftermath of the 1916 Rising (52).

The body of Terence MacSwiney is carried out of St. George's Cathedral, Southwark, London.

Cork Public Museum.

The deaths of Terence MacSwiney and Kevin Barry brought worldwide attention to the British presence in Ireland and helped to sway the propaganda battle in Sinn Féin's favour. Day-to-day life in Ireland, however, continued to be challenging. In Cork, as a reprisal for several IRA attacks, the Black and Tans set fire to the centre of the city, destroying St. Patrick's Street, City Hall, the Carnegie Library and other public buildings, as well as businesses and shops. A damning report into the burning of Cork was produced by the British Labour Commission, and former Prime Minister Asquith spoke out strongly: 'I say deliberately that never in the lifetime of the oldest amongst us has Britain sunk so low in the moral scale of nations ... things are being done in Ireland that would disgrace the blackest annals of the lowest despotism in Europe' (53).

By early November, the British Prime Minister felt that his forces were winning the war in Ireland and he confidently declared: 'We have murder by the throat in Ireland'. He was forced to revise this view following the 'Bloody Sunday' offensive on the morning of 21 November when the IRA, under the direction of Michael Collins, targeted British intelligence agents, killing fifteen people (not all intelligence agents) and wounding four. Michael Foy (2017) describes the event as 'a remarkable achievement by Collins [which] sent a seismic shock wave through

The ruins of Cork city after the fire of 11 and 12 December 1920.

Cork Public Museum.

the British political system, shaking public faith in the Government's Irish policy and forcing Lloyd George to reassess his goals in Ireland' (54). Retaliation was swift and brutal. That afternoon, at a Gaelic football match between Tipperary and Dublin in Croke Park, the Black and Tans and the RIC opened fire on the crowd. At the end of ninety seconds of frenzied shooting, fourteen people had been killed or mortally wounded. One of those who died was Jane Boyle, who was shot and trampled, her hand slipping from her fiancé's grip as the panicked crowd swept him away. She was buried in her wedding dress on the same day she was due to be married (55). Diarmaid Ferriter (2020) argues that the events of Bloody Sunday changed British attitudes to Ireland and it was clear to all that the maintenance of law and order had long crumbled in the country (56).

The following meeting of Dublin Corporation, on Monday 6 December, was interrupted by British armed forces who arrested six members of the council – Aldermen Staines and Lawlor and Councillors Lawless, O'Brennan, Lynch, and Clarke. The Lord Mayor was left with no choice but to adjourn the meeting. As if the year 1920 had not been difficult enough, the daily internal activities of the Corporation were made more problematic by a breakdown in the relationship between the councillors and the Town Clerk, Henry Campbell. Pádraig Yeates

Match ticket for the fateful football match between Tipperary and Dublin on 21 November 1920.

The GAA Museum.

(2012) describes Campbell as 'a pillar of the Irish Party establishment' who was 'always impeccably and even flamboyantly dressed, with a magnificent walrus moustache' (57). Campbell was less-than-impressed with the results of the local elections in January 1920 which gave Sinn Féin a majority in the council chamber. At the very first meeting following the elections, he argued that Jennie Wyse-Power was not a legitimate member of council as she had signed her electoral declaration in Irish. Throughout the year, Campbell had refused to record in the minutes any statements or resolutions that were made in Irish. He also disobeyed the order of the council not to submit the Corporation's financial books to the Local Government Board. He clashed

THE TOWN CLERK'S OFFICE,
CITY HALL,
DUBLIN, 13th. December, 1920.

To the Right Honourable the Lord Mayor,
Aldermen, and Burgesses of Dublin.

MY LORD MAYOR,
The attitude adopted by your Lordship at the meeting of the Council, on Monday last, has demonstrated to me that I would be wasting the time of the Corporation and my own if I were to remain any longer in the office of Town Clerk. During that meeting you stated that you would ignore the Town Clerk and his Assistant. In point of fact, you immediately took a greater plunge when, dealing with the Minutes of Council of the 4th. October last, you accepted an amendment, the effect of which, if it were to become a resolution of the Council, would make the Assistant to the Town Clerk and myself responsible for certifying and giving legal sanction to transactions of a so-called meeting of the Council which was held when neither he nor I was present.

I temporarily withdrew my letter of resignation in the hope, and with the desire, that my remaining in office might be of assistance to the Court and the Corporation in the proceedings instituted in connection with the audit of the accounts; but, in view of your Lordship's announcement, above referred to, I feel that my continuance in office would be futile; and, accordingly, I repeat my letter of resignation of the 15th. November ultimo in its exact terms, as follows:—

Town Clerk, Henry Campbell, had a fractious relationship with the elected members. He submitted two resignation letters in 1920, dated 15 November and 13 December. The councillors rejected his resignation attempts and fired him instead.

Minutes of the Municipal Council of the City of Dublin 14 December 1920, Dublin City Library and Archive.

frequently with Sinn Féin members and, at the meeting of 6 December which had been interrupted by armed forces, Councillor Jennie Wyse-Power remarked: 'The Town Clerk and his friends are here'. A furious Campbell rebuked Wyse-Power, stating, 'How dare you speak to me like that' (58). By the middle of December, the elected members and Henry Campbell both felt that they had had enough of one another. Campbell tendered his resignation but this was rejected by the councillors. Instead, they dismissed him. Campbell was soon employed by the Local Government Board and was later knighted as Sir Henry Campbell (59).

Campbell was now out of the equation and, on 20 December, so too was Dublin City Hall. Military authorities took possession of the building and removed the municipal flagstaff – 'The Government was making it brutally clear that the Corporation, by allying itself with the Republican rebels, could no longer be regarded as a reliable administrator of the needs of all the citizens' (60). The Corporation needed a new venue for its meetings and it used the Mansion House. Thus ended a very traumatic year for Dublin's municipal authority, a year which began with the election as Lord Mayor of a man, Tom Kelly, who never actually took up the position.

British troops take over Dublin City Hall in December 1920. A couple of weeks previously, a meeting of the Corporation had been interrupted by troops who arrested six councillors.

Dublin City Library and Archive, Birth of the Republic Collection.

Laurence O'Neill was once again elected as Lord Mayor of Dublin on 31 January 1921, during a council meeting held in the Mansion House. This followed on from an extraordinary series of letters between O'Neill and Éamon de Valera earlier in the month. Initially, de Valera wrote to O'Neill asking for his assistance in setting up a relief committee in Ireland, to be called the Irish White Cross. Its principle aim would be to distribute funds raised by the American Committee for Relief in Ireland. In reply, O'Neill stated that he would help in any way he could but he also pointed out that the Mayoral election was scheduled to take place at the end of the month. He noted: 'If I am not Lord Mayor, I would have very little weight and less influence in launching the scheme as suggested by you' (61). In essence, the Lord Mayor was asking the Sinn Féin leader if his party, the majority group on the Corporation, intended to nominate a candidate for the Mayoralty. In a very carefully crafted response, de Valera asked O'Neill if he could guarantee that, on political matters regarding relations with England, he could be relied up on 'to take counsel with and be advised by the responsible political representatives of the vast majority of the Irish people' (62). To some extent, it can be argued, that O'Neill was being asked to sacrifice his independence and align with Sinn Féin in order to maintain power as Dublin's Lord Mayor. On the evening of 27 January, four days before the meeting to elect a Lord Mayor, he wrote to de Valera confirming that he was happy to proceed as the Sinn Féin leader had suggested. Therefore, at the meeting, Laurence O'Neill was nominated by the Sinn Féin councillor, John Forrestal, and seconded by another Sinn Féin councillor, Hanna Sheehy-Skeffington. Dr James McWalter offered token resistance and queried why Sinn Féin was not putting forward a candidate of its own given its majority position in the Corporation. He speculated as to whether Laurence O'Neill was truly independent and he then nominated the Unionist councillor, Andrew Beattie. This came as a surprise to Beattie who informed the meeting that he was not willing to have his name go forward; Laurence O'Neill was duly elected Lord Mayor for 1921.

Pádraig Yeates (2012) states that 'violent death was ubiquitous in Dublin in early 1921' (63) and it is the case that the first six months of the year saw a period of intense warfare. The Lord Mayor had aligned himself to Sinn Féin and it became difficult for him to distinguish between local and national politics as Éamon de Valera had an office in the Mansion House at this time. Michael Collins was a regular visitor, often wearing different disguises. Corporation meetings in the Mansion House were dominated by votes of condolence and sympathy. One such meeting was held on Monday 7 March and it commenced with Councillor John Forrestal proposing a vote of condolence for the relatives of six men who had been executed in Cork Prison a week before. He asked his fellow Corporation members to place on record their 'admiration for the heroic fortitude with which they met their deaths' (64). A weary and despondent Lord Mayor lamented: 'One sad event follows another in this country' (65). He said that he had just received a telegram with the news that the Mayor of Limerick, Alderman George Clancy, and former Mayor, Councillor Michael O'Callaghan, had been murdered by the Black and Tans in the early hours of the morning. As a mark of respect, the meeting was adjourned for a week. The Lord Mayor attended the funeral services in Limerick and presided over the council meeting on 14 March, which had been adjourned from the previous week. A familiar patter ensued with a vote of condolence for the families of six men executed in Mountjoy Jail that morning. A sombre Lord Mayor told the meeting (66):

I am now more firmly convinced than ever that those who are attempting to rule Ireland with the sword should understand that the body of Ireland might be tortured, but until the whole Irish race is exterminated, the soul of Ireland will remain true to the traditions of the past. There can never be an absolute peace between England and Ireland until the Irish people are given the power, which by right belongs to them, to work out their destiny in their own way.

Councillor Patrick T. Daly declared that Britain was trying to 'out-Herod Herod' in endeavouring to kill the soul of a nation (67). After the condolence motion was passed in silence, the meeting was again adjourned. Thomas J. Morrissey (2014), the biographer of Laurence O'Neill, correctly points out that the Corporation, by this time, was not showing balance in its expressions of outrage and there were rarely motions of condolence passed for the relatives of British soldiers killed by the IRA. Another death, albeit a natural one, deeply saddened the Lord Mayor in the early months of 1921. The respected councillor Dr James McWalter – who had served in the First World War – passed away. Though McWalter sometimes clashed with the Lord Mayor, they were good friends and McWalter was a diligent councillor, latterly representing the Municipal Reform Association. Speaking in tribute at a meeting of the Corporation, Alderman William T. Cosgrave, noted: 'The city has lost a brilliant son, the Corporation a gifted colleague, the medical profession an able and generous practitioner, and we have lost a friend' (68).

Meanwhile, the War of Independence continued unabated. In May, the Custom House – headquarters of the Local Government Board – was destroyed by the IRA and all of its records were lost in flames. The LGB was now homeless. In the following month's General Election, Sinn Féin swept the boards and formed the second Dáil (69). Behind the scenes, tentative attempts to promote peace had started and the Lord Mayor of Dublin, Laurence O'Neill, was at the heart of them. In June, a public appeal for reconciliation by King George opened the door for Lloyd George to invite Éamon de Valera to a conference. First, de Valera sought to hold consultations with representatives of the Irish Unionists, and the Lord Mayor hosted the meeting in the Mansion House on Monday 4 July. At the end of the meeting, it was the Lord Mayor who addressed the press, stating that good progress had been made and that discussions would continue on Friday. At the regular meeting of Dublin Corporation that evening, the Lord Mayor was upbeat, declaring it to be the happiest day of his life. He told the council (70):

Peace is in the air. I am breaking no confidence in telling you that during the past three or four hours, in the drawing room close by, in my opinion, one of the most delicate and one of the most momentous conferences that has ever been held in this country has taken place. I am breaking no confidence in telling you that I have great hopes that a great deal of good will come out of it.

When the talks resumed on Friday, the Commander-in-Chief of the British forces in Ireland, General Nevil Macready, sat across from Éamon de Valera in the Mansion House and 'the principles governing a truce were agreed' (71). It was announced that the truce would commence at noon on Monday 11 July. The following day, Éamon de Valera led a delegation to London for talks with Lloyd George. Interestingly, the delegation included the Lord Mayor of Dublin, Laurence O'Neill.

Chapter 5
The Treaty, the Civil War and the power of dissolution

Though Lord Mayor Laurence O'Neill was part of the Irish delegation which went to London in July 1921, he was not an important player in the discussions which took place, many of which were private meetings between Éamon de Valera and Lloyd George. Thomas Morrissey (2014) describes O'Neill's role as 'a mixture of public relations and catering for the welfare of all the members of the party' (1). When the delegation returned to Ireland, the mood in Dublin was positive as people greeted the truce and the ongoing talks with a mixture of relief and hope (2). David McCullagh (2017) notes: 'Crowds flooded the streets, and overladen trams took tens of thousands of day trippers to the seaside. Members of the Auxiliary Division commandeered vehicles to join them. Ice cream vans sold "Gaelic ice cream", and the city's dealers laid out the fruit and vegetables on their handcarts in patriotic display' (3).

The proposals which emerged from the July negotiations were rejected by Dáil Éireann when the delegation returned home. However, they paved the way for

Welcoming party for Éamon de Valera at Kingston (Dún Laoghaire) after the July talks – from left to right, H. Friel (Chairman of Dublin County Council), Máire O'Donovan (acting Mayor of Limerick), Vincent White (Waterford TD), Kate O'Callaghan (Limerick TD), Donal O'Callaghan (Lord Mayor of Cork, Chairman of Cork County Council and Cork TD), and Liam de Róiste (Member of Cork Corporation and Cork TD).

National Library of Ireland.

Lloyd George to issue a further invitation for talks to see if the differences between both sides could be reconciled.

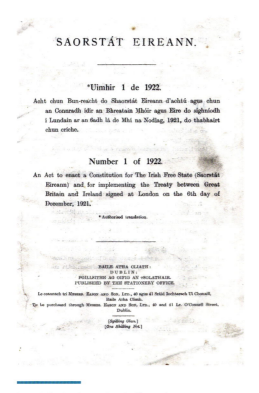

SAORSTÁT EIREANN.

*Uimhir 1 de 1922.

Acht chun Bun-reácht do Shaorstát Eireann d'achtú agus chun an Connradh idir an Bhreatain Mhóir agus Eire do sighníodh i Lundain ar an 6adh lá de Mhí na Nodlag, 1921, do thabhairt chun críche.

Number 1 of 1922.

An Act to enact a Constitution for The Irish Free State (Saorstát Eireann) and for implementing the Treaty between Great Britain and Ireland signed at London on the 6th day of December, 1921.

* Authorised translation.

BAILE ÁTHA CLIATH:
DUBLIN:
FÓILLSITHE AG OIFIG AN tSOLATHAIR.
PUBLISHED BY THE STATIONERY OFFICE.

Le ceannach trí Messrs. Eason and Son, Ltd., 40 agus 41 Sráid Iochtarach Uí Chonaill, Baile Atha Cliath.
To be purchased through Messrs. Eason and Son, Ltd., 40 and 41 Lr. O'Connell Street, Dublin.

[Spilling Glan.]
[One Shilling Net.]

Legislation implementing the Treaty between Great Britain and Ireland.

Dublin City Library and Archive, Birth of the Republic collection.

These talks commenced on 11 October and lasted for eight weeks, with scarcely a break. Critically, Éamon de Valera was not a member of the Irish negotiating group; he argued that as Head of State, he should be kept in reserve. William T. Cosgrave disagreed fundamentally with the decision as he felt that it was unwise to leave a man with de Valera's noted negotiating skills at home. He famously argued that the Irish 'team' was leaving its ablest player in reserve and now was the time to use him (4). The five delegates who formed the Irish negotiating team were Arthur Griffith, Michael Collins, Robert Barton, George Gavan Duffy, and Eamonn Duggan. After nearly two months of discussions, 'the delegates returned to Dublin at the beginning of December and brought with them a draft treaty proposed by the British' (5). The seven members of the Dáil cabinet met in the Mansion House and it was clear that they were divided. Ultimately, the cabinet rejected the proposals and the negotiating team was sent back to London for further negotiations. Robert Barton asserted again that de Valera should form part of the team but this was rejected. At quarter past two on the morning of Tuesday 6 December, the five Irish delegates – Griffith, Collins, Barton, Duffy, and Duggan – signed a treaty with the British; both the Irish and British sides agreed to recommend it to their respective parliaments.

The Treaty stated that the Irish Free State – comprising twenty-six of Ireland's thirty-two counties – would have the same constitutional status as Canada, Australia, New Zealand, and South Africa, that is, it would be a dominion of the British Empire. Members of the new Free State's parliament would be required to take an oath of allegiance to King George V, his heirs and successors. *The Irish Times* of 7 December took a positive view of the Treaty agreement (6):

> *The Irish situation has undergone a swift and almost bewildering change. Men rubbed their eyes like people who step suddenly from the darkness into sunshine. Forty-eight hours ago, a renewal of civil warfare seemed to be imminent. Today, we are offered, in Lord Birkenhead's words, 'the sure and certain hope of peace' ... We shall not indulge in premature felicitations. Though the whole outlook has been transformed, the future is still uncertain. It is possible that the Imperial Parliament may hold that the promise of Irish peace has been bought too dearly. It is possible that Dáil Éireann may raise objections on the question of allegiance ... One thing, however, is certain. If this Treaty is ratified, if Irishmen of all creeds and parties combine to administer it in a spirit of broad-minded patriotism, if it bridges the gap between North and South, if it reconciles Ireland to the Empire – if it gives us all these blessings, it will be one of the most fruitful and most glorious achievements of modern statesmanship. It will close a hideous era of strife and bloodshed and will open a new era of material and intellectual progress.*

An emergency meeting of the Dáil Éireann cabinet, comprising seven members, took place on 8 December to discuss the Treaty. The venue was the Mansion House and the meeting was hosted by Lord Mayor, Laurence O'Neill. Tensions were high, with Arthur Griffith, Michael Collins and Robert Barton speaking in favour of the Treaty, as opposed to a return to war. Collins expressed the belief that the Treaty, though far from perfect, would be a stepping stone to greater freedom. Éamon de Valera, Cathal Brugha, and Austin Stack were opposed, believing that more concessions could be gained through further negotiations with the British. William T. Cosgrave was uncertain and, as such, he occupied the unenviable position of the 'swing' vote. Writing nearly a decade later, Laurence O'Neill commented that Cosgrave called to see him in his study in the Mansion House during a break in discussions: 'Cosgrave was battling with his conscience, and talking to himself ...... Never again do I wish to see a human being struggling so much between love and duty' (7). Laurence O'Neill also wrote that, during the heated debate of 8 December, Cathal Brugha's pent-up animosity towards Michael Collins was let loose (8). After agonising for quite some time, and resorting to prayer, Cosgrave supported acceptance of the Treaty. With the cabinet split, but agreeing on a four-three basis to side with the Treaty, attention now turned to Dáil Éireann – would a majority of members ratify the Treaty? Debates were held in University College Dublin, over a fifteen-day period (with a short Christmas break), starting on 14 December.

Richard Aldous (2009) describes the debates as 'an intense, often high-minded, occasionally vitriolic battle not just for the hearts and minds of the deputies, but for those of the people' (9). Michael Collins addressed the Dáil on 19 December and argued that if the plenipotentiaries who had negotiated in London had not done a good job, then the fault lay with the Dáil for selecting them. He pointed out that he took part in the negotiations because of a sense of duty but he asked deputies to remember that he had protested against being part of the delegation. Collins stressed that the decision to be made was a straightforward one – reject or accept. He called on members to accept and pleaded: 'Don't let us put the responsibility, the individual responsibility, upon anybody else. Let us take responsibility ourselves and let us, in God's name, abide by the decision' (10). The Dáil finally voted on Saturday 7 January 1922 and ratified the Treaty by sixty-four to fifty-seven. After the result was announced, Éamon de Valera rose to his feet, pointing an accusing finger across the room, and declared: 'That document will rise in judgement against you' (11). Michael Collins stood up and appealed for public safety but he was followed by an impassioned Mary MacSwiney, sister of Terence, who declared that she had witnessed that night 'the grossest act of betrayal that Ireland ever endured' (12). De Valera immediately resigned as President of the Dáil but ran for re-election, only to lose by two votes. Arthur Griffith was elected as President and a new pro-Treaty cabinet was formed. The drama of the occasion was well captured by the report in *The Irish Times* the following Monday: 'The session was to end in a tragic vein. Mr. de Valera tried to speak a final word, but he could hardly speak, and, abandoning the attempt, buried his head in his hands. Tears were running down Mr. Harry Boland's cheeks' (13). The report concluded that Ireland was saved but that the tragic figure of the Republican President (de Valera) threw a gloom over the popular rejoicing. One of those who rejoiced was the Lord Mayor of Dublin, Laurence O'Neill, who savoured the historic days that followed when the Provisional Government met in the Mansion House and later took ceremonial possession of Dublin Castle. On 21 January, there was another momentous occasion when City Hall was handed back to the Government. William T. Cosgrave, Minister for Local Government and an Alderman in Dublin Corporation, raised the national flag over the municipal authority amidst much celebration.

Laurence O'Neill had more cause for celebration at the end of the month when he was re-elected as Lord Mayor. He had earned a reputation as a skilled mediator and someone who had the respect of all sides. Alderman Joseph MacDonagh seconded O'Neill's nomination and he noted: 'Alderman O'Neill has been Lord Mayor during the difficult years. We should now, as an act of grace, give him an easy year' (14). O'Neill did not have things all his own way, as Councillor John Forrestal was also nominated for the role of Lord Mayor. However, the motion to elect Forrestal was lost on a vote of forty-one to twenty-seven and O'Neill was returned once again as Dublin's first citizen. He did not, though, enjoy an easy year as had been forecast by Joseph MacDonagh.

The Treaty had effectively split the dominant Sinn Féin party into two bitterly opposing factions. Groups opposed to the Treaty began to mobilise, including Cumann na mBan, driven by the redoubtable Mary MacSwiney. On 11 January – just four days after the vote in the Dáil – the Cumann na mBan executive had voted by twenty-four to two to reject the Treaty. This was followed by a Special Convention of the women's movement on 5 February where delegates voted against accepting the Treaty by four hundred and thirteen to sixty-two (15). In March, anti-Treaty IRA held a convention in the Mansion House and rejected the authority of the Provisional Government and the Ministry of Defence. The following month, they occupied a number of buildings in the centre of Dublin, including the Four Courts (16).

With the outbreak of isolated incidents of violence and intimidation, and the threat of Civil War in the air, the Lord Mayor of Dublin, Laurence O'Neill, and the Archbishop of Dublin, Edward Byrne, took the step of convening a peace conference in the hope that leaders of the pro and anti-Treaty sides would come together to restore peace in advance of elections scheduled for June. The conference – which ran from 19 to 29 April in the Mansion House – was attended by Arthur Griffith, Michael Collins, Éamon de Valera, and Cathal Brugha; Stephen O'Mara was the agreed facilitator. Archbishop Byrne delivered a heartfelt opening address, stating: 'It is a strange thing that we should use the first instalment of anything like freedom to engage in fratricidal strife. Already hearts have been made sore enough by the British bullet and British bayonet without Irishmen bringing more sorrow to Irish homes' (17). Despite the best efforts of the Archbishop and the Lord Mayor, the conference ended in failure, with no agreement reached. The official report for the conference stated: 'No useful purpose would be served by prolonging it' (18).

A forlorn Lord Mayor reported the breakdown of talks at the Dublin Corporation meeting on Monday 1 May. At the meeting, the Town Clerk read a letter from the Minister for Local Government asking for the views of the elected members on parliamentary polling districts for the forthcoming district. Alderman Joseph MacDonagh objected to the letter - he argued that the council had previously pledged its allegiance to Dáil Éireann but this communication came from a different source, the pro-Treaty Provisional Government. The Lord Mayor conceded that MacDonagh was correct 'up to a point' and the letter was deemed out of order (19). Partly because of this issue, when the council met the following week, it took the step of approving a motion by Alderman William T. Cosgrave 'that it recognises and will conform to the lawful orders and decrees of the Provisional Government of Ireland' (20). This was comfortably passed by forty-four votes to eleven. Alderman James Hubbard Clark, leader of the Municipal Reform Association, was one of those who spoke in favour of the motion; he contended that the average man looked upon the Provisional Government as the Government of Dáil Éireann and that people were fed up with insincerity and play-acting (21).

Amidst the ongoing breakdown of law and order and with 'nightly gun battles on the streets of Dublin' (22), attention turned to the General Election of 16 June, in some respects a public vote on the Treaty. The majority of the incumbent candidates were Sinn Féin members but these could now be divided into pro-Treaty Sinn Féin and anti-Treaty Sinn Féin. In advance of the election, Michael Collins and Éamon de Valera agreed to enter a pact. As Eoin Neeson explains (1998): 'In

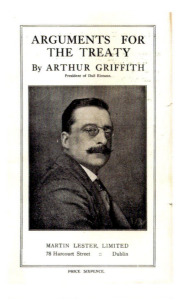

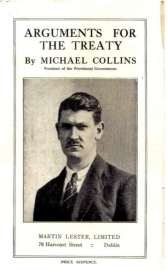

Pro-Treaty pamphlets were produced by Arthur Griffith and Michael Collins, as President of Dáil Éireann and President of the Provisional Government, respectively.

Dublin City Library and Archive, Birth of the Republic collection.

essence it provided that Sinn Féin – the original undivided party – would put forward a panel of candidates for election. A Government would be formed of both pro and anti-Treaty representatives in proportion to the respective numbers elected' (23). The election was a triumph for Collins and the Provisional Government, especially in Dublin. Anti-Treaty Sinn Féin candidates only won one of the twenty-two seats in the capital. The sole success was Seán T. O'Kelly who took a seat in the Dublin Mid-West constituency on the sixth and final count. Lord Mayor, Laurence O'Neill, topped the poll in the constituency ahead of Alfie Byrne, another Independent Nationalist (24). Amongst the high profile anti-Treaty Sinn Féin candidates who lost their seats in Dublin were Countess Constance Markievicz, Kathleen Clarke, and Margaret Pearse. With a decisive pro-Treaty result, the *Irish Independent* proclaimed that the people of Ireland had demonstrated their desire 'to replace the rule of gun by ordered Government' (25).

This optimism was misplaced and, by the end of the month, a Civil War had officially begun. On 27 June, the cabinet served notice on anti-Treaty militants (or Irregulars as they were called) to evacuate the Four Courts and surrender all weapons, or military action would ensue. In the early hours of 28 June, National Army troops of the Provisional Government attacked the Four Courts and the Civil War was underway. While the Civil War would continue until May 1923, the first phase – from 28 June to 5 July 1922 – was concentrated on the centre of Dublin. The Lord Mayor, recently elected as a TD, was heartbroken 'to see former friends in mortal combat and his much loved city, which he had largely protected under British Rule, now being destroyed by fellow Irishmen' (26). O'Connell Street, in the heart of Dublin city, was reduced to rubble for the second time in six years.

The Four Courts on fire in July 1922.

Dublin City Library and Archive, Dixon slides collection.

The Lord Mayor tried his best to broker peace. He facilitated a women's peace committee chaired by Maud Gonne MacBride which drew up proposals that hostilities should cease so that the conflict could be resolved at the July meeting of the new Dáil. Laurence O'Neill led a delegation to meet with both sides but the Government representatives of Arthur Griffith, Michael Collins, and William T. Cosgrave, refused the terms proposed unless the Irregulars agreed to give up their arms. Cosgrave affirmed that military action against the Irregulars would continue and the Government issued a statement declaring that the people had given them their trust and they were determined 'to protect and secure all law-respecting citizens without distinction' (27). John Dorney (2017) expresses the view that this was a reasonable argument: 'They did have a mandate to govern since the June election and the citizenry had long been crying out for a restoration of order' (28). Eoin Neeson (1998) argues that the Civil War need not have happened; it achieved nothing that could not have been dealt with by constitutional means; and, once started, it should not have lasted so long (29).

One of the great tragedies of the Civil War is that, in two months, it 'took the lives of more prominent members of Sinn Féin than had occurred in four years of armed struggle against British forces' (30). The minutes from Dublin Corporation meetings show that much time was devoted to votes of condolence and expressions of sympathy, as had been the case following the Easter Rising in 1916 and through the War of Independence. At the meeting of 17 July, a vote of sympathy was passed for Cathal Brugha who had died the previous week from a gunshot wound sustained during hostilities. Brugha had played a prominent part in the 1916 Rising and the War of Independence, he had chaired the historic first meeting of the Dáil in January 1919, and had subsequently taken a firm

Cataĺ bruġa
A ṗuaiṗ báṗ aṗ ṗon na h-Éiṗeann aṗ an 7aḋ Lá Iúil, 1822

Cathal Brugha died on 7 July 1922.

Dublin City Library and Archive, Birth of the Republic collection.

anti-Treaty stance. The Lord Mayor lamented his loss, stating: 'No greater epitaph can be written on the tomb of Cathal Brugha than that he was an Irishman who never asked any Irishman to do what he was not prepared to do himself' (31). At the same meeting, Hanna Sheehy-Skeffington proposed that prisoners captured by the National Army on behalf of the Government should be treated as prisoners of war and she evoked the names of Thomas Ashe and Terence MacSwiney. Importantly, the Lord Mayor, himself a pro-Treaty member of Dáil Éireann, seconded the motion and it was passed. Laurence O'Neill had always felt strongly on this issue, regardless of sides, and the treatment of prisoners would become a recurring theme for the Corporation over the months ahead. By now, the battle of Dublin had resulted in a comprehensive military victory for the Free State Government, but, 'since it inaugurated a prolonged Civil War, it was a hollow triumph in many ways' (32).

Prominent leaders on both sides of the conflict continued to pass away. In early August, the anti-Treaty TD, Harry Boland, died from gunshot wounds. On 12 August, Arthur Griffith, President of Dáil Éireann died of a brain haemorrhage and was replaced by William T. Cosgrave. Ten days later, Michael Collins, on the way to a meeting in Cork with the apparent intention of trying to bring an end to the war, was killed by a single shot to the head near Béal na mBlath, West Cork. He was thirty-one years old. A special meeting of Dublin Corporation was convened for eleven o'clock on Saturday 26 August in the Oak Room of the Mansion House, where Michael Collins had attended many meetings. Councillors, some still reeling from shock, paid glowing tributes to Collins, and the following resolution was passed (33):

THE LATE HARRY BOLAND

August 1922 was a tragic month, with the deaths of prominent leaders on both sides of the conflict, including Harry Boland at the start of the month.

Dublin City Library and Archive, Birth of the Republic collection.

> *That we, the Municipal Council of the City of Dublin, in special meeting assembled, place on record an expression of our deep sense of horror and grief on the untimely and tragic death of General Michael Collins TD, Commander-in-Chief of the National Army, and of the irreplaceable loss which it entails to the Irish Nation, and we tender our heartfelt sympathy and condolence to his relatives, and to his colleagues in the Government and Army, in their sad bereavement.*

Noticeably, the Lord Mayor, Laurence O'Neill, did not speak during the meeting. *The Irish Times* reported (34):

The Lord Mayor, who had been indisposed during the week, under the care of his physician, became deeply affected and moved to tears when it became his duty to put the resolution. He was so overcome that he could not trust himself to speak, and signified to the members by a motion of his arm to rise. The resolution was then passed in silence, the members standing in their places.

Though showing signs of faltering health, the Lord Mayor led the Dublin Corporation delegation at the funeral of Michael Collins and his burial in Glasnevin Cemetery on 28 August.

Laurence O'Neill attended the meeting of the third Dáil on Saturday 9 September but it turned out to be one of his last public engagements for the best part of a year. He suffered 'a serious break-down in health, a massive burn-out marked by physical and psychological exhaustion' (35). Given everything he had been through over the preceding years, it is little wonder that his health broke down. In the Lord Mayor's absence, different colleagues took his place, most frequently

The funeral of Michael Collins on 28 August 1922.

National Library of Ireland.

Alderman Alfie Byrne. The Civil War continued even though, militarily, the National Army was dominating. It should have been possible to negotiate an end to the conflict during the closing months of 1922 but, frustratingly, various peace attempts broke down.

Members of Dublin Corporation continued to regularly raise concerns about the treatment of prisoners and they established a committee to examine the issue, much to the annoyance of the Free State Government. The committee was created following the meeting on Monday 9 October at which Maud Gonne MacBride, though not a councillor, was permitted to speak. It turned out to be a stormy meeting and Alderman Alfie Byrne, deputising for the Lord Mayor, struggled to retain control in front of a boisterous public gallery. Maud Gonne MacBride alleged that there were between six thousand to seven thousand prisoners in jail, many in Dublin, and that the conditions were a disgrace to any civilised country (36). It was agreed that the Corporation's medical officer, Dr Matthew Russell, and a deputation of councillors should visit prisoners and report to the council.

> PUBLIC HEALTH COMMITTEE,
> 28 CASTLE STREET,
> DUBLIN, 14th. October, 1922.
>
> DEAR TOWN CLERK,
>
> As directed by the Municipal Council, I applied for permission to visit the prisons. I applied at the Wellington Barracks, and the O/C. informed me that he could not admit me without an authority from the Adjutant-General. I then visited Portobello Barracks and interviewed the Adjutant-General, and showed him a copy of the resolution passed by the Municipal Council directing me to visit and report on the sanitation of the prisons. He stated that there was a competent staff under a Director-General, Dr. Maurice Hayes, who were looking after the sanitation of the prisons, and that he would send me a written reply. Up to the time of writing I have not received any communication.
>
> I am,
> Dear Town Clerk,
> Yours faithfully,
> M. J. RUSSELL,
> Medical Officer of Health.
>
> John J. Murphy, Esq.,
> Town Clerk.

Letter by Dr Matthew Russell, the Corporation's Medical Officer, to the Town Clerk, John J. Murphy, explaining that he had been denied entry to Wellington Barracks.

Minutes of the Municipal Council of the City of Dublin, 23 October 1922, Dublin City Library and Archive.

At the next Corporation meeting on 23 October, elected members were furious when it was reported that Dr Russell and the deputation had been refused entry by the military authorities and the Government to inspect Dublin's prisons. Alderman Alfie Byrne, chairing the meeting, informed the councillors that he had received a phone call from William T. Cosgrave on 13 October. Cosgrave assured him that while the Government was not willing to permit the visitation of prisons by the Corporation deputation, he was happy to tell him that there was no ill-treatment of prisoners. He admitted that there was a problem of overcrowding but claimed this was not the fault of the Government (37).

Ironically, having spent much of the meeting on 23 October lambasting the

Government, councillors were then asked to consider another item on the agenda – the resignation of William T. Cosgrave from the council following his election as President of Dáil Éireann. Councillors paid glowing tributes to their departing colleague and recorded a vote of appreciation for his many years of service on the municipal authority. Alderman Alfie Byrne stated that Cosgrave had won the respect of all parties over the years by his courtesy and excellent manner (38).

In November, Dublin Corporation – which, according to John Dorney (2017) 'displayed marked neutral tendencies throughout the Civil War' – again incurred the wrath of the Government when it wrote to both sides to try and broker a ceasefire (39). The Government criticised the Corporation's intervention and issued a terse reply to the members of the municipal authority: 'Ill-considered resolutions and correspondence of this nature, far from being conducive to peace, tend to a prolongation of disorder inasmuch as they encourage the Irregulars to believe that by holding out they can force the Government to grant them better terms, than already offered' (40). The composition of the Corporation, though predominantly pro-Treaty, was interesting. An IRA intelligence report, dated 19 November 1922, broke down the fifty-two pro-Treaty councillors as follows (41):

10	Hard Pro-Treatyites, 'real bad eggs'
10	Treaty – including Laurence O'Neill and Alfie Byrne
32	Pro-Treaty, 'but not so bad'

The same intelligence report listed sixteen councillors as 'Republicans' and 'Anti-Treaty'. Without the steadying influence of Laurence O'Neill in the Mayoral chair, meetings of the Corporation became increasingly fractious. The meeting on Monday 6 November was again described by *The Irish Times* as 'stormy'. Members heard from another deputation about the treatment of political prisoners by the Government. Helena Molony urged the councillors to initiate an inquiry and stressed: 'We do not want this matter referred to the members of the Corporation who are members of the Dáil. To bring the matter before the Dáil is like going to the devil, who has a court in hell' (42). Mrs. Cathal Brugha also addressed the meeting and reiterated the call for the Corporation to establish an inquiry. After a debate, it was agreed that the members of the deputation appointed on 9 October would act with the Public Health Committee and with other councillors to receive evidence on the treatment of prisoners. One week later, the inquiry began in the Mansion House, with Councillor Patrick T. Daly presiding, in spite of the Government insisting that the Corporation had no power to hold a sworn inquiry on the issue. Councillor Daly told the people present at the inquiry that evidence would be given under oath. He stated that he would not allow the inquiry to become a farce and added that the Government would be asked 'to give safe conduct to any and all witnesses coming or going to and from the inquiry' (43). Inquiry hearings were typically held twice a week at the Mansion House for the remainder of November. At its third sitting, a letter was read from the Government in response to the request for 'safe conduct' to participants. In rejecting the request, the letter stated: 'I am to point out that a sworn inquiry, in the circumstances, is illegal, and if it is persisted in, the matter will be referred to the Chief State Solicitor, with a view to advising on a prosecution' (44).

Despite the threat of legal action, the inquiry continued. It heard evidence from Thomas Fisher who stated that his eighteen-year-old brother, James, had been executed the previous Friday. A few days prior, James had written a letter to his brother saying that he was well and that they would be together for Christmas. The Fisher family received no correspondence from the Government about James standing trial. Instead, they read about his execution in the newspaper and, later, received a telegram, as follows (45):

> *Remains of James Fisher have been coffined and buried in consecrated ground – Provisional Government.*

As the Government had pointed out, the Corporation inquiry was illegal and it did not have any power. Nonetheless, it attracted large crowds and received generous newspaper coverage. As such it served a useful purpose in exposing the systematic beating and torture of prisoners (46). Much of the evidence was graphic and harrowing and highlighted the brutality of three men in particular – Charlie Dalton, Joe Dolan, and Frank Bolster. The inquiry heard about Christopher Ferguson, an eighteen-year-old anti-Treaty guerrilla, arrested for shouting 'Up the Republic'. He was beaten by intelligence officers and, in his own words: 'They gripped me by the hair and banged my head against the wall again and again … I was told to go on my knees as I was going to be shot, a cocked revolver was put against my chest and a shot went off behind me. It was blank but I was told the next one would be death for me' (47). Ferguson was then beaten repeatedly around the head with pistols until a sergeant intervened. A report from the inquiry was presented to the full council but it did not go any further and no disciplinary action was taken against pro-Treaty forces for their abusive treatment of prisoners. The Provisional Government – led by William T. Cosgrave who had served as a councillor for many years – was not impressed by the actions of the Corporation. As John Dorney (2017) records: 'Legal action was not taken against the Corporation for its inquiry but local elections due to be held in January 1923 were postponed for six months and the Government would not forget what it considered to be the hostility of the Dublin Municipal government to it' (48). Thomas Morrissey (2014) notes the irony of the situation: 'In the past, the council perceived itself as speaking for the Irish people in supporting prisoners held by an alien power, now it was a local assembly protesting against the lawfully elected Government of the country on behalf of rebels who had taken up arms against that Government' (49).

Fresh Civil War atrocities in November and December 'saw the country sinking more deeply into the mire' (50). Erskine Childers, who was secretary to the Treaty negotiating team in 1921, had subsequently become a leading figure in the anti-Treaty campaign. After being arrested at home on 11 November and condemned to death, he was executed by firing squad in Beggars Bush Barracks on 24 November (51). At the end of the month, three more Dublin anti-Treaty Volunteers were executed at Beggars Bush. Even pro-Treaty supporters, and newspapers such as the *Irish Independent*, were appalled at the executions and questioned the need for the Government to act so severely. *The Irish Times* took an alternative perspective. Though mourning the death of Childers, an editorial the following day stated (52):

> *When the Wicklow elections put Erskine Childers at the bottom of the poll, he, like his leader, Mr. de Valera, repudiated the verdict of democracy and took arms against the State. Now he has paid the penalty ... Cannot Mr. de Valera and his followers consent even now to give the country the peace for which it craves?*

These executions at the end of November prompted Dublin Corporation to launch a peace initiative but, as recounted above, the Government dismissed the Corporation's efforts as 'ill-considered'. On 7 December, a day after the formal establishment of the Irish Free State, the pro-Treaty TD, Seán Hales, was killed on his way to the Dáil. The Government response was devastating with the execution the next day in Mountjoy Prison of Liam Mellows, Rory O'Connor, Joseph McKelvey, and Dick Barrett. A sombre mood enveloped the meeting of

Republican propaganda material describing difficult conditions in Mountjoy Jail, with the potatoes described as 'absolutely inedible'.

Dublin City Library and Archive, Birth of the Republic collection.

Dublin Corporation on Monday 11 December, at which Alderman Alfie Byrne moved a resolution of sympathy for the parents and relatives of Hales, Mellows, O'Connor, McKelvey, and Barrett. Councillors again discussed what role the Corporation might play in restoring peace but a despondent Alderman Byrne stated: 'For the moment, we have nothing to report of a favourable nature' (53). Alderman Andrew Beattie expressed the frustration of those in the room when he asked, 'Are we going to sit here from month to month and see awful happenings, without doing our utmost to bring about peace?' (54).

Two weeks later, the Corporation was mourning the untimely passing of another of its members. Alderman Joseph MacDonagh had started the year seconding the nomination of Laurence O'Neill as Lord Mayor. He had won a seat in the last General Election as an anti-Treaty candidate and was later arrested following the outbreak of the Civil War. He was removed from Mountjoy Prison on 23 December with a burst appendix and died on Christmas Day. 1922 ended with an increasingly pointless Civil War continuing and, amidst the ongoing turmoil, Dublin Corporation held no election at the start of the following year. This meant that Alderman Laurence O'Neill, recuperating from poor health and absent from the council, continued in office as the city's first citizen.

Accordingly, it was Councillor Patrick T. Daly who chaired the Corporation meeting on Monday 8 January 1923 and he proposed that the report of the inquiry examining the ill-treatment of prisoners should be printed for general information. The Corporation's Law Agent intervened to say that, as the inquiry itself had been illegal, the expenditure required to print copies of the report was not legal. A two-thirds majority of council was required to pass the motion but, much to his exasperation, Councillor Daly failed to achieve the target and the motion was not carried. However, a defiant Daly declared, amidst applause from the public gallery, that he would arrange to get the inquiry report printed privately. Whether the absence of Laurence O'Neill was a crucial factor or not, Corporation meetings were now increasingly poorly attended and more chaotic in nature. Alderman Alfie Byrne presided over the meeting on Monday 15 January, which was scheduled to start at three o'clock in the Mansion House. Thirty-five minutes later, only sixteen councillors were present and, as the quorum of twenty had not been reached, the meeting was adjourned. *The Irish Times*, a persistent critic of the Corporation, reported: 'A number of women who had been admitted to the gallery gave free expression to their opinion of some of the councillors'

(55). The mood of the council was pessimistic in the early months of 1923, and not just because of the continuing Civil War. Another factor is what Diarmaid Ferriter (2004) has referred to as the 'utter contempt' that had quickly developed at central Government level for local democracy (56).

Antrim-man, Ernest Blythe, had been appointed as Minister for Local Government and Public Health in 1922 by William T. Cosgrave and he wasted little time in stamping his authority (57). Officials of the Department of Local Government and Public Health were sent to audit and inspect many local councils and the difficulties of local authorities 'were viewed from the centre with exasperation' (58). The main official in the department was the Secretary, Edward (known as E. P.) McCarron. McCarron was a controversial appointment and he was 'greatly distrusted by many local authorities' given that he was a former Local Government Board official under the British regime (59). The attitude of Blythe, McCarron and other senior officials in the Department of Local Government and Public Health was both paternalistic and austere: 'They were less committed to local democracy than to notions of rectitude and efficiency' (60).

Ernest Blyth.

National Library Ireland.

Blythe had steered the Local Elections Postponement Act 1922 through the Dáil in December, in the midst of the Civil War – the first of many times central Government would defer local elections over the coming decades. The minister was also working on a significant piece of legislation, the Local Government (Temporary Provisions) Act. This legislation gave power to the minister to dissolve local authorities and replace them with a centrally-appointed commissioner. During a committee-stage Dáil debate on the proposed legislation in February 1923, Blythe singled out Kerry County Council for criticism. He stated that the council had not met over the previous eight months and that rate collection was at a standstill. He concluded: 'Local administration in that particular case [Kerry County Council] cannot be pulled together unless there are powers to appoint Commissioners to carry on the work of the local authority which has fallen to bits' (61). During the same debate,

Deputy Darrell Figgis took issue with the minister and argued: 'It is a power [the power of dissolution] that one could imagine, under circumstances that do not prevail, could be very dangerously used' (62).

While rate collection in counties such as Kerry was indeed a shambles, there was a feeling that one motivation behind the proposed legislation was to curtail the activities of troublesome local authorities, especially those who were showing support for the anti-Treaty side in the Civil War. Ultimately, despite criticisms, the Local Government (Temporary Provisions) Act was passed on 28 March 1923. The essence of the 1923 act, as contained below, was that the minister could dissolve a local authority having first ordered an inquiry into its performance. The reinstatement of the council, following a new election, would be decided by the minister with no timeframe indicated.

Suspicious of Blythe and McCarron, and having crossed swords with the Government on the treatment of prisoners' inquiry and efforts to initiate peace, members of Dublin Corporation again clashed with the Government early in 1923. The Government sent a letter to the Corporation directing that no monies should be paid to the dependants of Corporation employees held in military custody. This cut across a decision that the Corporation had reached on 22 January that dependants in such circumstances should receive half the salary. This meeting again proved a very difficult one for Alderman Alfie Byrne to chair due to a boisterous public gallery, with *The Irish Times* describing 'a running fire of comments and interjections' making debate difficult (63). With the Civil War moving inevitably towards a victory for the Free State Government, Dublin Corporation continued to aggravate them by expressing concerns about the treatment of Republican prisoners. When Maud Gonne MacBride was arrested on 10 April and interned in Kilmainham, she went on hunger strike and the Corporation called for her release. The Corporation also received a letter from one of its imprisoned members, Councillor Joseph Clarke, who wrote from the Curragh Internment Camp, alleging ill-treatment and torture. After the declaration of a ceasefire by anti-Treaty forces on 30 April, the Civil War was effectively at an end but Marie O'Neill (1994) describes the aftermath as 'long and bitter' with Republican prisoners kept in custody (64). Once again, the Corporation argued that a deputation from the municipal authority should be permitted to visit prisons. Once again, this was rejected by the Government, leading to the councillors 'protesting against the denial of a right which had been allowed even during the Black and Tan regime' (65).

Though the ending of the Civil War promised a period of peace and stability, this was not necessarily what the future held for Dublin Corporation. Relations between the council and the Free State Government were strained and rumours were circulating around the city that the Corporation might be dissolved under the provisions of the 1923 act.

Local Government (Temporary Provisions) Act, 1923

Section 12

(1) The Minister may at any time he thinks fit, order a Local Inquiry into the performance of its duties by any Local Authority.

(2) If and whenever (a) the Minister is satisfied, after the holding of such a Local Inquiry, that the duties of a Local Authority are not being duly and effectually discharged by such Local Authority, or (b) a Local Authority wilfully neglects to comply with any lawful order, direction or regulation of the Minister, or (c) a Local Authority fails to comply with any judgement, order or decree of any Court in Saorstát Éireann, **the Minister may, by Order dissolve such Local Authority, and either order a new election of members of such Local Authority or transfer the property and the several powers and duties of such Local Authority to any body or persons or person he shall think fit.**

(3) Whenever the Minister makes an Order under the foregoing sub-section dissolving a Local Authority he may appoint such and so many persons as he shall think fit to perform the duties of such Local Authority and may from time to time remove all or any such persons and appoint others in their place and may fix the tenure of office, duties and remuneration of all such persons.

(4) The remuneration of all persons appointed under the foregoing sub-section shall be paid out of the revenue of such Local Authority as part of its expenses.

(5) At any time after a Local Authority has been dissolved under this section the Minister may by Order cause a new election of members of such Local Authority to be held, and upon the completion of such new election all the property, powers and duties of the dissolved Local Authority shall vest in the body elected notwithstanding that the same body may have been transferred by the Minister under the section to any other body, persons or person.

(6) The Minister may from time to time by Order do all such things and make all such regulations as in his opinion shall be necessary for giving full effect to any Order made by him under this section.

The Local Government (Temporary Provisions) Act, 1923.

No sooner had the Civil War ended than the Government made the decision to dissolve Kerry County Council on 9 May. The council was replaced by a Commissioner, Philip Monahan, who was appointed by Minister Ernest Blythe. When Dublin Corporation met on 28 May 1923, Councillor George Lyons moved a motion that: 'The suggestion recently made to the Minister of Local Government for the abolition of this elective assembly is unwarrantable, unjustified and reactionary'. The suggestion referred to by Councillor Lyons had been made by the Dublin Citizens' Association and it enraged the elected members. In a lengthy and passionate speech, Lyons took aim at the Citizens' Association and the press (66):

> *In the press, the Corporation is continually misrepresented. Members of the council are represented as a lot of 'fat-bellied capitalists' with Regent Street hats and Punchestown coats. Only one member of the Corporation wears a tall hat, and that only on Sundays, and he is a member of the Citizens' Association … The citizens should remember that this is the Corporation that carried on the business of Dublin during all the trouble, defying the mighty British Government and refusing to send our books to audit, and yet the British never suggested that the council should be abolished.*

The resolution was passed unanimously, even though 'there was barely sufficient attendance to form a quorum' (67). The following day, the Government dissolved Leitrim County Council but would it take on Dublin Corporation, the oldest pubic body in the country? Councillor Lyons had drawn attention to the Corporation defying the British, this argument was being turned on its head by the Government, as Eunan O'Halpin (1991) explains (68):

> *[William] Cosgrave and [Kevin] O'Higgins learnt an obvious lesson from the use of local councils to subvert British rule: the more leeway such bodies had, the more these could embarrass and defy central government. After independence they took steps to thwart Republicans attempting to use the same tactics against them.*

Dublin Corporation was in the firing line. It was not a Republican local authority and had remained impressively neutral during the Civil War. Nonetheless, it had antagonised the Government whose view was that 'sovereignty and self-government was to be vested in central Government, accountable to an Irish parliament in Dublin, not dispersed or extended to local areas' (69).

Part 2: Dublin Corporation on Trial

Chapter 6
Preparing the pitch

The 1923 legislation - and its immediate use with the dissolutions of Kerry County Council and Leitrim County Council - not only worried the members of Dublin Corporation, it also emboldened the critics of the capital's municipal authority. Alderman Alfie Byrne presided at a special Corporation meeting in the Oak Room of the Mansion House on Monday 23 April 1923 to hear from a delegation of business interests in the city – the Dublin Chamber of Commerce, the Dublin Citizens' Association, the Dublin Mercantile Association, and the Merchant Drapers' Association. The meeting had been called for this specific purpose and it had been a custom of the Corporation for many years to hear from such delegations. Despite this, objections were raised by some elected members, led by an irate Alderman William O'Brien who told the meeting (1):

> We ought to consider whether we hear these gentlemen or not. As members of the Corporation, we are fairly well acquainted with their views, since they use the press to lecture the Corporation on what we ought to do. One body has gone the length of asking the Local Government Department to wipe the Corporation out and appoint a Commissioner. I don't see why they should come here now to lecture us further.

He received support from Councillor Tom Lawlor who claimed that the business deputation had no confidence in this Corporation, or indeed any Corporation. This view was countered by Alderman Andrew Beattie who said that the Corporation should hear from a large body of the city's ratepayers. He added that waste and excessive expenditure were still features of the Corporation. On a vote of twenty to eighteen it was agreed to receive the delegation, although there was a clearly some hostility in the room towards them, especially the Citizens' Association.

First to speak was John Charles Malcolm Eason of the Dublin Chamber of Commerce who stated that citizens and ratepayers were concerned with the burden of high rates in the city; they were 'alarmed and astonished' that the rates for the current year had been fixed at 19 shillings and 10 pence (2). Sydney Orr spoke for the Citizens' Association and, predictably, he was challenged by councillors during his presentation. Orr tried to reassure the elected members that he had not come to the Mansion House to lecture them but he did readily admit that his association had gone to the Local Government Department to get the Corporation dissolved and replaced by a commissioner. He asserted that all departments of the municipal authority were not working economically and he focused particularly on housing. He referred to a recent contract placed by Belfast Corporation for fifty-six kitchen houses at a cost of £351 a house; such houses, he claimed, would cost £1,500 in Dublin. Labour councillor, Tom Farren, objected strenuously – in his view, the figure was untrue and Orr should withdraw it. Eventually, Orr did withdraw his remark, following an intervention from the Acting Lord Mayor, Alfie Byrne, who said that no house built by the Corporation would cost £1,500 (3). Council members were in no mood to bow down, as was evidenced by Councillor Patrick T. Daly who challenged the President of the Mercantile Association as to how many members of his deputation had ever demonstrated enough civic spirit to stand for local election and give their time to the benefit of the city.

One week later, high rates and municipal maladministration were the topics discussed at a lunch meeting of the Rotary Club at Kidd's Restaurant. The main speaker was Dr Lombard Murphy who had been part of the deputation to the Mansion House. He complained that the motion to allow them to speak was only passed by two votes and he criticised the Labour councillors who had mainly voted against. Lombard also commented on the unwelcoming attitude of the elected members, stating that 'certain Corporation members seemed to treat us an invading army that should be repelled with fire and sword' (4). Figures were presented at the lunch meeting showing that Dublin Corporation labourers were paid far higher wages than their equivalents in Belfast, Liverpool, and Glasgow. Significantly, the political nature of the council was criticised by Sparkhall Brown whose view was that: 'Political matters ought to be left to the Dáil' (5). One of the outcomes from the meeting was an agreement that the business associations in the city should come together to contest municipal and parliamentary elections. To some extent, the Municipal Reform Association was already occupying this space.

During the summer, the Lord Mayor, Laurence O'Neill, made a welcome return to the Corporation. His calm leadership qualities had been badly missed over the preceding twelve months. With his health and self-confidence not fully restored, O'Neill opted not to contest the General Election of August 1923 and, so, his time as a TD turned out to be very brief. The election brought victory for the Government party, now called Cumann na nGaedheal, but there was also a strong Republican anti-Treaty vote. John Dorney (2017) claims that the rise of the anti-Treaty vote was perhaps sympathy for how they had suffered at the Government's hands in the Civil War, 'but could also conceivably be interpreted as a vote to encourage them to take peaceful lines rather than persist with armed struggle' (6). Under the Lord Mayor's stewardship, Dublin Corporation continued to raise the issue of the treatment of political prisoners, still detained despite the ending of the Civil War. At its meeting on Monday 24 September, the following resolution was approved (7):

> *That, in the opinion of the Council, the time has arrived when all prisoners, interned or otherwise for what are considered political offences, ought to be set free immediately; that the release of the prisoners will be an interpretation of the manifest desire of the electorate, which found definite expression in the recent elections; and that such a course of policy will do more to restore harmony and promote the national ideal than any other alternative now placed before the people of Ireland.*

The proposer of the motion was Councillor Michael Flanagan who said that approximately fifteen thousand men and women were currently imprisoned. The longer they were held in prison, the more bitter they would become, leading to a possible vendetta when they were eventually released. Councillor Michael J. Moran opposed the motion and described it as a waste of time: 'If the Government feels that it cannot release these prisoners, I am satisfied. The safety of the people is of far bigger importance than the release of these people' (8). The resolution, with the support of the Lord Mayor, was passed on a vote of nineteen to nine and a copy was sent to the Government.

Thomas Morrissey (2014) refers to the 'growing alienation' between the Corporation and the Government, and at its meeting on Monday 8 October, the municipal authority once again questioned the treatment of prisoners (9). The Corporation also met the following Monday for a brief meeting to express its outrage after the body of Noel Lemass, an employee of the local authority, was found in the Dublin Mountains. Lemass had taken an anti-Treaty stance in the Civil War and was arrested in August 1922, only to escape and move to Britain. He returned to Dublin and to the Corporation after the ending of the Civil War but was abducted in broad daylight on Exchequer Street Dublin in July 1923 (10). For three months, nothing was known of his wellbeing or whereabouts until the discovery of his body. In its resolution, the elected members of Dublin Corporation described Lemass as an 'esteemed and worthy officer of this Council who had been foully and diabolically murdered' (11). An addendum was added which condemned 'the system which organises and sustains those murder gangs' (12). The resolution was passed unanimously, with all members standing, before the meeting was adjourned. At its next meeting the following week, Councillor Hanna Sheehy-Skeffington alleged that a prisoner had died at the Curragh or Newbridge (this was denied by the military authorities) and the Corporation resolved once more to request that a delegation of its members be permitted to visit Dublin prisons. On Monday 29 October, the Lord Mayor read the response from General Richard Mulcahy, on behalf of the Government; it was a firm refusal.

ᴀɪʀᴇᴀᴄᴛ ᴄᴏsᴀɴᴛᴀ,
(MINISTRY OF DEFENCE),
ᴅᴇᴀʀʀᴀɪᴄ, Ρᴏʀᴄᴏʙᴇʟʟᴏ,
ᴅᴀɪʟᴇ ᴀᴛᴀ ᴄʟɪᴀᴛ,
25th. Oᶜᵗᵒᵇᵉʳ, 1923.

Fo-Chleireach na Cathrach,
Oifig an Ard-Chleirig,
Baile Atha Cliath.

A CHARA,

I am directed by General Mulcahy to refer to your letter of the 23rd. instant, requesting that arrangements be made to enable the Lord Mayor, the Medical Officer of Health, and the Chairman of the Public Health Committee to visit certain prisons in Dublin, and, in reply, to state it is not intended under present conditions to grant facilities for the inspection of prisons except to persons who may be appointed for the purpose under the provisions of the " Public Safety (Emergency Powers) Act, 1923." I am to add that arrangements in this connection are at present under consideration.

Beir Beannacht,
C. B. O'CONNOR,
Runaidhe.

Ministry of Defence letter, on behalf of General Richard Mulcahy, refusing to allow the Corporation's Medical Officer and members of the Public Health Committee from visiting prisons in Dublin.

Minutes of the Municipal Council of the City of Dublin 29 October 1923, Dublin City Library and Archive.

Councillor Hanna Sheehy-Skeffington proposed a motion, which was passed, criticising the reply and repeating the demand for councillors to visit prisons. Her motion ended with the following words: 'We remind the Free State Authorities that in refusing this right, they are acting in an arbitrary manner, and are depriving the representatives of the citizens of a right accorded to them even during the Black and Tan regime'. Councillor Lawrence Raul argued that the Lord Mayor, as Chief Magistrate, should go to the prisons and demand to see the men and women held in custody. This drew a protest from the Lord Mayor who commented: 'Would you like to put the Lord Mayor of this city in a humiliating position in the face of this letter?' (13). Councillor Michael J. Moran bemoaned that the issue was being continuously raised as it was wasting the Corporation's time.

As noted previously, Dublin Corporation had a clear pro-Treaty majority but, poor attendance at meetings, meant that anti-Treaty members were sometimes able to dominate proceedings. Other councillors, including the Lord Mayor, though pro-Treaty, were appalled by the heavy-handed actions of the military authorities and they had consistently spoken against the ill-treatment of prisoners. They had done so during the War of Independence and the Civil War and were now doing so in the post-Civil War period. *The Irish Times* reported that the ordinary business of Dublin Corporation, at the meeting on Monday 5 November, 'was interrupted three times in order that the treatment of political prisoners be discussed' (14). A resolution was passed calling for the release from prison of Éamon de Valera and all anti-Treaty deputies 'as the first step to national unity, peace and prosperity' (15). The councillors also came up with a novel proposal that the Lord Mayor should be allowed to go to the Dáil and present a petition on the issue of the treatment of prisoners. The privilege of presenting a petition to Westminster had previously existed. A predictable response was received from the Ceann Comhairle of the Dáil, stating that there was 'no procedure at present by which petitions can be presented to the Dáil' (16). The Government was becoming more and more irritated by the Corporation and this increased in December when the council criticised the Government's reduction of the old age pension.

The Corporation meeting of Monday 17 December heard an interesting debate on a proposed road improvement grant of £10,190 from the Department of Local Government, based on two conditions – the money should be spent on trunk roads and the men to be employed should, as far as possible, be former National Army men. Correspondence crossed between the Corporation and the department, with the local authority arguing that the money should not just be used on trunk roads. A response from the department indicated that the Minister was willing to consider that request but added that wages should not exceed £2, 10 shillings a week. A furious Councillor Patrick T. Daly described the letter from the Department of Local Government as impertinent, adding (17):

> *We were anxious to get rid of the English Local Government Board. We did get rid of them but, though the name has changed, the same Roman hand is controlling our affairs. Economy is to be everywhere, except in the salaries of the Ministers.*

It seems that even when trying to offer a grant for road improvements to the council, the Government was incurring the wrath of the councillors. As Thomas Morrissey (2014) notes: 'To President Cosgrave, so long a proud member of the Corporation, the hostility of the Municipal Council must have been difficult to accept with equanimity' (18).

1924 was an exceedingly difficult year for the Lord Mayor, Laurence O'Neill. It began with the death of his wife, Annie, on Wednesday 16 January at their home in Portmarnock. The funeral drew a large crowd to Baldoyle Church on Friday 18 January. *The Irish Times* reported that the President of Dáil Éireann, William T. Cosgrave, was one of the first mourners to arrive (19).[2] In the aftermath of his wife's death, it appears that Dublin Corporation did not have a Mayoral election and Laurence O'Neill continued in office. The previous year, he had remained in his post though ill and absent from the council. Perhaps, it was intended that a Mayoral election would be held in February but a letter, dated Wednesday 20 February, from the Secretary in the Department of Local Government, E. P. McCarron, to the Town Clerk of Dublin, John J. Murphy, changed everything. The letter stated:

> *I am directed by the Minister for Local Government to state that serious complaints have arisen concerning the administration of the Dublin Corporation. The Minister has found himself under obligation to order a local inquiry under Section 12 of the Local Government (Temporary Provisions) Act, 1923, into the performance of its duties by the Corporation. He has accordingly directed his Inspector, Mr. O'Dwyer, to hold such inquiry, the arrangement for which will be notified at an early date.*
>
> *Section 12 of the Local Government (Temporary Provisions) Act, 1923, authorises the Minister at any time to order an inquiry into the performance of its duties by any local authority. If and whenever the Minister is satisfied, after such inquiry, that the duties of a local authority are not being duly and effectually discharged, 'the Minister may, by Order, dissolve such local authority, and either order a new election of members of such local authority or transfer the property and the several powers and duties of such local authority to any body or person he shall see fit'.*

---

2 According to Thomas Morrissey (2014, p. 225), the biographer of Laurence O'Neill, 'President Cosgrave, it appears, did not attend the funeral, nor did any of his ministers'.

The press reacted in a triumphalist way to the news of the impending inquiry. An *Irish Independent* editorial stated that there would be no sympathy for the Corporation and referred to 'the gross mismanagement of the business and finances of the municipality, and the callous disregard of the ratepayers, and even of the unemployed ex-soldiers of the National Army' (20). The latter point related to the road improvement grant offered by the Government, on the condition that former National Army soldiers were employed. Dublin Corporation was in the process of negotiating terms and conditions with the Department of Local Government, especially on the issue of wages. It had not rejected the grant but the Government and the press had interpreted the councillors' reluctance that way. An editorial in the *Evening Herald*, under the heading 'Hope for Dublin Ratepayers' was particularly brutal (21):

HOPE FOR DUBLIN RATEPAYERS

Editorial in the *Evening Herald*
Friday 22 February 1924

The long suffering, over-burdened ratepayers of Dublin have read this morning, with a feeling of relief and satisfaction that the Minister for Local Government has decided to hold an inquiry into the administration of the Corporation. This decision has been conveyed to the Town Clerk in a letter from the Ministry stating, that in view of the serious complaints regarding the administration of the affairs of the Corporation an inquiry must be held.

Practically every department of municipal administration in Dublin has been mismanaged. The facts are notorious. Jobbery and corruption are rampant at the City Hall. An enormous sum is paid annually for the cleansing of the streets, and yet Dublin is in that sense the dirtiest city in Europe. When the inquiry comes to be held, it is hoped that the investigators will go fully into the circumstances of the cleansing of the thoroughfares, say, twenty-five years ago, and those of today; also, that they will exercise a little curiosity as to the circumstances of the appointments in this department and their relations, if any, to the 'Civic Fathers' of the present or the past time.

The members of the Municipal Council at the present stage of its deterioration are, for the most part, men of straw. They pay no rates except those which even the ordinary workingman cannot escape. They are not fitted in any sense to hold authority or to administer any municipal department. We hope that they have now arrived at the end of their tether, and that the Government will kick them out. All Dublin has been disgusted at the action of this gang in refusing to accept the Government grant of £10,000 for the benefit mainly of ex-soldiers of the National Army. Corrupt and unscrupulous brutes is the only description we can apply to a large proportion of the members of the Corporation. Although we fear and dislike bureaucracy, still we shall be glad to hear that the Government has put a term to the existence of the present Municipal Council of Dublin.

Minutes, with a list of attendees, from the Dublin Corporation meeting of Monday 25 February 1924.

Minutes of the Municipal Council of the City of Dublin 1924, Dublin City Library and Archive.

At the meeting of Dublin Corporation which followed on Monday 25 February, the normally placid Lord Mayor hit back at the *Evening Herald*. He informed his fellow councillors that he did so more in sorrow than in anger and he realised that attacking the press was foolish as they would have the last word (22). In a strong defence of the Corporation, the Lord Mayor claimed that the *Evening Herald* had over-stepped the line of decency and fair criticism; he was upset in particular by the description of the elected members as 'corrupt and unscrupulous brutes'. Unable to resist a comment about the President of the Dáil, William T. Cosgrave, Lord Mayor O'Neill argued (23):

> *With an experience of what my colleagues went through in the Black and Tan regime of three or four years ago, when the men and women of this Council faced prison, and even assassination, and when they loyally stood behind President Cosgrave, then a member of the Corporation and Minister of Local Government, it is my belief that if this Corporation faltered then, and did not take up a stand in giving a lead to the country, it is questionable whether you would have a Free State Government in power today.*

While the councillors supported the strong words of the Lord Mayor, it is interesting to note that some expressed concerns that the press might now become even more antagonistic towards the Corporation.

Two days later, the Government formally gave notice that the inquiry into the performance of the Corporation would commence in the Oak Room of the Mansion House at eleven o'clock on Tuesday 11 March. The notice was printed in the newspapers with the invitation that any person interested could attend and give evidence. A financial statement presented by the City Accountant, Mr. Mangan, at the next Corporation meeting on Monday 3 March did little to improve the mood of the councillors.

> Having referred to the disadvantages under which the Corporation had worked during the past few years, with its ranks depleted by death and tragedies, the Lord Mayor concluded :—'' Although I do not agree with many of the things done by my colleagues, not agreeing with the majority of my colleagues on their action in connection with this much-talked-of grant—and it does not follow that I am right and they are wrong—I must say that I have never yet found anything in their actions which would merit the designation applied to them by the *Evening Herald*, as being 'corrupt and unscrupulous brutes.' "

The Lord Mayor responded powerfully to the criticism of the *Evening Herald*. He was particularly upset by the description of the elected members as 'corrupt and unscrupulous brutes'.

Minutes of the Municipal Council of the City of Dublin 25 February 1924, Dublin City Library and Archive.

Mangan outlined that the financial situation was grave, mainly due to the inadequacy of the grants being paid by the Government, far less than what had been received by the local council under British rule. He also criticised the delays in grants being issued by the Government which sometimes did not come near to recouping the Corporation for the money it paid for school meals and public health services. The burden regrettably then fell on the hard-pressed ratepayers of the city. Councillor Patrick T. Daly argued that rural councils were benefitting hugely from generous agricultural grants and that the Corporation was at a disadvantage. He regretted that there did not seem to be any public spirit in Dublin to make itself heard on the issue (24).

Attention then turned to the upcoming inquiry. Lord Mayor, Laurence O'Neill, suggested that the wave of concerted attacks in recent months against the Corporation and its elected members led him to believe that 'the pitch was being prepared' for the holding of an inquiry. He vigorously argued: 'But I am sufficiently long in the Corporation to know that the charges are not true, nor half true, nor quarter true, nor true at all' (25). He proposed the following motion:

> *That for the purpose of safeguarding the rights of the Corporation, as representing the citizens of Dublin, a Committee be appointed to act on behalf of the Council, in conjunction with the Town Clerk, the Law Agent and the City Accountant, at the inquiry mentioned in the Ministry's letter; that authority be given to engage such legal and other assistance as may be found necessary, and to incur such expenditure as may be required for the proper presentation of the Corporation case; and that the Minister for Local Government be requested to furnish the Council with copies of the serious complaints referred to in his letter.*

The Lord Mayor then named the committee that would be formed, comprising the chairs of the Corporation's standing committees.

- Lord Mayor, Alderman Laurence O'Neill

- Alderman Michael Staines

- Councillor Patrick T. Daly

- Councillor Patrick McIntyre

- Councillor J. J. Murphy

- Councillor Lawrence Raul

- Alderman William O'Brien

- Alderman James Hubbard Clark

- Alderman Seán T. O'Kelly

- Alderman Tom Lawlor

- Councillor Hanna Sheehy-Skeffington

During a prolonged discussion with contributions from many councillors, one question arose time and time again – what were the 'serious complaints' referred to in the letter by E. P. McCarron, on behalf of the Minister Séamus Burke? In seconding the Lord Mayor's motion, Councillor Hanna Sheehy-Skeffington claimed that there was a prejudice for star chambers and secret inquiries. In a strongly-worded speech, she asserted (26):

> *The dice is loaded against the Corporation and Commissioners are already appointed to draw salaries when the Corporation is superseded. Neither I, nor my colleagues, will shirk a fair public inquiry, but we will resist a blindfold inquiry. We are entitled to know who has formulated the complaints and why, with such startling suddenness the Government, proverbially slow, has so eagerly responded to the pressing of the button. … It would be very fitting for the Free State Government to put its own house in order first. The Corporation is to be tried and found guilty, not for its deficiencies, but for its virtues, and the Dublin press and the Free State authorities are clamouring for its blood.*

Councillor Tom Farren maintained that the Corporation should have nothing to do with the inquiry until such time as an indictment was tabled containing the alleged complaints. In the absence of an indictment, the Lord Mayor should refuse the use of the Mansion House for the inquiry. In closing the discussion, the Lord Mayor stated: 'If you pass this resolution, I think you may safely leave it in the hands of the Committee I have named, to carry out your wishes. Personally, I will have nothing whatsoever to do with this inquiry until first I am in a position to know what are the charges against myself and against my colleagues. I give that undertaking to this Council' (27). The motion was passed unanimously.

When the Corporation met the following Monday, the day before the start of the public inquiry, it was clear that there was tension in the air and things were beginning to unravel. Letters were read from three elected members – Councillors George Lyons, R. Rooney, and Joseph McGrath – tendering their resignations. An irritated Councillor Patrick T. Daly proposed that consideration of the resignations should be postponed for three months. It was wrong, he believed, for three members of the council to try to resign the day before the inquiry. Councillor Daly's proposal was accepted and consideration of the resignation letters was deferred. Another letter also drew a sharp response from the elected members. The Town Clerk read aloud correspondence from Councillor Michael J. Moran to the Department of Local Government asking for an immediate inquiry into the workings of the municipal workshops in Stanley Street. Councillor Moran alleged mismanagement, waste and excessive expenditure.

Letter from Councillor Michael J. Moran to the Minister of Local Government, 19 February 1924

Minister of Local Government
Government Buildings
Upper Merrion Street

Sir,

I beg to suggest you should hold an immediate inquiry into the working of the Stanley Street Workshop for the reasons which I shall set forth.

Last week, the Streets Committee had under its consideration estimates for the Cleansing Department for the year ending March 31st 1925. They include an item of £1,400 under the heading of Harness. As there is a stud of 132 horses, and one set of harness for each, plus a reserve stock, this amount would appear to be excessive for repairs, even allowing for replacements.

The Superintendent said, when pressed, that he could do with half of the £1,400 if he were allowed to go outside and procure his requirements under this heading. Half the amount was allowed.

£1,400 divided by 132 works out roughly at £11 per horse, and I understand a set of new harness could be purchased for £12, 10 shillings. The expenditure to the end of the current year will be £1,377, 8 shillings. I also ask that an inspection of the harness be made by your Department and an inquiry held into the expenditure of this latter sum.

Similarly, an estimate of £3,000 was put in by the Superintendent for Refuse Tramway Wagons, the intention being to purchase ten new ones at £90 each and to spend the remainder on repairing the thirty in stock. This shows that while new ones can be purchased outside for £90, Stanley Street would require £70 each for repairing the old ones.

I claim this as an excessive figure for repairs, but, as in the case of the harness, the Superintendent stated if he could go outside for repairs he could put in a much smaller estimate. The current year's expenditure under this heading will be £1,871, 19 shillings, 5 pence.

As far as I am aware, this sum will be spent entirely on repairs.

I claim also that there should be an inquiry into this expenditure, as well as an examination of the wagons, to see if the condition is such as to justify this expenditure. A sum of £2,500 was agreed upon.

I make the same case regarding the estimated figure for Plant (carts, brushes, etc.); £5,000 estimated, £4,000 agreed on. At Stanley Street prices, the Superintendent stated, the work could not be done, but if allowed to go outside he could submit an estimate for the figure allowed.

Expenditure for the current year is £4,609, 10 shillings, 11 pence. I ask, as in the cases of harness and tramways, this expenditure, as well as the condition of this plant, should be inquired into.

I respectfully suggest that this is an urgent matter which should receive your immediate attention.

The annual estimates are now being considered, and if a reform is possible, it should be effected before the striking of the rate.

The Cleansing Estimates are bound to be exceeded next year by the amounts the Committee has reduced them if last year's prices are to prevail.

I ask the inquiry to be held for another reason. Various efforts have been made during the last seven years to get the Municipal Council to adopt the practice of competitive tenders. Every effort was unavailing, including the recent one where the Council is committed to an expenditure of about £6,500 on the City Hall and Municipal Buildings for alterations, repairs, and painting.

I am sending a copy of this letter to the Town Clerk.

Yours truly,
(Signed) M. J. Moran

In response, Councillor Lawrence Raul said that he found it 'extraordinary' for a member of the Corporation to go behind the backs of the council and the Finance Committee in such a way. He drew attention to the inquiry which would start the following day, saying that it would be run by a group of people who had badly mis-managed the affairs of the country for the past two years. It was his contention that central Government was 'squandering money in a fashion that a country as rich as America could not stand' (28). Alderman Seán T. O'Kelly also argued that it was an unworthy act of Councillor Moran to send his letter to the Department of Local Government and Public Health; it should first have been placed before the council for debate. Councillor Moran defended his actions, saying that everything in his letter was true.

It was against this backdrop that Dublin Corporation faced into the public inquiry, effectively a trial into its performance and competence. As a footnote, the councillors, at the meeting on Monday 10 March, passed a vote of condolence for the former Town Clerk, Henry Campbell, who had passed away. Campbell would have been an interested spectator at the public inquiry; he had clashed repeatedly with the councillors before being sacked in December 1920. In proposing the vote of condolence, the Lord Mayor paid Campbell a back-handed compliment: 'It is true that he [Campbell] made a great number of enemies, but it is equally true he made a great number of friends' (29).

The coming weeks would determine if Dublin Corporation had more enemies than friends.

Chapter 7
A false start

A large crowd packed into the Oak Room of the Mansion House on Tuesday 11 March for the start of the eagerly-anticipated inquiry into the administration of affairs by Dublin Corporation. Minister Séamus Burke had appointed Nicholas O'Dwyer, Chief Engineering Inspector in the Department of Local Government and Public Health, to conduct the inquiry. Twenty-nine year-old O'Dwyer was born in Rahan, County Limerick, on 20 February 1895 and had attended St. Colman's College in Fermoy, County Cork. He studied engineering at University College Dublin before becoming involved in the Independence struggle, in which he played an active role as brigade engineer and battalion commander in the East Limerick Brigade. In February 1921, he was appointed an engineering inspector in the pre-Truce Department of Local Government and retained his position in the same department when it was officially established after the Treaty. Interestingly, he would later go on to become a Commissioner in Kerry to administer the affairs of the dissolved County Council (1).

Inspector O'Dwyer opened the proceedings by formally declaring that the inquiry had been ordered by Minister Burke under Section 12 of the Local Government (Temporary Provisions) Act, 1923. He wanted to first reference a letter from Dublin Corporation's Assistant Town Clerk, dated 4 March, on foot of the meeting of the council the previous day. The letter, based on a resolution of the elected members, had sought for Minister Burke to furnish the Corporation with details of the complaints made against them. O'Dwyer explained (2):

Nicholas O'Dwyer chaired the local government inquiry in Dublin.

From Dissolved (2017) by Aodh Quinlivan.

> *From the terms of the letter, one would conclude that the members of the council are under the impression that the inquiry is being held to deal with some specific complaints. This is not the case. The inquiry is*

being held into the performance of its duties by Dublin Corporation. I have no further instructions than to hold an inquiry on these terms, and the report I will make on the inquiry will be absolutely and entirely based on the evidence that will come before me, and nothing else. I think this should satisfy the members of the council.

Having assured everyone present that he would conduct 'an absolutely impartial hearing' he then called on the Corporation's legal representatives to deliver opening remarks. The Corporation had assembled an impressive legal team, led by two senior barristers, Patrick Lynch and James Carrige Rushe Lardner. The Corporation's first choice barrister had been Senator Samuel Lombard Brown but he was unavailable, due to prior commitments. Brown was aligned to a largely ex-Unionist group of Independents in the Seanad and he supported Cumann na nGaedheal. He had a particular interest in the improvement of local government and spoke regularly on the topic. James Lardner was Brown's replacement at the public inquiry. The Corporation's barristers were supported by a solicitor, P. White, and instructed by Ignatius Rice, the Corporation's Law Agent.

Fifty-eight-year-old Lynch was the first to speak. Born in Newmarket-on-Fergus in county Clare, he had studied in the Royal University of Ireland and was admitted to the bar in 1888. He had served as Crown Prosecutor for county Kerry, and – as a noted Home Ruler - he contested the 1917 East Clare by-election for the Irish Party. He was defeated by Éamon de Valera after a fraught campaign during which Sinn Féin labelled him a 'Castle Place Hunter' who wanted to become an MP to grab some English gold (3). Within a year of the election, Lynch became a member of Sinn Féin and he defended many IRA activists in the 1920s and represented the widow of Tomás MacCurtain at the inquest which followed his murder in Cork in 1920. He took the anti-Treaty side in 1922 and, notably, he was the senior counsel at the court martial of Erskine Childers in the same year. Later in life, he served as a senator for Fianna Fáil and he was appointed Attorney General in 1936 by his former political opponent, Éamon de Valera.

Rising to speak, Lynch told Inspector O'Dwyer that he would limit himself at this stage to a few short remarks. Referring to the Inspector's opening words, he expressed surprise that no specific complaints had been formulated against the Corporation. He stated that the Corporation 'courted the fullest inquiry' and he guaranteed that the council would submit the fullest evidence and documentation needed to allow the Inspector to form his final judgement. His only request was that notice would be given if specific issues or the work of individual committees were to be discussed at the inquiry.

As the legal representative of the Dublin Citizens' Association, Norman Keough, next delivered his opening remarks. He wanted to assure the Inspector and those present in the Mansion House that the members of the Citizens' Association were not hostile towards the Corporation; however, they took the view that they 'were entitled to criticise and investigate any rate or any action of the Corporation which they thought should be questioned' (4). He argued the Association's members were angered by the 'enormous increase' in rates since 1892. He alleged that there was over-staffing and over-paying in the Corporation which contrasted with the salaries paid generally in Dublin. It was the view of those he represented that the Stanley Street workshops were uneconomical and there was bewilderment that the Corporation had turned down a Government grant in excess of £10,000 for road improvement works and the relief of unemployment. Keough conceded that the present Corporation had inherited mistakes made by its predecessors but he concluded by stressing that if rates continued to rise year on year as they had been doing, it would result in financial bankruptcy for many firms and shops in Dublin.

W. J. Larkin represented the Dublin Tenants' Association at the inquiry and he did not hold back in his opening comments, describing the Corporation as incompetent and inept. He asserted that 'a whole new council should be elected by the people' (5). To some extent this was missing the point, as the Government had chosen to postpone local elections; the outcome of the inquiry in Dublin would decide if the existing council should continue or else be replaced by an appointed Commissioner. Larkin's rambling opening statement ended with a declaration that his remarks were made free from all party politics, and based 'solely upon a Christian civic conscience and duty' (6).

At this point, Nicholas O'Dwyer called a brief adjournment and, when the session, resumed, Patrick Lynch – representing the Corporation – asked to speak. He drew attention again to the meeting of Dublin Corporation on 3 March at which the elected members had passed a resolution to form a committee to represent the views of the council at the inquiry, once it had been furnished with details of the complaints made against them. Lynch argued that – in the absence of charges or complaints being tabled – the elected members on the committee were now in 'a peculiar position' as they had no authority to proceed further without consulting the Corporation. On this basis, he called for the inquiry to be adjourned until such time as a special meeting of the Corporation could be held. James Lardner supported the call for an adjournment, as did Lord Mayor Laurence O'Neill who stated (7):

> It is not fair to such an old body as the Corporation, that undoubtedly does good work for the citizens, that specific charges have not been tabled. I court the fullest inquiry, as do my colleagues, but I think it is only fair that the application of counsel (to adjourn) should be granted.

The matter was discussed for a while before Inspector O'Dwyer made a judgement. Though frustrated, as he was anxious for the inquiry to proceed, he recognised the validity of the request brought forward by Lynch. Accordingly, he adjourned the inquiry until Wednesday 19 March, on the understanding that a special meeting of Dublin Corporation would be held the previous day. This brought the first day of the inquiry to a premature and rather anti-climactic end. Inspector O'Dwyer was entitled to feel frustrated but, equally, the Corporation was correct in its approach. The problem had been created by E. P. McCarron's letter (on behalf of Minister Burke) of 20 February which specifically stated that an inquiry was to be held arising from 'serious complaints' which had arisen. It now transpired that there were no such complaints.

When the members of Dublin Corporation met for the special meeting on Tuesday 18 March, the proceedings were animated. The Lord Mayor stated that, following the opening of the inquiry the previous week, he had received a report from the Corporation's committee asking for further instructions in relation to the inquiry. On that basis, the Lord Mayor proposed (8):

> That, as the fact has been disclosed and admitted by the Inspector at the opening of the inquiry, that no serious complaints were made to the Ministry as mentioned in the letter of the Local Government Board on 20 February, and as the Local Government Department have the power to hold the inquiry, we instruct the Town Clerk and Law Agent to take the necessary steps to have the Corporation represented to meet any charges made against the Corporation.

Alderman Seán T. O'Kelly strenuously objected to the proposal and called the inquiry 'nothing but a sham' (9). He argued passionately that there were no grounds for the inquiry, which was set up for political purposes, and that the whole process had been instigated by the Dublin press, which was 'as rotten as ever' (10). He tabled a counter-proposal that the council's officials be instructed to take no part in the inquiry because of the failure to produce the complaints alluded to. Many councillors contributed to the debate which followed and it was clear that the room was divided. The opinion expressed by Councillor John Stritch was that the rate-paying public did not hold the elected members in high regard and it would be fatal to the interests of the Corporation if the inquiry was not held. Corporation member and senator, Tom Farren, disagreed (11):

> *The Corporation has not been treated fairly. There has been a considerable amount of propaganda carried on for some years against the Corporation ... The Corporation now finds itself in the position that it has taken this scurrilous propaganda lying down, and there has been no serious effort made to combat it. The Government has taken advantage of this propaganda to hold the inquiry. In my opinion, the Government have made up their minds to make some charge in the personnel, or the removal of public bodies in the country, and they want to provide a reason for the holding of these inquiries. Unless I am summoned as a witness, with reference to any question in which I have been involved, I will have nothing to do with the inquiry.*

Councillor Lawrence Raul stated that the Corporation had a very satisfactory record, considering the terrible four years that they had been through. Like other elected members he believed that the inquiry was politically motivated: 'The reason for the inquiry, in plain truth, is that the Government's jobbers have not been installed, and they wanted to have them installed' (12). Councillor Raul was referring to the controversial Government grant, with the condition that employment would be given to former National Army men. At this point, Alderman Seán T. O'Kelly intervened and asked for his proposal to be amended, with the insertion that 'This Council resolves to take no further part, by itself or its officials, in the inquiry'. This provoked a strenuous response from the Lord Mayor (13):

> *For my part, I want to make my position clear with respect to the Council and to my colleagues, who have stood behind me so long. If*

this inquiry is held, no matter what this Council may vote, I am not going to allow fourteen or fifteen years, during which I was a member of this Council, go by the board. I am not going to let every Tom, Dick, and Harry come in and level charges against me. So I am going to the inquiry, and if any personal charges are made against me, I will be there to refute them.

Councillor Hanna Sheehy-Skeffington proclaimed that the inquiry was a waste of time as Commissioners to administer the affairs of the Corporation had already been appointed. She claimed to know the names of the Commissioners but did not provide them to the meeting when asked by the Lord Mayor. A vote was finally called on the motion put forward by Seán T. O'Kelly (to boycott the inquiry) but this was defeated by twenty votes to thirteen with the Lord Mayor abstaining. Accordingly, the initial motion of the Lord Mayor – that the Corporation would take part in the inquiry – was carried.

| Ayes | .... | .... | .... | .... | .... 13 ; |
| Noes | .... | .... | .... | .... | .... 20 : |

The following were the ayes :—

Alderman O' Kelly, T.D. ;
    „   Charles Murphy, T.D.;
Councillor Mrs. Sheehy-
          Skeffington, M A. ;
    „   Joseph Clarke ;
    „   Hynes ;
    „   Atkins ;

Councillor Raul ;
    „   Brennan ;
    „   John Lawlor ;
    „   Farrell ;
    „   Gordon ;
    „   O'Maoilfhinn ; and
    Senator Thomas
          Farren ;

The following were the noes :—

Alderman Staines ;
    „   J. Hubbard Clark,
          J.P. ;
    „   Shields, M.A. ;
    „   Alfred Byrne, T.D. ;
    „   Thomas Lawlor ;
Councillor John Farren ;
    „   McIntyre ;
    „   McCarthy, J.P. ;
    „   Michael J. Moran ;
    „   Stritch, J.P. ;

Councillor O'Callaghan ;
    „   Senator Mrs Wyse-
          Power ;
    „   Chase ;
    „   Doyle, T.D. ;
    „   Daly ;
    „   Brohoon ;
    „   John J. Murphy ;
    „   Michael T. Byrne ;
    „   O'Toole ; and,
    „   Maxwell-Lemon ;

Seán T. O'Kelly's motion to boycott the public inquiry was defeated by twenty votes to thirteen.

Minutes of the Municipal Council of the City of Dublin, 18 March 1924, Dublin City Library and Archive.

The press reaction to the meeting – and the attempts made by Seán T. O'Kelly for the Corporation to boycott the inquiry – was harsh. A blistering editorial in the *Freeman's Journal* stated (14):

Political passion explains a good deal of the hot air that was released in the Corporation yesterday. These gentlemen are prepared to turn municipal administration upside down for the purposes of anti-Treaty propaganda, and the knowledge that the Government will not tolerate performances of this kind in future lashes them into frenzied rage. Fortunately, there are sufficient members there who realise that noisy defiance of the central Government is not good business, though it was deplorable that yesterday, as on practically every occasion when critical matters come up for discussion, half the Corporation did not think it worthwhile to put in an appearance. Now that the boycotters have failed, we may expect the inquiry to proceed with its task. If it can introduce reforms which will save us from the sort of display to which we were treated yesterday, the citizens will be profoundly grateful.

Never someone to take criticism lying down, Seán T. O'Kelly fired off a letter to the *Freeman's Journal* in response to its editorial. He argued that he was not opposed to the inquiry which has been established 'by the so-called Minister for Local Government of the Free State' but he was not satisfied 'that the people in Merrion Street, judging by their record during their short period in office, are the people best qualified to show the Dublin Corporation how to administer its affairs economically' (15). O'Kelly again took the opportunity to criticise the fact that an inquiry was taking place in spite of the lack of charges or complaints made against the Corporation (16):

> *When we attended the inquiry [on 11 March], we demanded the production of these complaints, and, to our astonishment, the Inspector admitted that they did not exist. This speaks for itself in the matter of the honesty and good faith of the so-called Minister; he makes a bogus accusation which falls to the ground on the admission, under compulsion, of his own Inspector.*

Nonetheless, the inquiry did continue and a big crowd attended the proceedings in the Mansion House on Wednesday 19 March. It would prove to be another difficult day.

Chapter 8
No blows struck to damage the Corporation

Patrick Lynch began the second day of the inquiry by explaining the outcome of the meeting of Dublin Corporation the previous day. Despite the fact that Inspector O'Dwyer had admitted that no specific complaints had been made against the local authority to the Minister for Local Government, the elected members had decided to have the Corporation represented to meet any charges tabled at the inquiry. Lynch concluded his remarks by stating that the onus was now on Norman Keough, representing the Dublin Citizens' Association, to 'lay his charges on the table' (1). A flustered Keough – already on the back foot – asserted that it was his understanding that Dublin Corporation officials would be the first to be examined. By asking him to bring forward specific charges, he was being placed in an awkward position: 'The whole burden of the inquiry is being thrown on my shoulders' (2). Lynch immediately pounced and reasonably stated that nobody was making any complaints against the Corporation, bar Keough's clients who had asked for the inquiry. Keough weakly responded that he had no witnesses present as he believed that the Corporation witnesses would be the first to be examined. Dismissing this argument, Lynch stated that it had been made quite clear on the first day of the inquiry that it was up to Keough and the Citizens' Association to make its case as to why Dublin Corporation should be dissolved. This clash between Lynch and Keough represented a poor start to the second day's proceedings. Keough, in particular, was not impressing those gathered in the public galleries or indeed Inspector O'Dwyer. An irritated O'Dwyer agreed with the position taken by Patrick Lynch and called on Keough to make his case.

Though disconcerted and somewhat unprepared, Keough took to the floor to lay out complaints against the Corporation, focussing on wages. He criticised the incomplete nature of the information which had been provided by the local authority. In relation to street maintenance, the wages had not been segregated from the total expenditure. For 1922, a sum of £44,541 was paid for paving, and of that sum, there was £28,078 for wages. For 1923, the sum paid for paving had increased to £50,458, but it was not shown what portion of the total was paid in wages. Keough claimed that wages paid to Corporation employees was excessive and that the burden was ultimately falling on citizens through 'enormous increases in the rates' (3).

Warming to his task, Keough next shifted his attention to sick pay which had risen from £2,780 for 1922-1923 to £3,560 for 1923-1924. He argued that this was 'a considerable amount' for sick pay. He then stated that there was an item on the financial accounts submitted by the Corporation that he did not understand. An amount of £3,700 was listed under the heading of 'Holidays for Wages Staff'.

> *What are 'Holidays for Wages Staff'? I presume it is a category for holidays for the staff paid by wages and not by salaries. If a man is entitled to holidays in the year, surely the salary or wages should go into the ordinary figures and not be set out separately?*

Keough had recovered his composure quite well but the complaints he made against the Corporation were trivial and it could not be said that he had landed a significant blow.

After a short break, Inspector O'Dwyer called on W. J. Larkin, representing the Dublin Tenants' Association. Larkin was sworn in and his contribution was more forceful and hard-hitting than that of Keough. Larkin concentrated initially on the state of the streets – he described three laneways off Sheriff Street as being in a 'deplorable and shocking condition'. They had not been cleaned for a very long time, 'except for the removal of diseased dead dogs' (4). Repeating part of Keough's testimony, Larkin argued that the citizens were paying far more for the services of the Cleansing Department than they should and he described the levels of sick pay as 'a damning indictment' against the Corporation.

Larkin was now in full flow, as he went on to state: 'The streets and lanes are a disgrace to civilisation, thanks to the lack of care and duty by the Cleansing Department, backed up by the callousness of the Corporation, who are not doing their duty' (5). He then made the staggering claim that, prior to Independence, due to things being so bad, he had written to Lord French and to Dr Matthew Russell, Medical Officer of Health, asking for the city's curfew to be suspended so that citizens in certain localities could be allowed to clean the lanes and streets near their tenements.

He described the condition of North Lotts as 'criminal' due to the defects in the sewerage system and he informed Inspector O'Dwyer that he had forty-eight specific points relating to the neglect of duty by the Corporation with regard to street cleansing and sanitation. In addition, he would provide the inquiry with letters from seventeen different doctors as to the prevailing conditions.

> *It is my view, and that of the Dublin Tenants' Association, that the Corporation has neglected its duty. The people's representatives have failed to see that the officials do their jobs. There is a lack of supervision by officials in the different departments, and yet their salaries have been enormously increased (6).*

Larkin next criticised the addition of five and-a-quarter pence in the pound to the public water rate, though the statutory limit of the increase was three pence. He drew howls of laughter from the galleries when he alleged that it was very difficult for people to get the books they wanted from the public libraries and that the reading rooms 'were packed with betting men and toughs of all descriptions' (7). Larkin concluded by stating that the Cleansing Department was not doing its job and promised to deal with the other departments as the evidence came up.

It was clear that Patrick Lynch, barrister for the Corporation, had a tough opponent in W. J. Larkin. Lynch had opted not to cross-examine Keough after his weak testimony, but he decided to challenge Larkin. However, Larkin responded strongly to Lynch's questions and asserted that, as the President of the Tenants' Association, it was his view – and that of his members – that the council appeared to have a general licence to spend as much as it liked, and how it liked.

Councillor Patrick McIntyre, Chairman of the Streets Committee, was then sworn in. Before the questioning of Councillor McIntyre commenced, barrister Patrick Lynch interjected with a familiar question: 'Is there any specific charge formulated against the Streets Committee?' (8). Inspector Nicholas O'Dwyer replied: 'Not that I know of' before turning to Norman Keough. Keough stated that the Citizens' Association was making no charges, other than the wages and cost of materials being uneconomical. Lynch jumped to his feet and argued that if definite charges were not being made, then Keough should not be permitted to question witnesses. Inspector O'Dwyer quickly ruled against Lynch and called on the inquiry to continue with the evidence of Councillor McIntyre.

Councillor McIntyre did his best to defend the activities of the Streets Committee, noting that there were sixteen members on the committee and, since he had taken over as Chairman, no meeting had fallen through due to the want of a quorum.

> *I have given my best attention to the work of the Cleansing Department. I am often up at six o'clock in the morning and go around to the various depots to see how work is being carried out. Whenever I find a dereliction of duty, I do not hesitate to report it and see that the matter is put right (9).*

Under cross-examination from both Keough and Larkin, Councillor McIntyre admitted that certain streets had been in a poor condition three or four years ago, but their surfaces were much improved in the last two years. It was his contention that the roads had been in bad repair due to military operations. When Larkin asked if the British War (War of Independence) or the Irish War (Civil War) was responsible for the disrepair, McIntyre replied: 'Both'. He continued his evidence by stating that the British Government had provided a grant of £11,000 for road repairs in 1922; accordingly, the cost of the improvement works had not been taken from the pockets of ratepayers. McIntyre stressed that Dublin could hold its own with most other cities with respect to roads, adding: 'Of course, if we had more money, we could do more work' (10).

At this point, Inspector Nicholas O'Dwyer adjourned the day's proceedings until the following morning, saying that the questioning of Councillor McIntyre would continue at that point.

The third day of the inquiry in the Mansion House, on Thursday 20 March, started with a clarification by the Inspector, Nicholas O'Dwyer. O'Dwyer called attention to a statement contained in a recent press report of the previous week's special Corporation meeting. As contained in the report, he was alleged to have said that 'no serious complaints [against Dublin Corporation] were made to the Ministry'. O'Dwyer's recollection was that he had said that no serious complaints had reached himself.

> *I am not called upon to enter into any matters between the Dublin Corporation and the Minister for Local Government. I will only deal*

with complaints that have reached me. I felt that the matter was made fairly clear before, but I thought it was desirable to draw attention to it today (11).

In reply, the Lord Mayor, Councillor Laurence O'Neill, stated that he had personally drawn up the motion for the Corporation meeting and he very was sorry to impute anything to the Inspector that he did not say or mean. However, the Lord Mayor added that the impression left on his mind was that the Inspector had stated that no serious complaints had reached the Ministry. He was sorry if he had misunderstood. Accepting the apology, Inspector O'Dwyer announced the continuation of the inquiry and called upon Councillor Patrick McIntyre, Chairman of the Streets Committee, to resume his evidence. McIntyre was well prepared and he proceeded to give a very detailed account of the activities of various departments under his authority. In the Sewers Department, he noted that there were one hundred and thirty-seven men currently employed, as against one hundred and twenty-eight in 1914. The increase was accounted for by the transfer of nine men from the main drainage section. In other sections of the Corporation, under the control of the Streets Committee, the number of staff employed had decreased. His committee was constantly seeking cost savings and efficiencies and were presently examining the possibility of saving £900 by eliminating some staff from the workforce.

Councillor McIntyre then referred to newspaper reports about nuisances that were alleged to exist at Hill Street and Glenville Street: 'If these nuisances exist at all, they exist on private property over which my committee has no control. If complaints were made that nuisances did exist on public property, we would see to it that these were remedied' (12). In response to a direct question from the Inspector, McIntyre explained that he was not in a position to give any information about estimates for the current year, as his committee was not finished with them yet. He added: 'Generally speaking, I find that the workmen give pretty good value for their money. In both cleaning and paving, the Corporation is anxious to have the most up-to-date methods adopted' (13). Councillor McIntyre had delivered a very polished performance in the witness box and this continued during cross-examination by Keough and Larkin. In response to a question from the former, McIntyre pointed out that the hours of unskilled labour were forty-four per week and the average minimum wage was sixty-four shillings a week. At the same point the previous year, the weekly minimum wage was seventy-three shillings. He was not able to say if the Corporation's minimum wage was more than the trade union rate.

Answering questions about the Paving Department, Councillor McIntyre said that there were twenty-six more men employed now than in 1914 and the number of horses was about the same. Up to 1908, refuse from the streets was removed by the barge 'Eblana' but, since then, carts were being used. After the present Corporation was elected into office in 1920, the use of the barge was discontinued; they now had six motor sweepers on the streets, as well as carts. At a recent Corporation meeting, a demand had been made for another motor sweeper and fifty men for night work. The fifty men had been taken on to deal with extra work.

Inspector O'Dwyer asked a few more direct questions, each of which was dealt with expertly by Councillor McIntyre. He repeatedly stressed that the departments under the auspices of the Streets Committee were doing their utmost to do work as economically as possible. For the current year, the estimate was £98,000 – compared to £95,500 for 1922/1923. The increase was due to the extra number of men employed. The estimate for paving for the year to March 1924, was £50,430, compared to £47,270 for 1923 and £49,250 for 1922. After a day of little drama, during which Councillor McIntyre had represented the Corporation very well, the inquiry was adjourned until the following morning.

The fourth day of the inquiry, Friday 21 March, saw Dublin Corporation officials present detailed evidence. First up was Norman Chance, Assistant Borough Engineer, who answered some gentle questions posed by Patrick Lynch. Chance maintained that the city's paving had improved considerably over the past four or five years. There were improvements also in the principal thoroughfares and in residential streets, such as those off South Circular Road. Chance did acknowledge that there were some areas where the work could be better and also that the Corporation's workers had not yet been through all of the city's streets to effect the improvements necessary. Answering a question by Norman Keough, Chance stated that the paviors employed were a mixture of half-temporary and half-permanent staff.

W. J. Larkin stood up and declared that he would like to examine the witness in relation to workmen's compensation claims set out in the estimate for 1923 under the heading of 'General Expenses'. This drew a sharp rebuke from Patrick Lynch, who appealed to Inspector O'Dwyer:

> *If we are to have a roving inquiry, the sitting will never end. When workmen are compensated, it is done under Act of Parliament, and the Corporation, or anybody else, cannot prevent it. It is not fair for people to come in here pretending to be friends of the poor and questioning the payment of compensation, though it has to be paid under Act of Parliament (14).*

Much to Larkin's annoyance, Inspector O'Dwyer sided with Lynch's argument; however, this did not stop the Inspector asking Norman Chance about pensions. Chance explained that workmen were not anxious to go out on pension, as a man of twenty-five years' service would drop about thirty shillings a week.

Next into the witness box was George Harty, the Corporation's engineer in charge of sewers and main drainage. He calmly explained the work of his department in which one hundred and thirty-six men were employed. There were two carpenters, eight bricklayers, one painter, a rodman, and one motor driver – all others were labourers. He felt that all of his staff did efficient work and he considered them to be 'some of the best tradesmen and labourers in Dublin' (15).

At this stage, the inquiry was interrupted by a member of the public gallery who rose from his chair to speak. John Landy from Rathfarnham stated that he wanted to give evidence as a citizen. Inspector O'Dwyer explained that he would be happy to hear the man's evidence but it would have to be at a later stage as that day's schedule was full. He then called forward John Devine, the Corporation's Superintendent of the Cleansing Department. Devine had a staff of five hundred and sixty-three, divided into eleven sections, each of which had an overseer. Like his fellow officials who had already given evidence, Devine was confident and unruffled in the face of questions. He dealt with a query about excessive expenditure by telling the inquiry that the Cleansing Department had one hundred and thirty-six horses, and a harness cost about £18 or £18, 10 shillings per set. The cost of repairs and maintenance of a harness worked out at about £7, 14 shillings, 3 pence per set.

Devine was followed by Mr. Keegan who was introduced as the Corporation official in charge of trees. His evidence was succinctly and impressively delivered, leaving little scope for cross-examination. Keegan had seventeen men under him, and a carter. They were responsible for approximately three thousand trees standing on the streets, of which they did not lose more than twelve in any given year. Each tree was planted in a footway and had to be watered for two years after planting and protected during this period. The trees also had to be pruned continuously, so as to leave plenty of room for pedestrians and people in carts who were passing. Given the number of trees under his control and the budget under which he operated – the estimate for the year was £3,500 – Keegan contended that he and his staff did very good work.

The final witness of the day was the Corporation's Town Clerk, John J. Murphy, who said that under an Act of Parliament, the Corporation could give a pension to any employee on a service of twenty years and on the age of sixty. The limit of the pension was two-thirds of the salary, taking the average of the preceding three years. The minimum wage was seventy-three shillings a week. Murphy further explained that no man over thirty was appointed on the permanent staff, and no man was employed unless the doctor certified him physically fit. When asked about the large burden on the ratepayers in respect of pensions, Murphy stated that this could be attributed to want of care in the selection of men appointed many years ago. In his view, the Corporation was now acting under a much more efficient system but a historic burden still existed. He added his opinion that there was no reason why employees should contribute to a pension fund (though this might be desirable in the interests of ratepayers) when Acts of Parliament made the payment of pensions compulsory.

At the close of Murphy's evidence, Nicholas O'Dwyer adjourned the inquiry for the weekend, until the following Monday morning. After four days of evidence, little had been produced to damage the Corporation. The council's officials had performed well in the witness box and were clearly well prepared. In addition, the barrister hired by the local authority, Patrick Lynch, was outperforming both Norman Keough, representing the Citizens' Association, and W. J. Larkin, representing the Tenants' Association. Keough had appeared as hapless and under-prepared while Larkin made bold and sweeping statements but lacked the forensic and methodical approach of Lynch.

Chapter 9
An ignominious end for W. J. Larkin

The inquiry recommenced after a weekend break for a short session on Monday 24 March. The reason for the brevity of the proceedings was to accommodate a special meeting of Dublin Corporation in the evening. Town Clerk, John J. Murphy, resumed his evidence and claimed parts of his testimony the previous Friday had been misrepresented in the press. He asked for the record to show that the Corporation minimum weekly wage was sixty-three shillings per week, not seventy-three shillings as reported. He was also reported as saying that pensions were fixed on the average salary for the past three years, but this was not the case. Patrick Lynch, representing the Corporation, excused the press by saying that acoustics in the room were poor and mistakes could easily happen. He noted however that it was best to quickly rectify these mistakes. Speaking in agreement, Inspector O'Dwyer asked the press to amend its reports and he then called upon W. J. Larkin to continue his questioning of the witness. Rather than ask specific questions, Larkin took the opportunity to deliver a short speech during which he criticised the Town Clerk and charged the Corporation generally with incompetence.

Respected councillor, Patrick T. Daly took to the witness box next, in his capacity as Chairman of the council's Public Health Committee. Daly provided details of the organisation of the committee and the number of officials under its control and he said that everything done by the committee was subject to the sanction of the Local Government Board. His committee and the Local Government Board did not always agree, but they always avoided a deadlock situation. W. J. Larkin raised some specific issues about people being incorrectly registered as owners of tenement properties before he asked about conditions at the Asylum Yard at Mark's Court, off Mark's Lane.

Councillor Daly admitted that conditions at the Asylum Yard were regrettably bad. He recalled the 'Belfast Pogrom' from 1920-1922 which saw many people move from Belfast to Dublin, with some of them residing in difficult circumstances in the Asylum Yard. The 'Belfast Pogrom' had brought a brutal period of violence, with urban rioting and the forceful removal of thousands of Catholic workers

This photograph is one of those taken by John Cooke in 1913 to illustrate the dreadful living conditions in Dublin. The 1911 census listed over one hundred people living in Asylum Yard.

Dublin City Library and Archive.

from the shipyards of East Belfast (1). While this resulted in some workers moving to Dublin, it hardly explained the state of affairs in the Asylum Yard.

After asserting, with some validity, that Councillor Daly had deflected the question, Larkin asked the witness if he recalled that Dr Oliver St. John Gogarty had charged the Corporation with corruption under the Public Health Acts. Councillor Daly denied any knowledge of this, adding: 'If Dr Gogarty has any such charge to make against the Corporation, now is the time to bring it forward' (2).

On this note, Inspector O'Dwyer ended the fifth day of the inquiry after what was effectively a half-day. A few hours later at the same venue, the Mansion House, Lord Mayor, Councillor Laurence O'Neill presided over a meeting of Dublin Corporation. The meeting was called to express the outrage of the council about the gun attack the previous Friday by a group of IRA men on unarmed British soldiers in Queenstown (Cobh) in county Cork. The British had retained a base at Spike Island after the Anglo-Irish Treaty of 1922 and a small group of anti-Treaty Republicans opened fire on a party of British soldiers and civilians as they arrived onto the pier in Queenstown. The attack resulted in eighteen of the soldiers suffering injuries, and one died. He was eighteen year-old Private Herbert Aspinall from Rochdale. In Dáil Éireann, William T. Cosgrave described the attack as 'a dastardly outrage' without parallel 'in its deliberation and savagery' while one British MP suggested in the House of Commons that what Ireland needed was another Cromwell (3).

Opening the special meeting of Dublin Corporation, the Lord Mayor stated that he was 'appalled and dismayed at the cowardly and brutal murder that was perpetrated in county Cork' (4). He expressed the wish that the 'fiends' responsible for the attack would be brought swiftly to justice and he called on his fellow councillors to pass the following motion:

> *That we, the Municipal Council of the City of Dublin, desire to express our horror and indignation at the brutal and cowardly outrage which occurred at Cobh on 21st March, the shooting upon unarmed and defenceless men, women and children; and we beg to express our deep sympathy with the relatives of the killed and injured, and with the people of county Cork.*

Alderman James Hubbard Clark, High Sheriff, seconded the motion and expressed horror at the death and suffering caused by 'wild barbarians' (5). Alderman Seán T. O'Kelly described the attack as 'a treacherous act which does not do any credit to Ireland' (6). He contrasted the unprovoked shootings in Queenstown with the War of Independence: 'When we went to war with England, we told her that we were at war with her, and gave her and her troops every chance of defending themselves, according to the laws of war' (7). Hanna Sheehy-Skeffington was one of the many councillors who spoke at the meeting and she joined the condemnation of the 'cruel and stupid outrage' (8). After the councillors had spoken, they unanimously passed the Lord Mayor's motion and stood in silence for a minute as a mark of respect for Private Aspinall.

The following morning, Tuesday 25 March, people gathered in the Mansion House for the sixth day of the inquiry. Entering the historic building that morning, nobody realised that the most dramatic day of the inquiry to date was about to unfold. In its report on the day's proceedings, *The Irish Times* headline read: HEATED SCENE AT INQURY, under which it ran a sub-headline, MR. LARKIN SILENCED BY INSPECTOR. The day began with an unexpected appearance by a new solicitor, Christopher Friery. Friery explained that he was representing the owner of a certain property on the north side of the city who, it was suggested by W. J. Larkin, was in collusion with some officials of the Corporation regarding the repair and maintenance of the property. Inspector Nicholas O'Dwyer agreed to hear the issue, and allowed Friery to call the property owner to the witness box where she was sworn in. Under questioning from Friery, she vigorously denied the allegations of collusion between her and Corporation officials. In fact, she maintained that the reverse was the case: 'I think that I have been rather severely dealt with by the sanitary officials of the Corporation as regards the houses I own' (9). The witness was examined at great length by W. J. Larkin but she maintained her story and insisted that she was not colluding with Corporation officials in the Sanitary Department. As Larkin continued to aggressively question the property owner, Patrick Lynch rose to express his displeasure at the line of inquiry being pursued by Larkin, and his tone. Lynch protested that charges were being made against Corporation officials, 'without a shred of proof' being brought forward to support the claims.

Turning to Lynch, Larkin angrily called on him to put the Corporation officials in the witness box. Lynch replied that he would not be dictated to by any blackguardism from Larkin. Larkin loudly repeated his refrain: 'Put up the Corporation witnesses'. Lynch pleaded: 'I must insist that every person, who is treated with courtesy and consideration by the Inspector, will behave himself with common decency … if he knows how' (10). Larkin's indignant response was: 'Put up the Corporation witnesses'. With Inspector O'Dwyer struggling to maintain control, barrister James Carrige Rushe Lardner, also representing the Corporation, asked to speak. He stated that he would stand for no imputation or impertinence. Turning to face Larkin, Lardner issued a direct admonishment to his legal rival: 'If you come here, you must conform to the ordinary rules of decency' (11). Growing visibly more irate with every passing minute, Larkin retorted that he would take no dictation on decency from Lardner. At this point, Inspector O'Dwyer valiantly tried to intervene and he called upon Larkin to sit down. Larkin refused, leading Lardner to protest: 'These charges are being bandied about under the shelter of a court of inquiry. It is time that Mr. Larkin should withdraw charges that he cannot prove' (12). Larkin burst into laughter and declared: 'You are getting sick of it. Put up your witnesses!' before sitting in his seat.

Lardner was struggling to maintain his own composure and, addressing Larkin, he stated: 'We are not going to put up witnesses for a cock-shy for your abuse. It is cowardice to make charges that are not proven' (13). Larkin's period in his seat did not last long, with *The Irish Times* reporting that he 'jumped up excitedly' before aggressively responding: 'For the first time in my life, I have been accused of cowardice by a man who asserts that the only dose for a man named Larkin is acid. I have never been known to run away from anything, and I will go to the extent of my life in defence of myself or the people I stand for. Why do you accuse me of cowardice?' (14).

After a momentary silence descended on the room, Lardner calmly gave his answer: 'Because you are acting in a cowardly way'. After Larkin again insisted that Lynch and Lardner should put the Corporation officials in the witness box, Inspector O'Dwyer managed to restore order temporarily and he permitted Friery to recall his witness. She claimed that she had been a member of Larkin's organisation – the Tenants' Association – but severed connection with it the previous year. It was since then that all the annoyance had started, she said. Rising once again to his feet, Larkin explained that when the witness had trouble in relation to one of her properties, he had fought her case in court. He asked how she could possibly now claim that he had done nothing for her. The witness, who was not named during the day's proceedings, then made a sensational claim. She said that when Larkin had asked for a subscription of £2 for the Tenants' Association she had put it in a box and handed it to Larkin, only for him to take it out and put it in his pocket. She was effectively accusing him of stealing money from the Tenants' Association.

By now, Larkin was fit to combust and he loudly protested his innocence: 'You are a contemptible perjurer. You tried to bribe me, and I refused to take it'. Inspector O'Dwyer intervened and twice asked Larkin to withdraw his last remark. Larkin declined to do so, adding: 'She is a perjurer. I won't withdraw my remark. She is a damned liar'. Responding, Inspector O'Dwyer said that he would hear from Larkin no longer and he ordered him to resume his seat.

Norman Keough, representing the Dublin Citizens' Association against the Corporation, interjected but he made no attempt to support or defend his colleague. Rather, the opposite was true. Keough asked the press to note that the charges of collusion were being made by Larkin alone and they had nothing to do with the Citizens' Association. He wished to disassociate himself from the unseemly row which had dominated the inquiry over the previous hour. Though lacking support from any quarter, Larkin once again asked if the Corporation officials were going to be called as witnesses. When Inspector O'Dwyer answered that the matter was closed, Larkin remarked: 'Yes, it has been closed by guilt'.

Resuming the inquiry, Thomas F. Cuffe took to the stand. He was the inspector in Dublin Corporation in charge of prosecutions. Though he was not one of the officials against whom Larkin was making an accusation, Cuffe began by stating that he had given twenty-five years of service to the Corporation and there never was any suggestion of collusion or impropriety against him. When Larkin asked if he could cross-examine the witness, Inspector O'Dwyer curtly replied 'No'. Larkin asked if he was allowed to question any witnesses. Inspector O'Dwyer's response was: 'You cannot, until you withdraw the remarks you have made' (15).

Larkin asserted that he stood by his remarks and pointedly asked the Inspector if he was now debarred from taking any further part in the inquiry. There was little ambiguity about the Inspector's answer: 'I have told you my decision, and I have no intention of altering it'.

The Corporation's Medical Officer, Dr Matthew Russell, was then called forward to testify, which drew an ironic remark from Larkin: 'You are safe now, Matt.' Larkin clearly felt that he had been unfairly silenced and that the Inspector was protecting the Corporation witnesses. Before Dr Russell presented any evidence, the Lord Mayor, Councillor Laurence O'Neill, was asked to speak. After being granted permission, he appealed to the Inspector to use his power to prevent citizens and witnesses from being grossly insulted by Larkin. The Inspector repeated that he had made his ruling and Larkin would not be heard from further until he apologised. Larkin, though, was a difficult man to silence and he caustically commented: 'You are safe too, Lord Mayor. I had a few pointers for you too, if I was allowed'.

Dr Russell proceeded to give evidence about the work being done by the Corporation's Public Health Committee. He claimed that the death rate in the city in 1918 was twenty-five per one thousand of the population. This had been reduced to fifteen in 1923. The Corporation had also been active in bringing convictions against people under the Food and Drugs Act. In 1923 alone, there were three thousand three hundred and thirty-six samples taken, one hundred and eighty-nine convictions, and fines imposed totalling £404. When Dr Russell had finished speaking, W. J. Larkin asked if he was permitted to cross-examine the witness. Inspector O'Dwyer said that he was not; this led to Larkin putting his papers in his briefcase, standing up, and leaving the room – much to the amusement of those in the public gallery. With the day nearing its conclusion, Councillor Jennie Wyse-Power told the inquiry that during her chairmanship of the Public Health Committee, Dr Russell had proven himself to be an excellent officer. The committee had progressed with a policy of abolishing private slaughterhouses and it had also done a great deal of work in the city with regard to child welfare.

A tired-looking Inspector O'Dwyer then announced that he was adjourning the inquiry for the day. There was much animated chatter in the public gallery after a dramatic day which had led to W. J. Larkin leaving the inquiry. Many questions hung in the air – would Larkin return the following morning? Would he apologise to Inspector O'Dwyer? Would the Tenants' Association have new legal representation? Did the entire case against the Corporation now rest on the shoulders of the hapless Norman Keough? As well as the extraordinary departure of Larkin, the sixth day of the inquiry had seen James Lardner come to the fore for the first time. Monaghan-born Lardner, now aged forty-four, was a formidable barrister of both Gray's Inn, London, and King's Inn, Dublin. He became a King's Counsel in 1921 and a bencher of King's Inn in 1924. He was also a well-known political figure as a Nationalist member of the House of Commons, taking a seat in a by-election in 1907 and retaining his seat in the two general elections of 1910. After the eight-year electoral gap, he chose not to contest the 1918 election. Lardner out-manoeuvred Larkin on day six of the inquiry and he certainly provoked the latter's ill-tempered outburst.

An even larger crowd than usual attended the inquiry the following morning, Wednesday 26 March. At the outset, W. J. Larkin was not present and the first witness called was Councillor John J. Murphy, as chairman of the Corporation's Housing Committee. He stated that over three thousand houses had been built during the past few years but, for financial reasons 'no marked impression had been made on the housing problem' (16). Replying to a question posed by the Inspector, Councillor Murphy explained that, in his estimation, the Corporation needed to build one thousand houses per annum for the next twenty years in order to cope with Dublin's housing crisis. Following a brief mid-morning break, excitement levels rose when W. J. Larkin strode purposefully into the room and walked directly to Inspector O'Dwyer before handing him a letter. With the Inspector's permission, Larkin read his letter aloud. He stated that, for the sake of the poor, and in order to avail of the privilege so kindly extended to him at the inquiry, he wished to amend the record of the previous day. If the Inspector would allow it, he wanted to add the phrase: 'The statement made by the witness is not true' and remove the words 'contemptible perjurer' and 'damned liar'. Larkin added: 'I am seeking this amendment to the record out of respect to womanhood generally and respect for the Inspector's position as adjudicator at the inquiry' (17). Attention now turned to Inspector O'Dwyer who thanked Larkin for the amendment and said that he had no objection to the new formula of words being inserted into the official minutes of the inquiry. If Larkin was relieved by this judgement, his relief did not last long. The Inspector continued and explained that, as Larkin had not apologised for his behaviour the previous day, he had no intention of altering his decision. Accordingly, he was not permitting Larkin to be heard at the inquiry. As a ripple of excitement, and some applause, spread through the room, Larkin left. He did not appear again at the inquiry.

After calling for order, Inspector O'Dwyer invited Councillor Patrick T. Daly to the witness box, in his role as the current chairman of the Public Health Committee. Councillor Daly presented the work of his committee and outlined the intention to install up-to-date machinery in the abattoir. In response to questions from the Inspector, he claimed that the work of the committee was very well done and he believed it could not be improved. This opinion was contradicted somewhat by Dr Matthew Russell who next resumed his testimony. The Corporation's Medical Officer was in a more critical mood than he had been a day earlier. He began by saying that he did not want the public to understand from his previous testimony that he or the Public Health Committee were at all satisfied with the prevailing conditions in the city. In his view, the housing conditions at the present time were appalling, and getting worse each year. Dr Russell's criticism, however, was largely directed at the national Government: 'If there is not a great housing policy brought forward by the Government, private builders and others, it is terrible to contemplate the over-crowding in Dublin in a couple of years' (18). Dr Russell continued by describing a particular problem faced by the Corporation and the Public Health Committee 'We do our best but, unfortunately, the worst class of tenements are owned by the poorest landlords and – with high unemployment – people want the cheapest places they can get. If the Public Health Committee proceeds too heavily against this class of landlord, they will simply abandon the houses and then the committee will have to go to a great deal of expense in keeping them clean' (19). He then added that he often wondered why workmen and tradesmen did not do more to expedite the building of houses, when the scarcity of them 'affected most of all their own class'. By now, it was noticeable that Inspector O'Dwyer was taking the lead with questioning, due to Larkin's absence and Keough's indifference. The Inspector asked if conditions were getting worse; Dr Russell's answer was emphatic: 'Yes, they are getting worse and worse' (20).

Town Clerk, John J. Murphy, was the last person to give evidence on the seventh day of the inquiry. He stated that the Corporation's aim was to provide affordable housing for the city's working classes. The economic rents would be about ten per cent of the cost of a building; therefore, the rent on a £650 house, which was a cheap one, would be £65 a year. Inspector O'Dwyer disputed the notion that £650 was cheap for a house, but the Town Clerk explained: 'The idea is to get those who can pay economic rent into the houses that we are building, and so make room for others in the houses that they leave' (21).

The Inspector called a halt to the day's proceedings and announced that they would resume the following morning at eleven o'clock. The inquiry had now sat for seven days and little damaging evidence against the Corporation had been produced. The local authority's officials and the chairs of its various committees were performing well in the witness box, appearing calm, professional, and well-briefed. On the legal side, the professionalism and thoroughness of barristers Patrick Lynch and James Lardner was very obvious. They had seen off W. J. Larkin and were easily out-performing Norman Keough.

Chapter 10
The business capacity of the elected members is challenged

As the inquiry reconvened on Thursday 27 March, it did so against the backdrop of two stories which were in that morning's newspapers. It was reported that Dublin Corporation would meet the following Monday to consider a report of the Finance Committee which recommended the re-grading of Corporation officials. The Finance Committee report noted:

> *If all the officials – numbering one hundred and ninety-one – dealt with in all of the re-grading scheme were to remain at their present salaries, and if their war bonuses were to be reduced to the Civil Service scale on 1 April next, the reduction would amount to £1,633. If, however, all the recommendations in the re-grading scheme are adopted, the total increase in salaries, as compared with 1923-1924, for the one hundred and ninety-one officials will amount to £1,729, as against which the change from Corporation war bonus to Civil Service bonus will result in a saving of £629, so that the adoption of the re-grading scheme, together with the substitution of Civil Service for Corporation war bonus, will result in an increase of £1,000, as compared to 1923-1924 (1).*

The timing of this issue and the report of the Finance Committee was interesting, given that a consistent criticism against the Corporation was the salary levels of officials. In the same edition of *The Irish Times*, Town Clerk, John J. Murphy, was quoted on the matter of the rate. It had previously been reported that the rate for the coming year would be reduced from 19 shillings and 9 pence in the pound to 17 shillings and 6 pence. The Town Clerk, denied this, telling the newspaper's reporter that such a reduction would necessitate economies in the Corporation of £120,000. Murphy proclaimed that there was not the 'slightest possibility' of this happening (2). As an aside, that morning's edition of *The Irish Times* contained a copy of an order from the Department of Local Government, stating that the Government had fixed 15 July as the date for the holding of local elections.

Questions surrounding the city's municipal rate and the salaries paid to Corporation officials featured prominently at the eighth day of the inquiry as the morning session was dedicated to a delegation from the Dublin Chamber of Commerce. The four-man delegation from the Chamber was made up of Dr W. Lombard Murphy (President), William Crowe (Vice-President), John Charles Malcolm Eason (Chairman of the Law, Parliamentary, and Municipal Committee), and G. N. Jacob. A similar delegation from the Chamber had appeared before Dublin Corporation in April 1923 and, as on that occasion, the talking was left to Eason. He began with the assertion that the rates in Dublin were too high and that the charges on individual businesses were excessive. The Chamber took a Dublin-wide view and it was anxious that the city should hold its head as high as any other municipality. Accordingly, the delegation was not at the inquiry to make an aggressive statement; rather, it wanted its contribution to be helpful.

Acknowledging the appropriateness of this approach, Inspector O'Dwyer asked Eason if he had specific matters he wished to raise. Eason gladly took the opportunity: 'At the moment, the burden of taxation is against the development of industry, and the city cannot go on as it is without something being done as regards wages and other costs, such as salaries and pensions. The Chamber thinks that the Corporation should get the best interest possible for every penny of the public money it spends' (3). Eason was an impressive and articulate witness and, without any theatrics, his testimony was hard-hitting. He alleged that the Corporation had failed in its duty as an employer and he cited a number of issues in relation to terms of employment, wages, and holidays. He felt that conditions and terms in City Hall should be the same as those in outside industries and he pointedly commented: 'The Chamber would like to know something of the position of the boys in the Corporation who, it is felt, are being paid in an extravagant fashion' (4). Now in full flow, Eason recommended that the Corporation's pension scheme should be revised and also that more information be made available regarding the Stanley Street Workshops, as well as the electricity accounts. Concluding, he stressed that the business men of Dublin city, represented by the Chamber, wanted the inquiry to be a thorough investigation of the Corporation as the rates were too high. Eason was cross-examined by Patrick Lynch but he was able to deal expertly with the questions put to him. Eason explained that he had nothing to say against the integrity of the Corporation's elected members but his concern was 'the want of business capacity amongst them' (5).

After Eason's evidence, Inspector O'Dwyer announced a lunch break, with the session to continue in the afternoon. Certainly, this had been the most difficult morning of the inquiry so far for Dublin Corporation due to the detailed, methodical and calm approach of the witness. Forty-three year-old John Eason joined the family business of Eason & Son after graduating from Trinity College Dublin in 1901. In 1916, he took charge of the wholesale news department and, from 1920, effectively took control of the whole business from his father. Heavily involved in the Dublin Chamber of Commerce, he became the first President of the Association of Chambers of Commerce of Ireland. Eason was a member of various Government bodies on Workingmen's Compensation (1925-1926); Bankruptcy (1927-1929); Currency (1927-1933); Banking and Credit (1934-1938) and he was a member of the Road Traffic Advisory Board in 1939. Along with other prominent industrialists and businessmen of the period, he was a founder member of the Irish Management Institute in December 1952. He died in Dublin in 1976, at the age of ninety-six (6).

The afternoon session was dominated by Councillor Michael J. Moran who testified about the Stanley Street Workshops. Though an elected member of the council, he spoke against the Corporation's management of the workshops. In March, at a meeting of the Corporation, Councillor Moran had alleged mismanagement, waste and excessive expenditure and – much to the dismay of many of his fellow elected members – he had written to the Department of Local Government seeking an immediate inquiry into the workings of the municipal workshops. Given his background on the issue, Moran's comments in the witness box were not a surprise. He stressed that the Stanley Street Workshops had 'not given satisfaction for a long time' (7). Moran instanced a specific case where an old, established firm in the city tendered for work at one pound less than the Stanley Street Workshops, but the latter was awarded the contract. It was Moran's view than the staff in Stanley Street were unable to do the work properly, which resulted in the project exceeding its budget to the extent that the Corporation had to put a sum aside in its estimates for 1922-1923. Answering the Inspector, Moran said that he attributed the high prices at Stanley Street to mismanagement, although he did acknowledge that competition and mass production were other factors. Moran then strongly criticised his fellow councillors for voting down a motion he had tabled to hold a meeting with representatives of the various unions to discuss wages.

Representing the Corporation, barrister Patrick Lynch took the lead on the cross-examination of Councillor Moran and he unmistakably had done his homework. He forced Moran to concede that the £5,000 deficit in the 1922-1923 estimates for the Stanley Street Workshops was largely due to a fire in the works at that time. Regarding a loss on a contract for blocks, Moran said that he would not contradict Lynch's statement that the loss was occasioned when Stanley Street tendered at £19, 10 shillings, and not when an outside firm tendered lower than the workshop. In studious fashion, Lynch continued to dismantle Moran's testimony. Picking up a document from his desk, Lynch stated that the report in his hand clearly explained that the deficit in the workshops was due to hostilities in 1922, when material was destroyed there. A sum of £9,316 was claimed for the loss, but only £5,836 was awarded, leaving a deficit of £3,480. There was also a sum of money paid to the employees of the workshops for holidays during the same period of hostilities. Lynch contended that these were the justifiable reasons for the deficit at the Stanley Street Workshops, rather than mismanagement. A chastened Councillor Moran agreed that such was the case. This ended the eighth day of the inquiry. In the morning, the Corporation had been hurt by the evidence of John Eason, but a strong performance in the afternoon by Patrick Lynch had reduced the damage, especially in relation to the Stanley Street Workshops.

The Corporation's Chief Veterinary Officer, J. Dolan, started proceedings the following morning and he described his duties under mild questioning by Patrick Lynch. Dolan noted that there were now seventy-five butchers using the Corporation's abattoir and one hundred and twenty using private slaughter-houses. To deal in a proper manner with the private slaughter-houses, he would need ten times his current staff. Dolan pointed out that in 1921, the number of tubercular cattle dealt with in private slaughter-houses was seven; it was nineteen in 1922, and then rose dramatically to eighty-nine in 1923. During the latter year, when four extra inspectors had been employed, there were forty-four cases found between October and December. The Corporation's policy was ultimately to abolish the private slaughter-houses, of which there were forty-nine spread over the city from Fairview to Inchicore. An ante-mortem and post-mortem of each animal should be made, and all the slaughtered beasts inspected. However, a shortage of staff in the Veterinary Department made this extremely problematic. On the question of milk, Dolan claimed that supplies coming from the country into Dublin were not sterilised or pasteurised.

Dolan was followed by John Devine, the Corporation's Superintendent of the Cleansing Department, who was making his second appearance in the witness-box. Devine criticised the police for not doing more to abate the dumping of refuse by people in laneways and other places. The Corporation could not monitor illegal dumping in every part of the city. Answering a question about the slimy nature of the street after rain, Devine explained that this was due to the nature of the subsoil. Representing the residents in Fitzwilliam Square, Mrs. Crofton then told the inquiry that refuse should be removed in covered cars earlier in the mornings.

In the afternoon, the inquiry returned to the Stanley Street Workshops, with evidence provided by Councillor Patrick McIntyre, who sat on the Corporation's Cleansing Committee. McIntyre's contribution was measured; while stressing that the staff in the workshops were doing a decent job, he acknowledged that, with regard to certain items, the work could be done more cheaply elsewhere than in Stanley Street.

Next to give evidence was Henry Thunder, Chief Clerk of the Stanley Street Workshops, and he predictably offered a staunch defence of the work which was undertaken there. Thunder outlined that, aside from himself, there were six other administrative staff members – a cost clerk, a storekeeper, two girl clerks, a typist, and an attendant. There were also one hundred and sixty workers employed there, of which only thirty-four were permanent. Thunder argued that the work turned out in Stanley Street was good ('in fact, too good') and the prices were not unduly high. The vehicular stock of the department was about two hundred and fifty and it would be difficult to say how improvements could be carried out with a view to economy. Regarding the wood block contract, it was Thunder's view that the estimate was too low in every respect, and he could not particularise that the loss of £7,910 was due to errors in costing.

Patrick Lynch skilfully led the witness through a series of questions which gave the latter the opportunity to explain that the loss of £5,000 for 1922-1923 was due to extraordinary circumstances and the hostilities that obtained at the time, including a fire at the workshops. Reference was again made to the fact that the Corporation had only been awarded £5,836 from its claim of £9,316, leaving a significant deficit. Under questioning from Norman Keough, Thunder stated that the majority of his suggestions over the years about running the workshops more efficiently had been implemented and he was satisfied with the system of reporting to the Chairman of the department concerned.

Inspector O'Dwyer announced that the inquiry was ended for the day and would resume after the weekend. Entering what would be the final week of proceedings, no knockout blow – or even damaging jabs – had been landed against Dublin Corporation.

Chapter 11
Bribery allegations, senile decay and salary increases

The public inquiry resumed on Monday 31 March, in what was a lively day of testimony which included allegations of bribery against the Corporation members on the Markets' Committee. The allegation was made by Patrick Leonard, the former President of the Cattle Salesmasters' Association. He provided evidence in relation to the Dublin Market, which was under municipal management. Leonard complained vociferously of the way in which cattle pens were allocated to the salesmasters. He asserted that the allocations were made by the Markets' Committee without the people immediately concerned being consulted. This led to genuine salesmen being squeezed out. Leonard continued by claiming that when the Markets' Committee was asked to put up a new weigh-bridge and make the existing ones accurate, it had failed to do so. Despite this, the Markets' Committee raised the tolls by over three hundred per cent. Leonard had written to the committee on these matters but to no avail. The witness then made the accusation that members of the committee had received money to influence their decisions on the allocation of cattle pens. This immediately brought Alderman Michael Staines to his feet. Alderman Staines was the Chairman of the Markets' Committee and he asked Leonard to clarify if he was testifying that members of his committee had accepted bribes for the allotment of pens. If this was the case, Staines demanded that Leonard inform the public inquiry of the names of the people making the accusation. When Leonard declined to do so, an irate Alderman Staines noted: 'When it is put to the witness to give the names of any persons who made the allegation, he runs away and does not give them. It is only fair to the members of the Markets' Committee that the whole thing should be thrashed out' (1).

Answering a question from Inspector O'Dwyer, Leonard weakly replied that he had not taken any steps to find out whether the information given to him was correct. Barrister Patrick Lynch refused to let the matter rest and he again pressed the witness to state who had provided him with the information that members of the Markets' Committee were receiving bribes for allocating pens in the market. A flustered Leonard replied that 'a big butcher in Dublin' had come up to him and said: 'You lost your pens in the Cattle Market because you did not do what other people have been doing' (2). Leonard then stated that the butcher was a former member of Dublin Corporation. This led to much excited murmurings in the public gallery. Having restored order, Inspector O'Dwyer asked Leonard to continue. He did so by adding the extraordinary claim that a current member of the Corporation had approached him on foot of his letter to the Markets' Committee. According to Leonard, the councillor had told him that he was 'absolutely right' in the allegations of bribery contained in the letter. For good measure, Leonard commented that a cattle dealer from Meath had spoken to him to the same effect.

Patrick Lynch asked the witness if he would say that some members of the Markets' Committee were honourable men. Leonard replied: 'I thought they were all honourable men' (3). Lynch then asked Leonard to specifically name the people who were making, or seemingly confirming, the bribery allegations – the former councillor, the current councillor, and the Meath cattle dealer. With Leonard again refusing to do so, Lynch argued that it was grossly unfair to charge men at a public inquiry in such a vague fashion. Leonard countered: 'I am not charging anybody. I was given certain information which I considered to be trustworthy' (4).

Inspector O'Dwyer intervened and explained that he regretted the fact that he did not have the legal power to compel the witness to answer the questions put by Patrick Lynch. He noted that bribery was a very serious charge to make against public men. For the first time at the inquiry, solicitor James Fallon rose to speak. Fallon was the legal representative of the Lord Mayor and he only had one question to ask of the witness: 'Do you make any charge against the Lord Mayor?' Leonard replied: 'Absolutely not'. Other members of the Markets' Committee who were present at the inquiry, including Aldermen Michael Staines and Alfie Byrne, asked if any charges were being laid against them. To each query, Leonard answered: 'I am not making any charge against anybody' (5). Directly addressing the Inspector, Patrick Lynch described the situation as unsatisfactory and stated that the matter could not be allowed to rest there, with unsupported allegations of bribery hanging in the air. He called Alderman Michael Staines, as chairman of the Markets' Committee, to the witness box.

Answering questions posed by Lynch, Staines said that the committee met with the Cattle Salesmasters' Association as far as possible, but the committee members did not want to allow the salesmasters to have all the say in the allocation of pens. He confirmed that, as chair of the committee, he had received the letter of complaint written by Patrick Leonard and he had referred it to the Corporation's legal department as he wanted the matter to be dealt with in a court of law. When asked by Inspector O'Dwyer if he had met with Leonard, Staines responded: 'No, I did not. I do not believe there is a word of truth in the statements he has made. I think it is a case where the committee should have taken Mr. Leonard into court and made him give the names and prove his charges. I think it is very unfair that people coming in here and doing public business should have these charges bandied about, and, if you want redress, you must have your own legal assistance' (6). Staines said he regretted that the committee had let the matter drop, following the advice of the Corporation's Law Agent, Ignatius Rice, not to pursue Leonard in court. Continuing his testimony, Staines outlined in great depth, the work of the Cattle Market, which he said was the biggest in Great Britain and Ireland. The market was very well maintained and the problems identified by Leonard regarding the weigh-bridges had been remedied.

As the inquiry was finishing early that day to accommodate a meeting of the Corporation, Inspector O'Dwyer moved quickly through two other witnesses. Both were officials of the Corporation – Mr. Sherlock (secretary to the Markets' Committee) and M. A. Moynihan (engineer to the Waterworks Committee). Sherlock provided fairly bland evidence regarding the finances of the Markets' Committee and the Cattle Market and he confirmed the testimony of Alderman Staines that the committee had reluctantly not brought Patrick Leonard to court, on to the advice of the council's Law Agent. Moynihan stressed that pensions were not given too freely to Corporation staff and that the men working for him were as any contractor could get in Dublin. Inspector O'Dwyer adjourned the inquiry for the day and, a couple of hours later, the elected members convened for a special meeting of Dublin Corporation.

The meeting had been called to discuss a report of the Finance and General Purposes Committee about the re-grading of officials and the fixing of remuneration levels accordingly. It is interesting that the elected members chose to deal with this contentious matter in the midst of the public inquiry, but the committee had been working on the report over a number of months. The report was presented and moved for adoption by Councillor Michael J. Moran.

Councillor Moran explained that there were one hundred and six officials not dealt with in the report, whose war bonuses would be reduced to the Civil Service scale from 1 April, leading to a reduction of £1,500. However, the proposals overall in the report were based on salary increases. Moran outlined that the increase over last year's total salaries would be £442, owing to the increased cost of living. He was mindful of the present circumstances in which the Corporation found itself with the public inquiry and he did not want to recommend changes that would lead to increasing local taxation. However, the present salary scales had been fixed twenty-five years earlier and his view was that a readjustment, based on modest increases, was warranted. He called on his fellow councillors to approve the report.

In response, Councillor John Lawlor argued that the time was not right to deal with the recommendations in the report. He called for consideration of the report to be postponed for six months, a suggestion that was seconded by Councillor William McCarthy. Councillor Patrick T. Daly agreed with the proposal to postpone consideration of the report, noting: 'The present council is suffering from senile decay. It has been in office for a long period, and this question should be left to the new council which – if no Commissioners are appointed – will be elected in July' (7). Alderman James Hubbard Clark argued that it was 'remarkable' that they were facing a proposal to increase the salaries of officials. In his view, there were two outstanding features of the report. The first was that there were over one hundred officials not included in it; the other was that there were no recommendations to reorganise the departments in the Corporation. His conclusion was that unless all clerical staff were included, the report was practically useless. Therefore, any decisions should be postponed until all staff were included and the reorganisation of departments was undertaken.

A vote was then called and the motion by Councillor Lawlor to delay consideration of the report for six months was defeated. A second motion was proposed by Alderman Shields that the report should be sent back to the Finance and General Purposes Committee with the instruction from council that the committee should make the total proposed remuneration, consisting of salary and Civil Service bonuses, not greater than the current total remuneration. This motion was also defeated and the report was adopted by thirteen votes to ten.

The remainder of the meeting was taken up with a thorough discussion on issues raised by Councillor Patrick T. Daly about central Government contracts. In particular, Councillor Daly wanted to know if Government contracts for supplies embodied the clauses in Corporation contracts regarding the employment of local and trade union labour and payment of standard wages. Town Clerk, John J. Murphy, explained that Government contracts included a fair wage clause, but conditions relating to trade union and local labour were generally not included. The whole question of supplies was under review by the Housing, Workshops, and Supplies Committee. The Town Clerk noted that the council had adopted a report in 1922, to the effect that the Corporation should take into consideration the prices of supplies quoted in the contract guide of the Department of Local Government. Instructions were accordingly issued directing Corporation officials to compare the prices in the Government list with those in the Annual Supplies Report, so as to ensure that the purchases would be made on the most economical terms. In practice, the Town Clerk noted, it had been found that the duplication of price lists did not work satisfactorily. There were also cases where the quality of supplies in the Government list was inferior to the Corporation standard. The elected members thanked the Town Clerk for his work on the matter and asked for recommendations from the Housing, Workshops, and Supplies Committee.

When people gathered the next morning in the Mansion House for the continuation of public inquiry, those with a copy of *The Irish Times* at hand would have seen a letter to the editor from the Corporation official, M. A. Moynihan. Moynihan wished to set the record straight in relation to Patrick Leonard and a loan from the Cattle Salesmasters' Association to the Corporation.

To the Editor of *The Irish Times*

Sir,

Yesterday, I listened to Mr. Patrick Leonard give evidence at the Local Government Inquiry in the Mansion House, during which he contended that his firm had put the Corporation under an obligation in consequence of the fact that, on the laying out of the Cattle Markets, they had joined with other cattle salesmen in advancing to the Corporation the sum of £500. On cross-examination, he stated that this sum had been repaid, and that during the time when it was out, the mortgages had received six per cent interest. It may be of interest to Mr. Leonard and other critical ratepayers to know that the cattle salesmen were not the only people to come to the assistance of the Corporation.

In 1921, during the fight against the British Local Government Board, when the usual grants-in-aid were withheld, the workmen and officials, in order to help the Corporation out of its difficulties, voluntarily paid in instalments from their wages and salaries £6,162 and 12 shillings, being the sum estimated by the Finance Committee required as interest on a loan from the bank to meet the deficit caused by the withholding of the grants. Neither the workmen nor the officers have been paid interest on this sum, nor has it been refunded.

Yours, etc.

M. A. MOYNIHAN
Deputy Borough Surveyor
City Engineer's Department
Castle Street, Dublin,
April 1st 1924

Moynihan's letter provided the backdrop for a morning that was again dominated by issues to do with the Dublin Cattle Market. At the outset, Inspector O'Dwyer made a statement to clarify the position with reference to the matter of a witness declining to answer a question (as had happened the previous day with Patrick Leonard): 'The position is that, if the subject matter of the question and answer are considered evidence, I can press for an answer, but if they are not considered evidence, I have no authority to press for an answer' (8). The Inspector then called forward the first witness of the day, James O'Brien, secretary to the Cattle Market Committee. He stated that the allocation of cattle pens was made each May and, as far as possible, unless there was a grave depreciation in the number of cattle, no person holding a stand was disturbed. O'Brien put on the record that he had 'no knowledge whatsoever' of any corruption or bribery in the allocation of pens. The first he had heard of such charges was the previous day during Patrick Leonard's testimony.

James Lardner asked a few benign questions, which O'Brien dealt with comfortably. He stated that, in his view, the market should be enlarged and there needed to be more accommodation for fat cattle. The Dublin Cattle Market and other smaller markets were regularly inspected by officials from the Department of Agriculture and there were no complaints. Replying to a rare question posed by Norman Keough, representing the Citizens' Association, O'Brien said that if any new market was to be established, it should be near the docks, where there would be shipping facilities.

The first witness in the afternoon was Patrick Blake, Superintendent of the Iveagh Market. He acknowledged that the market was not paying its way, but it did confer incalculable benefit on the poor people in the part of the city served by it. All the salaries and expenses in the market had traditionally been subject to the approval of the Local Government Board. John Egan, a Corporation official in the Weights and Measures Department, asserted that the department was run on efficient lines and was not over-staffed. He stated: 'The department exists for the protection of the public and it was never intended to be a commercial concern' (9). By now, Inspector O'Dwyer was moving briskly through witnesses. Captain John J. Myers, Chief of the Dublin Fire Brigade, and Mr. Fitzgerald, Superintendent of the Food Market, were examined and presented fairly anaemic evidence with respect to the workings of their departments. John J. Myers was a legendary figure. He attended at the fires in O'Connell Street in 1916, in Cork City in 1920, at the Custom House in 1921 and at the Four Courts in 1922. Though he received little acknowledgement for his bravery at the time, he earned a footnote in Ireland's literary annals with a mention in *Ulysses* when the author fantasises: 'Lieutenant Myers of the Dublin Fire Brigade, by general request, sets fire to Bloom' (10).

Councillor John J. Murphy was next to testify, in his capacity as chairman of the Housing Committee. He maintained that five-roomed houses, with accommodation for families consisting of from five to fourteen members, were favoured by the Corporation. There were about three thousand houses either occupied or reaching completion, and further houses were in contemplation. The yearly rental for two thousand, two hundred and seventy-nine of these occupied houses was £31,744 and the estimated receipts were £31,495. The final witness of the day was the City Architect, Horace Tennyson O'Rourke. He served the Housing Committee and stated that the committee had adopted the Scottish Guild system, with some variations. The Guild was registered as a Friendly Society. The Corporation bought the materials and paid the wages, and had not suffered any loss so far.

Inspector O'Dwyer brought the day's proceedings to a close in the late afternoon. It had been another day when Corporation officials and elected members performed creditably in the witness box, and were largely untroubled by the questions of Norman Keough or the Inspector.

Chapter 12
The inquiry tamely ends

The twelfth day of the inquiry, Wednesday 2 April, was dominated by three witnesses – Patrick J. Dillon, Councillor John Farren, and Alderman Thomas Lawlor. Dillon, Superintendent of Housing, was first to give evidence and he stated that he had over sixteen years of experience in housing matters. He explained that Corporation houses were allocated by the Housing Committee, who selected the most deserving applicants. In the specific case of the Donnelly's Orchard scheme, there was a ballot amongst the selected applicants for the larger old houses. An applicant, to be qualified, had to have at least three children, and five people was the minimum level to be living in the household. Dillon stated that he respected the decision of the elected members on the Housing Committee but he did not personally agree with the ballot system as there was a danger that one deserving tenant might get preference over another. Answering a series of questions from Norman Keough, Dillon expressed the view that most of the Corporation's tenants were satisfactory and looked after the houses well but added: 'The civic sense is not as highly developed amongst them as I would like' (1). Dillon readily conceded that there was a dearth of houses in the city as the population was increasing on a daily basis. The Dublin Artisans' Dwellings Company was making a profit, but it charged higher rents than the Corporation and selected 'what might be called a better class of tenant' (2). Pressed by Keough, the witness maintained that he was always fully satisfied by any work done by the Stanley Street Workshops and he did not think that the Corporation could get better value by having the work done by outside contractors. His personal experience of contract work was that there was a great deal of supervision required, and the best materials were not always used. A very strict watch was kept on the Stanley Street workmen, and he was content with the quality of their work. In response to questions from James Lardner, Dillon admitted that some of the Corporation houses were sublet by the tenants to relatives. This was not allowed under the rules but it was very hard to prove these cases. He remarked: 'Every care is taken in the selection of tenants but, in some cases, they get the loan of children in order to qualify' (3). This comment drew loud laughter from the public galleries.

Labour Party councillor, John Farren, spoke next, as the chairman of the Electricity and Public Lighting Committee. He presented detailed evidence, explaining that the public electricity supply was inaugurated in Dublin in 1892. From 1904 to 1910, the undertaking was run at a loss, but from 1911 to the present time, it was run at a profit. The exceptions to this were 1917 and 1918 when a small loss was sustained, owing to the fact that wages and the cost of materials had increased very substantially, and a corresponding increase in the price of electricity had not been passed onto the citizens. Farren was a very confident witness, armed with the figures from his committee. He outlined that the profit for the year 1922-1923 was £45,327. Electricity had shown a smaller increase in price than practically any other commodity in recent years. A sum of £25,000 went from the undertaking for the relief of rates the previous year. Farren was adamant that his department could supply any customer with electricity at a price that would compare favourably with the price charged for the same supply elsewhere. The final witness for the day was Alderman Thomas Lawlor, who chaired the Dublin Tuberculosis Committee. He praised the work of his committee and the Corporation officials who served it. The number of tuberculosis cases in the city had fallen substantially between 1915 and 1923. In 1917, there were one thousand and sixty-three cases which was down to six hundred and sixty-six in 1923.

Day thirteen commenced with testimony by Professor Bernard Francis Shields, chairman of the Corporation's Technical Instruction Committee. Professor Shields, or Barney, as he was affectionately known, was a fascinating man. After the establishment of a Faculty of Commerce in University College Galway, he was appointed the first Professor of Commerce and Accountancy in 1914. This was the earliest full-time Chair in the United Kingdom with 'accounting' or 'accountancy' in its title (4). In October 1918, Shields was appointed to the (vacant) Professorship of Commerce in University College Dublin. In the 1920 local elections, Shields was elected as Alderman for Dublin City Council for the new Kilmainham and Usher's Quay Wards. Standing as a Municipal Reform candidate, he was easily elected on the first count having exceeded the quota (5).

In presenting his evidence to the public inquiry, Professor Shields stated that the Corporation had made every effort to popularise technical instruction and the teaching of domestic economy and science. In the Parnell Square schools, there were one thousand, six hundred and thirty-nine students; in the Bolton Street schools one thousand, three hundred and eighty-five; in the Kevin Street Schools eight hundred and eighty-two; and, in the School of Music on South William Street, there were three hundred and thirty-five. Classes were held continuously from half-past nine in the morning until ten o'clock at night and, at the present time, they had twenty-five classes in Irish. Under questioning, Professor Shields expressed the view that the day-apprenticeship system was satisfactory, but there was scope for improvement. In his opinion, employers should be compelled to send their apprentices to the Technical Schools for at least one hundred and thirty hours per session. Shields disagreed strongly with Inspector O'Dwyer who asked if young people were being educated at the expense of the ratepayers for export purposes: 'In my own particular branch of the university, only two students taught by me have left the country. One went to Wales to teach and the other went to India, to take up an appointment in his native state' (6). Professor Shields was followed in the witness box by L. E. O'Carroll, secretary to the Technical Instruction Committee. He supported the previous testimony and pointed out that when technical instruction was first started, they had one school and one thousand pupils. Now, they had four schools and five thousand pupils.

In the afternoon, the Lord Mayor of Dublin, Alderman Laurence O'Neill, took centre stage and he provided a passionate and staunch defence of the Corporation. He stated that he was a member of the council for sixteen years, and for a period of seven years was Lord Mayor of the city. He kept himself as far aloof as possible from sectional differences in the city and the country. He could only recall two meetings that had fallen through due to the want of a quorum. The Lord Mayor asserted that there had been so many national crises, labour troubles, and demands on him that he had devoted very little of his time over the previous seven years to his own private business. He did not regret this sacrifice and he was proud of the work of the Corporation and its elected members: 'There is no body in the three kingdoms better served by the chairmen of the different committees than the Corporation of Dublin' (7). Lord Mayor O'Neill was equally fulsome in his praise for the Corporation's officials who served the citizens well and took a deep interest in their work. He defended the Corporation's recruitment system, arguing that examinations were held for clerical appointments and these were open to everybody, from Derry to Cork.

Conceding that the municipal authority was not perfect, the Lord Mayor recommended that the Corporation offices should be centralised: 'The present scattered system is inconvenient and expensive. It would be better if we had one municipal building in which all of the work can be concentrated' (8). Challenged by Norman Keough, the Lord Mayor said he did not possibly see how there could have been any corruption in the Corporation. He was glad that the public inquiry was taking place as it was a chance to clear the air of suspicions which had been created, principally by the press. The Lord Mayor's final point of the day was an extension of the city boundary would be beneficial for Dublin. Rather than being dissolved, Dublin Corporation should be expanded.

Friday 4 April 1924 marked the fourteenth and final day of the public inquiry into the performance of Dublin Corporation. Financial matters were to the fore, with Town Clerk, John J. Murphy, going through the Corporation's accounts. He claimed that when the new council was elected in March 1920, there was a debit balance in the revenue account of £18,791, and in the capital account of £31,229, giving a combined total debit of £50,020. The position as of 31 March 1924 was that there was a debit balance on the capital account of £126,000. Answering questions from Patrick Lynch, the Town Clerk explained that the Corporation's revenue account was £105,800 better than when the new council had taken over, but the capital account was worse by £95,000. It was the practice of the Corporation to keep down the taking up of loans, even when authorised, until the very last moment, in order to save interest. When Patrick Lynch queried if the Corporation's revenue account could afford to sustain this practice, the Town Clerk replied: 'Quite so. We have only the one account in the bank and, so long as we keep a credit balance in the bank, we are quite satisfied to allow our capital account to be overdrawn. In that connection, I should say that within the last three or four years, more than £20,000 in interest has been saved' (9). In the course of further evidence, the Town Clerk stated that the policy of the Corporation over the last twenty years had been to borrow less than they had previously done.

As regards rates collection, the Corporation had instituted a new method of collection, with a larger number of collectors, covering smaller districts. The result for the first year of the new method was that a sum of £10,000 in excess of the previous collections had been obtained. Town Clerk Murphy continued by presenting the percentage of rates collected over the previous years.

1920-21	95.80%
1921-22	96.57%
1922-23	96.29%
1923-24	98.35%

Given the difficult period that the city had endured, the Town Clerk claimed that the percentage of rates collected was impressively high and compared favourably with the collection rates in any other Irish local authority.

Hugh McCarthy, secretary to the School Attendance Committee, testified that the average school attendance in Dublin for the previous year was eighty-four per cent, which represented a big increase from the figure of sixty-three per cent at the turn of the century. The salaries of the entire staff under the committee amounted to £4,458 and 12 shillings. Detailed, if bland, testimony was then provided by Corporation official, Mr. McGinley, about the work done in the Crossling Sanatorium, and by the Assistant Town Clerk, J. Walsh, about the activities of the Libraries Committee.

The Lord Mayor, Alderman Laurence O'Neill, was the final witness at the public inquiry. He gave evidence regarding the work of the Finance Committee, in the absence of the committee's chairperson, Senator Jennie Wyse-Power. He agreed with the Town Clerk as to the economies achieved by the committee since the last municipal election and said that he ruled out of order every proposal to increase officials' salaries, giving as his reason that the time was inopportune. Inspector O'Dwyer interjected and asked what relation, if any, should exist between the wages paid by the council and the rate of wages paid by the private individuals who financed the council through rates.

The Lord Mayor replied: 'It has often occurred to me in discussions about wages that a body like the Corporation should be, if not the best, at least one of the best employers in the city. On the other hand, I am not going the length of saying that the Corporation should outstep the ordinary rate of wages paid in the city by a large percentage' (10).

This was a fitting note on which to end the formal evidence provided to the public inquiry into the affairs of Dublin Corporation, with the Lord Mayor defending the wages paid to officials. Drawing the proceedings to a close, Inspector Nicholas O'Dwyer thanked the legal representatives and all of those who had appeared before the inquiry. He reserved special praise for the citizens of Dublin who had attended the inquiry in large numbers over the full fourteen days that they had been in session. It was now his duty to write a report in as fair a manner as possible, knowing that he could not please all parties. Ultimately the fate of Dublin Corporation rested with the Minister for Local Government, Séamus Burke TD, and the Government.

Part 3: The Commissionership Years

Chapter 13
The axe falls on a dying body

Business continued as usual for Dublin Corporation after the inquiry as it awaited the verdict from Minister Séamus Burke TD. The elected members were satisfied that the inquiry had gone well and that the Corporation had received a fair hearing. The onus had been on Norman Keough, representing the Citizens' Association, and W. J. Larkin, representing the Dublin Tenants' Association, to make the case for the dissolution of the municipal authority. The councillors felt that the case had not been made. Norman Keough's performance over the fourteen days of the inquiry was feeble and W. J. Larkin had bowed out controversially midway through the proceedings. Apart from an uncomfortable day on Wednesday 27 March, when the delegation from the Dublin Chamber of Commerce had criticised the council for its lack of business capacity, the inquiry had seen a procession of elected members and officials take to the witness box and deliver strong performances in defence of the Corporation. Even the evidence provided by Councillor Michael J. Moran in relation to the Stanley Street Workshops had not hurt the Corporation due to the expert cross-examination skills of Patrick Lynch. Lynch had forced Moran to concede that there were justifiable reasons for the losses suffered by the workshops and that the root cause was not mismanagement. The legal battle between Keough/Larkin and Lynch/Lardner had resulted in a decisive knockout victory for the barristers representing the Corporation. Though the council's elected members were happy with the inquiry, this did not translate to confidence about the likely outcome. Many felt that the inquiry was a charade and that a decision had already been made to dissolve the local authority.

When the council met on Monday 7 April, the elected members returned to a familiar theme – the treatment of prisoners. Alderman Charles Murphy, TD (a Sinn Féin anti-Treaty member of Dáil Éireann), moved the following motion: 'That this council demands that all political prisoners, whether sentenced or interned, should be at once released' (1). Alderman Thomas P. O'Reilly seconded the motion and many members spoke in favour of it. Councillor John Lawlor claimed that if the Republican Party came to power the following day and arrested people of the Free State, he would take up the same attitude on the question. There were three parties to be held responsible, according to Councillor Hanna

Sheehy-Skeffington, namely, the British Government, the parliament in Northern Ireland, and the parliament in Dublin. She called on her fellow councillors to endorse the motion. As usual, Councillor Michael J. Moran's contribution to the debate, was controversial. He stated: 'This is a matter for the Government and not for the Corporation. The Government was elected only six months ago, and therefore knows the minds of the people better than the Corporation, which is a dying body' (2). Alderman Seán T. O'Kelly took offence at Councillor Moran's comments, stating that members of the Corporation intended to live a long time yet and needed to make themselves heard in trying to bring back a little Christianity to the minds of partisans (3). He added: 'The sentences are farcical, and we know that the Government in whose name the sentences were made will not last another six months' (4). The motion was passed by twenty-eight votes to four. As ever, the members of Dublin Corporation were not shying away from national political issues.

Much of the remainder of April was spent discussing the estimates for the 1924/1925 year. At a special Corporation meeting on Thursday 24 April in the Mansion House, the Lord Mayor proposed the adoption of the estimates in the amount of £1,064,264, 5 shillings, and 10 pence with a rate of 19 shillings and 1 pence in the pound. Members raised the issue of £81,000 due to the Corporation by the Free State Government and the British Government. The Lord Mayor stated that they could be confident of receiving a portion of the money owed, but not all. Alderman James Hubbard Clark suggested that the Free State Government would not be able to pay the money because it did not have it (5). The meeting heard from Howard Hely, a leading member of the Dublin Citizens' Association. Hely presented a memorial praying for a reduction in the rates from what was proposed. He urged the councillors to take 'immediate steps' to reduce the wages of municipal employees to the agreed standard rates paid outside. As an example he stated that the rate for a builder's labourer was 58 shillings and 10 pence, but the Corporation was paying its labourers at a rate of 64 shillings. In addition, Corporation labourers had the advantage of no broken time and the benefits of sick pay and pension. In a strong presentation which would not have been out of place at the public inquiry, Hely called for the immediate closure of the Stanley Street Workshops in the interests of economy.

The elected members debated different aspects of the estimates which had been placed before them and objections were raised about the fact that outside parties were not invited to tender for the renovation of City Hall and municipal buildings which was estimated to cost £6,000. Alderman Seán T. O'Kelly took the opportunity to again criticise the Free State Government and the press. He noted that the Government owed money to the Corporation and that citizens deserved to be informed that if they were not getting a bigger reduction in the rates, it was the fault of those 'who have taken over the finances of the country' (6). He insisted that the Dublin media who had attacked the Corporation 'at the inspiration of Merrion Street' needed to accurately report the issue.

Towards the end of the meeting, the councillors discussed claims on behalf of P. J. Monks, former manager of the municipal workshops, and John J. Flood, former Assistant Town Clerk, for payment of pensions stated to be due to them by the Corporation. The Finance Committee had decided not to make provision for these pension payments in the estimates. Law Agent, Ignatius Rice, advised the members that the Corporation was obliged by law to pay the pensions. He added that the Department of Local Government had directed the Corporation in writing to provide for the pensions payable to Sir Henry Campbell, S. J. Hand, P. J. Monks, and John J. Flood. He noted that Campbell and Hand, however, were now deceased. Councillor William McCarthy proposed a motion to provide for the pension payments in the estimates. The members, though, in defiance of the Department of Local Government and the Corporation's own Law Agent, voted against the pension payments for Monks and Flood. The meeting was then adjourned until the following day.

When the councillors retuned to the Mansion House the next day, they spent two hours debating various amendments and moving money between different categories in the estimates. Alderman James Hubbard Clark drew attention to the fact that £10,000 had been provided to subsidise the building of new houses and that the Streets Committee had allocated £1,600 for roads in connection with these houses. He suggested that the Town Clerk should have the details published. The response of the Lord Mayor drew laughter from his fellow elected members when he stated: 'I am afraid we shall have to fall back on the press to do this for us' (7). A recurring theme at the meeting was criticism of the Government for its failure to pay money due to the Corporation. A frustrated Lord Mayor stressed: 'It is very unfair that the Corporation should be called upon to pay this money to carry on the business of the country, while the Government owes us so much money' (8). Alderman Seán T. O'Kelly raised a protest against the collection of the Poor Rate, in view of the fact that the Government had abolished the Dublin Board of Guardians. Consideration of this matter was deferred, and the meeting was adjourned for the weekend.

On the resumption of the estimates meeting on Monday 28 April, Alderman Seán T. O'Kelly re-stated his grounds of objection to the payment to the Commissioners who had replaced the Dublin Board of Guardians. Perhaps with one eye on what would happen if the Corporation was dissolved, he stated: 'We should not quietly give in to the demands of the gentlemen calling themselves Commissioners, who have asked for the sum of £182,000. I hold to the historic principle: "No taxation, without representation"' (9). Eventually, the elected members agreed to withhold the payment after voting in favour of a motion by Councillor Patrick T. Daly that no payment would be made until the Local Government Department received a deputation from the Corporation's Finance Committee and the subsequent report of the depuration had been considered by the council. Despite being faced with the prospect of its own dissolution, the Corporation was continuing to make life difficult for the Government and the Department of Local Government.

This trend continued when the members debated the proposed payment of £35,000 as a contribution to the Dublin Metropolitan Police. Councillor Hanna Sheehy-Skeffington maintained that the council should return to the course followed for some years under the British regime of refusing to make the payment. She argued that the elected members should do this as a protest against the 'irresponsible police force'. She referred to the provocative actions of the police in breaking up political meetings which had recently been held in Sackville Street. The amendment was carried by nineteen votes to thirteen. The revised estimates, as a whole, were then adopted and members moved on to discuss the plans of the Dublin United Tramways Company to run buses in the city. Alderman Michael Staines argued against giving the company the power to run buses, as it was already providing citizens with a poor tram service. It was his view that with motor traffic increasing, the tramway system would die out in time. He complained of insufficiency of cars at lunch-time, and of the continued use of cars with what he called 'pneumonia tops' (10). The matter was eventually referred to committee and the Lord Mayor ended the meeting. The councillors had successfully passed the estimates for the coming year, but would they be in place to see their plans come to fruition?

Though rumours and speculation were in plentiful supply, there was no official word from the Department of Local Government about the future of Dublin Corporation, and the elected members continued to meet in May. They also continued to irritate the Government. At a meeting on Monday 5 May, Councillor Patrick T. Daly spoke against the Government's Railway Bill, the primary aim of which was to amalgamate the railway systems and companies in the Free State. Lord Mayor, Councillor Laurence O'Neill, convinced his colleagues to defer the motion for a week, in light of the fact that the second reading of the bill was due to take place that week. When the Corporation met again the following Monday, Councillor Daly formally moved a motion which called on the Government to postpone consideration of the legislation until the people of Ireland were consulted, and the Lord Mayor was given the opportunity to convene a public meeting in the Mansion House. Daly argued that the proposed amalgamation of railways would have a disastrous effect on Dublin, as well as other port cities such as Cork and Waterford. He claimed that traffic would be diverted to Rosslare and the Port of Dublin would practically be wiped out (11). Councillor Peadar Doyle TD criticised the motion, stating that he failed to see how the legislation would negatively impact on employment in Dublin. Hitting back, Councillor Daly contended that all monopolies were bad and that the Free State Government was passing far too much 'express legislation' without proper consultation (12). His motion was passed by the council, with Councillor Doyle dissenting.

The members were more supportive of the Government's proposed legislation for the development of the water-power of the Liffey for electricity generation. A resolution was adopted authorising the application of the funds of the city for the purpose of promoting the bill. Law Agent, Ignatius Rice, informed the councillors that the principal object of the bill was to obtain land to enable them to construct reservoirs on the Liffey at Poulaphouca and Leixlip, and to erect generating stations at which electric power would be generated for distribution not only to the city of Dublin but also portions of counties Dublin, Wicklow, and Kildare. At the same meeting, a motion tabled by Councillor Laurence Raul was passed. It called for the inauguration of a municipal omnibus service. As had been discussed at a previous meeting, the Dublin United Tramways Company had announced plans to establish a bus service. The Corporation not only opposed this plan, it intended to establish its own bus service. The Town Clerk was instructed to take the necessary steps to make this happen. Interestingly, Senator Jennie Wyse-Power, remarked that out of the council's sixty-three members, only twenty-two or twenty-three were present. 'At the moment, we represent nobody. We should be showing a better civic spirit by applying ourselves to the work we have on hand and leaving the question of a municipal omnibus service, which is of great importance, to the new Corporation, which will be elected in July' (13).

The Corporation's plan to create its own bus service, in opposition to the Tramway Company, was not met with widespread enthusiasm. One critic was Thomas Picton Bradshaw who wrote a stinging letter to *The Irish Times*, published on 17 May. He accused the Corporation of trying to add another white elephant to its municipal menagerie, and he drew attention to 'the past history of the Corporation's extravagant expenditure and heavy loses' (14). Bradshaw concluded his letter with the recommendation that the Dáil should take over the management of the Corporation and appoint managers to the different departments who would run their units on business grounds.

At the following week's Corporation meeting, on Monday 19 May, the elected members were edgy – with good reason. The purpose of the meeting was to pass the resolutions necessary to strike the city rates for the year ahead, thereby giving effect to the estimates. Alderman Seán T. O'Kelly objected, saying that the councillors had agreed that a statement should be prepared showing the alternative rate which would have to be struck if the Corporation's claim for Government grants was not met in full. O'Kelly wanted the citizens of Dublin to know that, in this circumstance, the Government would be responsible for the high rates in the city. When the Town Clerk responded that the statement had not been prepared, Alderman O'Kelly proposed that the meeting be adjourned for a week. The Lord Mayor objected to this suggestion, maintaining that if the rates were not struck for another week, it could mean that services in the city would have to be stopped. The Town Clerk confirmed that a delay of a week would cause great financial difficulties for the Corporation. Councillor Patrick T. Daly addressed the elephant in the room, which everyone else was avoiding. He stated that he had heard that the Government was planning to postpone that year's local elections, until municipal administration was sorted out in Dublin: 'We are to be held up as the reason why no elections should be held in Ireland. The sooner we face our constituents the better. If elections do take place on 15 July, there ought to be no necessity for putting in Commissioners for a few months, unless the Government has a few more idle ones on the list to provide with jobs' (15). With a sense of foreboding, the councillors voted on the motion of Alderman O'Kelly to postpone the striking of rates for one week. O'Kelly's motion was defeated by

LETTERS TO THE EDITOR

Civic Administration

TO THE EDITOR OF *THE IRISH TIMES*,

Sir – The various trading departments of the municipality of Dublin run on lines which no ordinary business man would adopt. Housing, electricity, water, markets, municipal workshops etc. incur an annual loss of something like £100,000; which loss is levied in the shape of increased taxation on the ratepayers, whose poundage rate within the last eight years has doubled. This is notwithstanding the fact that this increased rate is assessed on a valuation also increased within that period by probably 50 per cent. Not satisfied with these municipal failures, the Corporation in their capacity of trustees now propose to speculate in two fresh undertakings.

The Tramway Company, one of the largest contributors to the city exchequer, has not alone to pay the increased rate on its valuations, but also pays a heavy annual sum for wayleaves over the streets, and in addition is bound to spend vast sums in maintaining and repairing the greater part of the roads over which the trams run. Now when they propose to link up outlying districts by an omnibus service, the Corporation propose to spend the ratepayers' money in opposition, and seek to run the service themselves.

Again, a syndicate which is prepared to speculate by investing private capital, amounting to a considerable sum, in harnessing up and developing the waste water power of the surrounding districts, is opposed in the same way by the Corporation, which is thus trying to add two more white elephants to the municipal menagerie.

The past history of the Corporation's extravagant expenditure and heavy losses and delay in dealing with the Vartry water reservoir extension, and the apparent failure of the motor traction already adopted by them, should teach them to let others speculate, with probably more advantage to the rates as well as benefits to the district. Recently, large sums have been expended on motor sweepers, tractors etc. to cleanse and repair the streets, for the cleansing of which the ratepayers provide something like £150,000 a year, with deplorable results.

It is the clear duty of the ratepayers, property owners, and all who are interested in the welfare of the city to prevent waste. If necessary, the Dáil itself should prevent it by taking over the management of the Corporation affairs, and appointing managers for those different trading departments who will, no doubt, show different results and will make them not only self-supporting, but paying propositions.

Yours etc.
T. Picton Bradshaw
May 16th 1924

Letter by Thomas Picton Bradshaw, *The Irish Times*, Saturday 17 May 1924.

Bradshaw severely criticised the Corporation, which he felt was being run 'on lines which no ordinary business man would adopt'.

'Dublin Corporation Abolished' was the lead story in the *Evening Herald* on Tuesday 20 May 1924.

twenty-three votes to nineteen, and the rates were adopted. This was to be the last decision taken by an elected municipal council in Dublin for six and-a-half years.

The following day, the much-anticipated news broke – Dublin Corporation was dissolved. The banner front-page headline of the *Evening Herald* read 'Dublin Corporation Abolished'. The sub-heading was: 'Corporation Gone: Local Government Order Now in Force'. The story noted that the Town Clerk, John J. Murphy, had received notification from Minister Séamus Burke that the properties, powers, and duties of the Corporation would transfer to three Government-appointed Commissioners from six o'clock that evening, Tuesday 20 May. The three Commissioners were Séamus Murphy, Dr William C. Dwyer, and Patrick J. Hernon. Murphy and Dwyer already held the positions as Commissioners of the Dublin Union; Hernon was an inspector in the Department of Local Government who, for some months, had been the chairman of the Commissioners of the Cork Union. Murphy had worked directly under William T. Cosgrave in a variety of capacities since 1919 (16).

The letter to the Town Clerk came from E. P. McCarron on behalf of Minister Burke.

The Town Clerk, City Hall, Dublin
20 May 1924

A Chara,

I am directed by the Minister for Local Government to state that, having given careful consideration to his obligations under Section 12 of the Local Government (Temporary Provisions) Act, 1923, and to the administration generally of the Dublin Corporation, as detailed in the report of the recent public inquiry, he has conceived it as his duty to dissolve the Corporation.

An order to such effect, and appointing Commissioners to perform the duties of the Corporation, accompanies this letter.

The Minister desires me to add that he has been impressed by the sense of duty and civic spirit displayed by individual members of the Corporation. It was evident, however, that the efforts of such members to secure efficient and economical management of the business of the city were unavailing in the absence of support from the majority of the Council.

In recent years the statutory functions of the Council have largely extended, and at the present time the efficient administration of the city, as the capital of the Free State, has become a question of national interest. It is proposed to have the problem of the city government examined adequately, and without avoidable delay, in the light of the results achieved elsewhere in modern experiments in city management.

Mise, le meas,
E. P. McCarron
Runaidhe

The accompanying ministerial order confirmed that Séamus Burke was using the provisions of the 1923 legislation and that he deemed that the members of Dublin Corporation had not discharged their duties effectively. The order stated the names of the three Commissioners who would replace the elected members from six o'clock on 20 May. Minister Burke added that the three Commissioners would hold office 'until I shall otherwise determine' (17). The report in *The Irish Times* which carried the story of the dissolution noted that the Charter of Dublin Corporation was granted by King John in 1192 and, accordingly, the decision of Minister Burke was an historic one.

The newspaper's editorial struck a triumphalist tone:

> *The people of Dublin cannot but welcome this decision. The fact that their Corporation for many years has been inefficient and extravagant is very humiliating, but also indubitably true. The rates and the streets bear melancholy witness to the failure of the Corporation to perform the tasks which were its duty, and a majority of its members seem to have had very little sense of responsibility to the citizens who returned them to office. A feeling of civic proprietorship seems to have grown up within the Corporation of recent years. The people of the city counted for nothing; the ratepayers merely existed for the purpose of footing the annual bill, and criticism of any kind was resented bitterly. The rake's progress of the Dublin Corporation could not be allowed to continue. No Government worthy of the name could have ignored the flagrant flaunting of public opinion in which members of the City Council indulged, and it was the obvious duty of the Ministry for Local Government to insist upon the proper administration of the ratepayers' money (18).*

The editorial noted that the rates were 'preposterously high' and that the streets were in a condition of 'chronic filth'. The thoroughfares were 'a disgrace to a Lancashire mining village' (18). In an effort to provide at least some small modicum of balance, the newspaper conceded that the citizens of Dublin had a right to elect their municipal representatives and that the Corporation should be 'reconstituted at the earliest possible moment' (19).

The *Irish Independent* was more generous to the municipal authority and accepted that some members of the Corporation 'strove to serve the citizens with fidelity and efficiency' (20). It added however, that unfortunately these members were outnumbered in City Hall. The *Belfast Newsletter* described the suppression of the Corporation as 'a humiliation for the city, but so far as the majority of its members are concerned, it has been thoroughly deserved' (21).

On the streets of Dublin, the decision to dissolve Dublin Corporation was broadly welcomed. Though the Corporation members and officials had fought hard to save the municipal authority, the writing was on the wall from the moment that Minister Séamus Burke called the public inquiry. A new era was about to begin, with three Commissioners at the helm and the elected members of the council forced to watch from the side-lines.

Chapter 14
A king without a kingdom

On the night that Dublin Corporation was dissolved, Lord Mayor, Councillor Laurence O'Neill gave an interview to *The Irish Times*. His anger towards the Government was apparent: 'I think the Government has made a mistake, in this age of democracy, so-called democracy, in depriving the citizens of the right to elect their own representatives. In my opinion, it is just as easy to hold a municipal election as a parliamentary one. I think it is a gross insult to the citizens of Dublin that their voice in the election of their own representatives should be taken from them' (1). At this point, the Lord Mayor dropped a bombshell, revealing that the President of Dáil Éireann, William T. Cosgrave, had asked him to stay on board as Chairman of the Commissioners running the Corporation. The Lord Mayor had declined the offer in writing, on the grounds that it would be disloyal towards his colleagues on the council (2).

> **Extract of Letter from Lord Mayor, Councillor Laurence O'Neill, to the President of the Executive Council of the Irish Free State, William T. Cosgrave, TD.**
>
> *Although appreciating very much the compliment you have suggested paying me, I regret that I cannot see my way to accept same. I presume if the Order is issued, you have no objection to me making it known the compliment you have paid me.*
>
> *With kind regards,*
>
> *Laurence O'Neill*
>
> *Lord Mayor of Dublin*

The letter was dated 16 May 1924, four days before the dissolution. Therefore, at the council meeting which he chaired on 19 May, the Lord Mayor knew the fate that was to befall the Corporation. During his interview with *The Irish Times*, O'Neill also addressed the legal status of the Lord Mayor: 'I intend to remain as Lord Mayor until I hand my trust back to the people's representatives, even if I am a king without a kingdom … The Mayoralty extends back over so many hundreds of years, and there are so many charters attached to the office, and the Lord Mayor is elected until his successor takes office. Therefore, the position of the Lord Mayor is a very moot question at the moment' (3). O'Neill defiantly stated that he would remain in residence in the Mansion House and added that he would summon a meeting of his fellow elected members within a few days.

The *Evening Herald* similarly questioned the status of the Lord Mayor following the dissolution of the Corporation. The newspaper had sought advice from 'a competent legal authority' who expressed grave doubt as to whether the Lord Mayoralty of Dublin could be abolished under section 12 of the Local Government (Temporary Provisions) Act, 1923 (4). The unnamed legal expert suggested that the difficulties of the situation were known to the Government and its advisers and that is why the offer had been made to Laurence O'Neill to remain in office as the Chairman of the Commissioners. The *Evening Herald* highlighted the possibility that the Lord Mayor and Aldermen of the city might be permitted to stay nominally in office to discharge certain civic duties such as the reception of distinguished visitors and the carrying out of functions associated with hospitality.

Though there was no public outcry against the dissolution, the matter was raised regularly in the Dáil over the coming weeks. On the day following the dissolution, Labour Party TD for Cork, Thomas Nagle, asked Minister Séamus Burke when he proposed to publish the report of Inspector O'Dwyer, on which he had based his decision to dissolve the Corporation. The Minister replied that the report was a voluminous document and he was hesitant to publish it, having regard to the expense involved. Labour Party leader, Thomas Johnson TD, responded strongly to the Minister's answer: 'The decision which has been taken to dissolve Dublin Corporation should have behind it some definite reasons, and presumably those reasons are contained in the report of the Inspector. In such a case, is it not obvious that the report should be published?' (5). Johnson was a consistent critic of the decision to dissolve the Corporation, describing it as 'a very extraordinary and unprecedented action which suggests that we are rapidly going towards oligarchy and dictatorship' (6). Minister Burke relented somewhat and said that he would circulate the report if it was the general view of the Dáil to do so.

Unsurprisingly, the Dublin Citizens' Association rejoiced in the demise of the Corporation. The Association's Secretary, Howard Hely, welcomed the scrapping of the present system of municipal government which he said had outlived its usefulness and which had undoubtedly been abused (7). He called on the Commissioners to be transparent in their work and said that they would be judged on whether they would be able to reduce the burden of taxation on citizens.

Three days after the dissolution, the Lord Mayor wrote to his former Corporation colleagues, asking them to attend a meeting in the Mansion House the following Monday at three o'clock. In a typically theatrical way, the Lord Mayor's letters had a thick black border of mourning (8). Around forty of the elected members attended the meeting. As there were no Corporation officials present, Councillor John O'Callaghan was appointed to act as secretary. An emotional and fired-up Lord Mayor was the first to address the meeting, stating: 'To the council, and the council alone, will I hand in my gun. I do not come before you with a swan song, but I would be false to my position if I sat down without protesting in the strongest manner possible the gross insult that has been offered to the citizens of Dublin' (9). The Lord Mayor argued that he had sat through the full inquiry and could not understand how the evidence presented had led to a decision to dissolve the Corporation. He called on the Government to announce municipal elections: 'This will give the council an opportunity of rendering an account of its stewardship to the citizens. It is for the citizens, and the citizens only, to decide' (10).

Councillor Patrick T. Daly then moved the following motion:

> *Whereas the passage of the Local Government Act of 1898 was the result of fifty years of agitation, imprisonment, and suffering for the establishment of the democratic right of local representation; and whereas the Free State Government, at two hours' notice, dissolved the most ancient Corporation in Ireland and, in our judgement, have grossly insulted the citizens of Dublin, this meeting instructs the Lord Mayor to call a public meeting of burgesses to consider the situation arising out of the undemocratic action of the Government and to press for an immediate election for members of the Corporation; and further, to take such steps as may be considered necessary to place the facts before our fellow countrymen.*

Speaking to his own motion, Councillor Daly had harsh words for the President of the Dáil, William T. Cosgrave: 'In what way does the council differ from the time when Alderman Cosgrave was a member of the Corporation? We have gone on exactly the same lines and have endeavoured to carry out the policy laid down by him as the leader of the majority party in the council at that time … It is said that we are extravagant, but when the President of the Free State was Chairman of the Finance Committee, the budget he proposed was far in excess of that recently adopted' (11). Councillor Daly also lambasted Minister Séamus Burke who he said knew nothing about Irish local government or its functions. Councillor Michael J. Moran seconded the motion and called for immediate municipal elections. His questioning of the suitability of the Commissioners drew applause and shouts of 'Hear, Hear' from those present. Alderman Seán T. O'Kelly described the order of dissolution as 'humiliating' and called upon his colleagues to stand up as one against the indignity put upon the city. Councillor Hanna Sheehy-Skeffington stated that the permanent officials of the Free State Government were pulling all of the strings behind the scenes. She added: 'The three inexperienced young men appointed as Commissioners will, no doubt, eat up every public body in the Free State' (12). There was a humorous interlude when the Lord Mayor tried to check an interruption and retain order. Having searched for a few moments, he eventually rapped his desk with a pencil and remarked, 'They have even taken my hammer away from me' (13).

The motion was passed unanimously, and Councillor Patrick Medlar then proposed the appointment of a committee of nine members to act with the Lord Mayor to draw up a statement to be sent to all public bodies in the country and to summon a conference of those bodies, to be held in Dublin. The Lord Mayor stated that he was not against the proposal but he reminded the meeting that, following dissolution, they had no funds with which to embark on an elaborate campaign. However, another motion was passed, expressing the opinion that the members of the dissolved Corporation should withdraw from the boards and committees of other public bodies on which they sat as representatives of the Corporation.

The protest meeting by the Corporation's elected members did not receive much publicity; nor did it lead to the citizens of Dublin speaking out against the dissolution. One reason for this is that on the evening that the meeting was held, the Government released the report of the public inquiry to selected newspapers. It is unclear if this was O'Dwyer's full report or an abridged version of it – the newspapers described it as containing sixty-six pages, hardly the 'voluminous document' that Minister Séamus Burke had referred to in the Dáil?

Whether it was the complete document or not, Nicholas O'Dwyer's report occupied many column inches in the newspapers over the days which followed. The majority of the report summarised the evidence presented at the inquiry, before Inspector O'Dwyer drew a series of conclusions, which he linked to the work of specific Corporation committees. Interestingly, the Inspector referred to 'a rather extraordinary change' which had occurred in the performance of the Corporation. When the elected members had taken office in 1920, O'Dwyer reported that they had 'accomplished great things for the better management of the city administration'; however in the past twelve months they had made little effort to suit their administration to prevailing economic conditions (14). Though O'Dwyer made no direct reference to it in his report, it is perhaps worth reflecting on the fact that for the best part of a year from September 1922, Lord Mayor, Councillor Laurence O'Neill, had been absent from the council due to ill-health. There is no doubt that the Corporation was somewhat rudderless in his absence.

Notwithstanding the neglect of the previous year, O'Dwyer noted: 'The administration has in general maintained a very high standard, and many members, including the chairmen of the standing committees, have diverted much time and energy to their public duties' (15). In describing the work of the Corporation's committees, O'Dwyer's report demonstrated an inconsistency of performance. He praised the Streets Committee for its work and for obtaining materials at economical prices. He criticised the Cleansing Committee, stating that there was no evidence that the quality of its work had improved, despite the introduction of better machinery. He recommended that the technical staff maintaining the sewerage and drainage system could be reduced by at least one engineer, without endangering the efficiency of the administration.

O'Dwyer maintained that the Public Health Committee was carrying out its extremely onerous duties to a high standard, though he did note that attendance of members at meetings was poor. He recommended that the equipment in the City Abattoir required immediate attention to cater for a larger proportion of meat trade in the city. The present practice of killing in private slaughter houses needed to cease due to public health risks. Turning to the Waterworks and Markets Committee, the Inspector pointed out that spending had increased considerably and had exceeded the estimates, but to a great extent, this was due to issues outside of the control of the committee.

O'Dwyer's harshest criticisms of the Corporation were centred on four issues. First, he asserted that the rates were too high. This was not so much due to the work carried out by the committees, but was the responsibility of the municipal council as a whole. The second issue that O'Dwyer highlighted was linked to the first one; a reason for the high rates was that work carried out through the council's committees was directed to the Stanley Street Workshops, without more competitive and economical solutions being sought. O'Dwyer recommended that the manufacturing department at Stanley Street should be shut down immediately. The business methods of the repairs shop should be altered and its activities curtailed. Thirdly, O'Dwyer focussed on the housing problem, though he did concede that the Corporation was not solely to blame. He stressed the evils of overcrowding in tenements and stated that if one thousand houses were built each year, it would take twenty years to put Dublin in a safe position in the matter of housing. However, the Corporation was falling well short of building one thousand houses per year and, at the present rate, it might take a century to complete. O'Dwyer also condemned the method of selecting tenants for council houses. The fourth, and perhaps most damning criticism made by O'Dwyer, related to wages. Referring to unskilled labour employed by the council, he noted that the men were paid £3, 10 shillings, 4 pence, with pensionable rights, municipal Bank Holidays, and a forty-four hour week. O'Dwyer stated in his report that the workers spent two hours of the forty-four 'going for their wages'. Compared to the rates paid by other bodies in the city and accepted by the unions, the Corporation rate was excessive by three pence per hour, for which the citizens were taxed eleven pence in the pound. A motion requesting the Corporation to inaugurate a conference with employee representatives regarding a revision of the war wage payable was turned down by a vote of twenty-two to fourteen. O'Dwyer reported that he found this decision to be 'absolutely unjustifiable', adding: 'If the interests of the workers had been the motive, one would expect a motion providing that any sum whereby the wages were reduced should be devoted to providing houses' (16).

Overall, the report produced by Inspector Nicholas O'Dwyer – at least the version covered in the newspapers - was balanced and fair. It drew attention to the good work being done by the council in some areas, while also criticising the municipal authority in relation to rates, wages, housing and the Stanley Street Workshops.

While issues of mismanagement and poor use of resources were highlighted, there was no suggestion of corruption or deliberate maladministration. O'Dwyer made no clear recommendation that the Corporation should be dissolved and it is hard to justify this course of action over the holding of municipal elections. An editorial in the *Irish Independent* described the report as 'temperate' and 'moderate' and stated: 'The Inspector cannot be accused of showing any bias against the Corporation or of having gone out of his way to make a case for its dissolution' (17). The *Evening Herald* concentrated on the negative aspects of the report, commenting: 'The glaring waste of money by the Corporation destroys any chance of sympathy going out to that public body so ignominiously turned out of office' (18).

On the same day that Nicholas O'Dwyer's report was covered in the newspapers, Minister for Finance, Ernest Blythe, was replying in the Dáil to a question on behalf of the Minister for Local Government. He said that the order dissolving Dublin Corporation and appointing Commissioners was not a permanent arrangement, and it was not the intention of the Government to deprive the citizens of Dublin of their ancient rights to elect their local public representatives. 'As a matter of fact,' Minister Blythe added, 'the Minister is considering the best means of safeguarding the interests of the citizens in matters of public administration'.

It was against this backdrop that the three Commissioners who had replaced Dublin Corporation - Séamus Murphy, Dr William C. Dwyer, and Patrick J. Hernon – faced into their historic first meeting in the Council Chamber of City Hall, on Thursday 29 May.

Chapter 15
Municipal strike disrupts the start of the Tailteann Games

It was significant that the first meeting of the Commissioners took place in the council chamber of City Hall. It had not been used by the Corporation as a meeting place since British forces had occupied it on 22 December 1920 and removed the municipal flagstaff. The Corporation had held its meetings since then in the Mansion House. Even after the City Hall was handed back by Britain, it had been in the possession of the Provisional Government and was not used for local authority meetings. *The Irish Times* painted an evocative picture of the first meeting (1).

Stripped of its upholstered seats, and of the large oil paintings of former Lord Mayors which adorned the walls, the council chamber presented a strangely unfamiliar appearance. Even the Lord Mayor's oaken chair had disappeared, and the three Commissioners and a few officials seated at a table carried on the business of a Corporation of eighty members. There was no room for speech-making in the Commissioners' programme, and the sitting occupied twenty-five minutes only!

County Borough of Dublin.

The first meeting of the Commissioners who had replaced the elected members of Dublin Corporation.

From the minute book of Dublin Corporation, 29 May 1924.

Minutes of a Special Meeting of the Commissioners of the County Borough of Dublin, held in the Council Chamber, City Hall, Cork Hill, on Thursday, the 29th. day of May, 1924, at 11 a.m.

Present :—

Mr. Commissioner Seamus O'Murchadha.
Commissioner Dr. W. Dwyer.
Mr. Commissioner P. J. Hernon.

320. On the motion of Commissioner Dr. Dwyer, seconded by Mr. Commissioner Hernon, Mr. Commissioner Seamus O'Murchadha was appointed Chairman of this meeting.

The meeting began with Dr William Dwyer, seconded by Patrick Hernon, proposing that Séamus Murphy chair the proceedings. This was to happen religiously at every meeting for the next six years. E. P. McCarron's letter of 20 May was then read aloud, as was the accompanying ministerial order which appointed the three Commissioners to replace the Corporation. The Commissioners then settled down to business, under the watchful gaze of two members of the public who sat in the gallery.

The Commissioners efficiently dealt with motions which had been tabled by elected members prior to the dissolution order. They also took care of outstanding correspondence. One such letter was from Sarah Cecilia Harrison (the first woman to be elected to Dublin Corporation in 1912) asking for permission to address the council on the subject of the request of the Art Advisory Committee of the Municipal Gallery of Modern Art to the effect that the council should take action regarding Sir Hugh Lane's French pictures. The Commissioners directed the Town Clerk to notify Harrison that since the council had been dissolved, she would not be able to address the elected members.

The focus of Chairman Séamus Murphy, was on the unemployment situation in Dublin. He explained that the Commissioners had already spent some time considering what schemes they could introduce with a view to taking on a large number of the unemployed at once. Details of the schemes had been forwarded to the Department of Local Government and, if the Government facilitated the Corporation by making an early payment of money, it was hoped to start employing people within the month. It was clear that the Commissioners were men on a mission who were keen to stamp their authority and achieve some early success. Their first meeting was met with a positive reaction in the press.

In contrast, the Lord Mayor and the ousted elected members were struggling for relevance. Their protest meeting in the Mansion House on 26 May had not been well received and had been overshadowed by the publication of Nicholas O'Dwyer's report. In an effort to turn the tide of public opinion, the Lord Mayor called a public meeting in the Mansion House on Friday 6 June. He described it as a rally in support of the principle of democratic control and popular representation.

PROTEST

AGAINST THE DISSOLUTION OF THE DUBLIN CORPORATION

A MEETING

will be held in the Mansion House on

TONIGHT (FRIDAY)

at 8 p.m. The Lord Mayor will preside.

CITIZENS,

Rally in support of the principle of Democratic Control and Popular Representation. Members of the Corporation are requested to attend at Mansion House at 7.30 p.m.

Recreation of advertisements that the Lord Mayor ran in the newspapers promoting the meeting of 6 June as a protest against the dissolution of the Corporation.

The meeting was a disastrous one. The omens were bad from the start when the Lord Mayor pulled out due to illness. In his absence, the meeting was chaired by P. T. McGinley, President of the Gaelic League, and he called upon Thomas Irwin of the Dublin Workers' Council and Councillor Michael J. Moran to propose a motion protesting against the dissolution of the Corporation. When Irwin rose to speak, he was drowned out by a raucous crowd. McGinley appealed for Irwin to be heard but the interrupters were unrelenting (2). A defeated Irwin resumed his seat and the meeting - with Constance Markievicz, Maud Gonne MacBride and Dr Kathleen Lynn in attendance – was off to a bad start.

Having restored a degree of order, P. T. McGinley delivered an ardent speech in which he stated that Dublin Corporation had been dissolved because it had sinned against three parties over the years. First, it had antagonised the representatives and friends of English power in Ireland. Secondly, it had riled 'the capitalists, profiteers, and exploiters' and, thirdly, it had annoyed the Free State Government (3). This latter point was met with loud hisses and groans from the crowd.

Councillor John O'Callaghan then spoke and called on the Dublin Dáil deputies to lobby for municipal elections to proceed on 15 July, as was initially intended. He used the refrain popular with many of his fellow elected members that the dissolution of the Corporation was 'an insult to the citizens' (4). The chair of the meeting, P. T. McGinley, next invited Thomas Irwin back to the stage. Irwin's second attempt to address the crowd was no more successful than the first. His opening words were: 'As a representative of the workers here tonight …' and he was then drowned out by shouts of: 'You don't represent us' (5). McGinley made a number of attempts to calm the crowd and he appealed to them to allow Irwin to speak. However, the shouting and hissing grew louder from the floor and, once again, Irwin resumed his seat.

With the meeting descending into chaos, Councillor Patrick T. Daly came to the podium, only to be greeted with a shout of 'Up de Valera' from a man in the public gallery. Daly retired from the podium having not delivered his remarks, leading to an impassioned Alderman Thomas Lawlor criticising the crowd. He said: 'If the Government wanted to organise an effort to destroy the effect of this meeting, they could not have done it better than you have done it' (6).

Chairman McGinley made a third valiant attempt to allow Irwin to speak but he was 'loudly hissed and groaned at, and eventually retired amid cheers and applause' (7). The same fate awaited Councillor Michael J. Moran who was unable to make his speech.

At this point, it looked certain that the meeting would break up, but Councillor Hanna Sheehy-Skeffington managed to make her voice heard and she asked a direct question of the crowd: 'Do you approve of the illegal dissolution of the Dublin Corporation by the Free State Government?' The response was 'No, no' and, on this basis, the meeting approved a resolution condemning the dissolution of the local authority. In spite of the fact that the resolution was passed, the rowdy meeting could not be deemed a success. A strange atmosphere prevailed, with much personal anger directed at Thomas Irwin. Perhaps this reflected the fact that as a representative of the Dublin Workers' Council he was prepared to speak in favour of the Corporation, though it paid its labouring staff at a higher rate than was available outside. The fury towards Councillor Michael J. Moran was likely based on the belief that he was partly responsible for the dissolution, given that he had written to the Department of Local Government calling for an inquiry into the workings of the municipal workshops in Stanley Street. Though the resolution was passed and there were strong sentiments expressed against the Free State, the meeting was unsatisfactory and failed to achieve what the absent Lord Mayor had hoped it would. The newspaper coverage delighted in the shambolic nature of the gathering and it did not reflect well on the Corporation or the councillors present.

In the meantime, the actions of the Commissioners received positive comment. At their meeting on 12 June, they resolved: 'That the Munster and Leinster Bank and the Bank of Ireland be, and are hereby, requested to accept the signatures of any two of the Commissioners of the County Borough of Dublin to make payments out of funds of the Corporation of Dublin' (8). A practical reason for this decision was that the Chairman of the Commissioners, Séamus Murphy, fell ill. On 19 June, *The Irish Times* carried a report that Murphy was 'progressing favourably in the private home attached to St. Vincent's Hospital' (9). The story noted that he had been 'rather seriously ill for some days'.

Murphy was back in City Hall, however, for the next meeting of the Commissioners on Thursday 3 July. The main business conducted was to rescind decisions taken by the elected members in relation to Stanley Street.

'That the resolution adopted by the Municipal Council on the 27th November 1916, directing that no work be ordered from outside firms unless the Municipal Workshops staff is incapable of carrying such work out, and the resolution of Council of 18th February 1918, directing that competitive tenders shall not be asked for any work that can be carried out in Stanley Street, and all other resolutions to the same effect, be, and they are hereby rescinded' (10).

The Commissioners were wasting no time in ending the protected monopoly status of the Stanley Street Workshops, as recommended by Nicholas O'Dwyer. In the Dáil, Minister Séamus Burke was receiving frequent criticism for the decision to dissolve the Corporation but he was largely unperturbed and unapologetic. The Government also comfortably had legislation passed postponing local elections until the following year.

It was not all plain sailing however for the Commissioners. An attempt to reduce wages of municipal staff and labourers was resisted. A letter dated 21 July from the Irish Municipal Employees' Trade Union gave notice of strike action from the following Saturday afternoon on behalf of municipal workers. Two days before the strike, one of the Commissioners – though not named – gave an interview to *The Irish Times* claiming that the wages paid to Corporation employees were too high: 'The wages of labourers in the Corporation represents a percentage over pre-war figures of one hundred and ninety per cent. Should the strike take place on Saturday, the number of Corporation staff affected will be approximately one thousand, five hundred' (11).

The strike did start, as promised, on Saturday 26 July. *The Irish Times* noted: 'The city sewage was turned into the Liffey, the streets remained unswept since Friday, while in the suburbs neither gas lamps nor electric lights were turned on in the streets, and towards midnight, the darkness reminded one of the early days of the curfew in 1920. Happily, there was abundance of rain on Saturday and Monday, and the elements largely discharged the duties of the strikers in cleansing the streets' (12).

The Commissioners acted quickly and convened a conference for the Monday. In a little over two hours, the conference delivered an agreement that the dispute would be settled by a Court of Arbitration. The unions and the Commissioners agreed to be bound by the decision. On the day of the conference, the President of the Executive Council of Dáil Éireann, William T. Cosgrave, staunchly defended the Commissioners and sharply criticised the municipal staff who had gone out on strike. Labour TD, John Thomas O'Farrell, asserted that Dublin Corporation 'might have done many silly and nonsensical things' but that it would not have been guilty of the folly which had led to the industrial dispute (13). Cosgrave did not accept O'Farrell's charge, saying that it was irresponsible of municipal staff, before any formal proposal to reduce wages had been tabled, 'to throw down the gauntlet of war'. He claimed that citizens were not getting value for the heavy rates they were paying and it was wrong to commence strike action just as Dublin was about to boom with the Tailteann Games and the Horse Show (14). Labour Senator and former Corporation member, Thomas Farren, alleged that the Commissioners had been sent to the Corporation in place of the elected members for the sole purpose of reducing wages. President Cosgrave curtly replied: 'On behalf of the Government, I deny that' (15).

With an ongoing industrial dispute awaiting a judgement from the Court of Arbitration, the Commissioners would not have been best pleased by a letter from E. P. McCarron which was placed on the agenda for the meeting of Thursday 31 July. The letter was accompanied by an order from Minister Séamus Burke, detailing the remuneration of the Commissioners, back-dated to May 1924, as follows:

Séamus Murphy	£1,000 per annum
Patrick Hernon	£800 per annum
Dr Dwyer	£500 per annum

Much to the annoyance and embarrassment of the Government and the Commissioners, municipal employees continued their strike action pending the decision of the Court of Arbitration. This caused some disruption to the first Aonach Tailteann (Tailteann Games) which started on 2 August and ran until 17 August. The list of sporting events covered by the Tailteann Games was notable and included athletics, weight throwing, decathlon, swimming, diving, cycling, rowing, boxing, rounders, golf, tennis, gymnastics, wrestling, motor cycling, car racing, billiards, chess, Gaelic football, hurling, handball and camogie (16). Soccer, rugby, cricket and hockey were excluded due to the ban imposed by the Gaelic Athletic Association. As well as sporting events, there were competitions in Irish dancing, poetry, prose, drama, oratory and story-telling.

The hosting of the Tailteann Games was massive for Dublin and an estimated crowd of twenty thousand people attended the opening ceremony in Croke Park. Competitors entered the stadium representing Ireland, England, Scotland, Wales, the United States of America, Canada, Australia, New Zealand and South Africa (17). After the Games were officially opened by William T. Cosgrave, a banquet was held in the Metropole Hotel. William Butler Yeats, Chairman of the Aonach Tailteann Distinguished Visitors Committee, addressed the crowd at the banquet but he and Cosgrave were both embarrassed by the fact that the municipal strike meant that there was no electricity in the building. It was reported that diners had to make do with candles (18).

With thousands of visitors in Dublin for the Games, Cosgrave was desperate to end the municipal strike and he wanted to do so before Monday 4 August which was a Bank Holiday. It was also an extremely busy day for competitions in the Tailteann Games. Accordingly, at one o'clock on the afternoon of Sunday 3 August, it was announced that the strike had ended and municipal workers had returned to work: 'Within three hours, the electricity supply was almost restored; in the evening the cinema halls re-opened; and by nightfall a serious effort to resume the services which are vital to the public health of the city had begun' (19).

The Commissioners had sought a wage reduction of six shilling per week, in three 'cuts' of two shillings starting in September 1924. Under the terms of the agreement reached after the strike, it was approved that there would be no reductions in salary until January 1925. At that point, there would be a cut of one shilling per week, followed by a further cut of one shilling in March. After a three-hour meeting in the Mansion House, the strikers voted for acceptance of the terms of the settlement. The agreement was signed by Commissioners Séamus Murphy and Patrick Hernon but the man who received the most praise for brokering the deal was Michael J. Moran, the former chairman of the Corporation's Finance

Committee. When the Commissioners met in City Hall for a meeting on Thursday 7 August, Séamus Murphy stated that he was pleased the dispute was at an end but he did not regard the reduction in wage levels as adequate. However, he added: 'The terms on which the strike has been settled were dictated solely by the necessity for carrying on the essential services of the city, and the avoidance, at a very critical time, of the spread of the trouble which any strike invariably brings' (20). The wage cuts proposed by the Commissioners may have led to strike action at any point but Murphy, Hernon and Dwyer got their timing wrong by trying to force the issue through before the start of the Tailteann Games. The strikers had the upper hand as the Government could not allow a situation where there was no electricity or refuse collection while thousands of people visited Dublin for the Games. It is little wonder that *The Irish Times* reported that the strikers returned to work completely satisfied (21).

Chapter 16
The Dublin Commissioners make their mark as Cork is used as a guinea pig

August 1924 was also the month when eleven of the now former councillors came together and published a thirty-one page booklet entitled *A Vindication of the Municipal Council of the City of Dublin*. The driving force behind the document was Seán T. O'Kelly and the other ten signatories were Séamus Ó'Maoilfhinn, Patrick Gordon, Laurence Raul, John O'Callaghan, Joseph Mooney, Charles Murphy, Thomas Atkins, John Lawlor, Patrick T. Daly and Joseph Clarke. Noticeably, the Lord Mayor, Laurence O'Neill, was not associated with it.

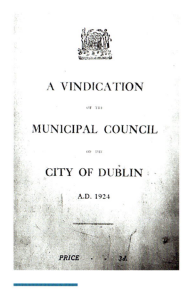

Seán T. O'Kelly was the primary architect of the *Vindication* document; the detail contained in it was impressive but it did not make an impact on the citizens of Dublin.

Old Dublin Society Library, RDS.

The first chapter of the booklet drew attention to the ancient status of Dublin and claimed: 'For many centuries have the citizens enjoyed and maintained the right to govern their own city' (1). The decision to dissolve the Corporation was described as unjust and unwise, and an act unprecedented in the history of the country: 'There could be only one justification for such an action; that is, namely, proof that the body so treated was guilty of notorious, dangerous, and infamous corruption. No such proof was forthcoming against the Dublin council' (2). Inspector O'Dwyer was subjected to harsh criticism: 'No report from the Government official who held the inquiry was issued to enlighten the citizens as to the result of his investigation. Like Pontius Pilate, he found no cause, washed his hands, and dried them with his report' (3).

In the second chapter, Seán T. O'Kelly and his colleagues examined different aspects of the council's work – housing, roads, cleansing, water works, public markets – and defended the policies approved by the elected members. In relation to the controversial Stanley Street Workshops, the document noted: 'This municipal undertaking is the great bugbear of the plague of "Civic Reformers" which this city has been afflicted with for the past ten or fifteen years. These workshops were organised for the purpose of having the principal work done for the council carried out by direct labour, and with the best material and workmanship, so that the right value would be given for the money spent. This certainly was the intention of the promoters, at first. Unfortunately, interested opposition was discernible from the start' (4). The authors made a valid point about wages paid to labourers in Stanley Street, stressing that the rates were set after an arbitration process chaired by Sir John Griffith. The arbitration ruling by Griffith was printed in full, with his conclusion that the municipal workshops could not be classed as contractors' shops and therefore employees were entitled to the same wages as had been agreed for municipal staff generally.

The problems associated with the Corporation's overall financial ill-health were laid at the door of the British and Free State Governments. It was asserted that the two Governments owed the Corporation a combined total of £82,496. If this money was received, it would have enabled the councillors to reduce the rates paid by citizens and businesses. Alas, the eleven former councillors noted: 'Whether these large sums will ever be paid, we cannot say' (5).

The third chapter was largely an attack on the press. The authors claimed that there were no noble-minded men connected any longer with the Dublin press and that the Corporation was not treated fairly. In particular: '*The Irish Times* and *Daily Express*, being of that complexion of politics known as Unionist, nearly always allowed their political bias to outbalance their judgment in dealing with Corporation affairs' (6). The *Freeman's Journal* had traditionally done the Corporation justice but, recently, 'had opened its columns to some of the most unfair criticism' (7). The *Irish Independent* was described as evil on the basis that it had 'thrown even decency aside' in reporting on the Corporation (8). The former councillors argued that the unduly negative attitude of the press had created an unwholesome impression amongst citizens: 'They [the citizens] believed when they saw this constant and continual reiteration of half-lies and half-truths concerning the Corporation that there was something wrong, but that the wrong was so cleverly obscured as to baffle investigation' (9).

The concluding chapter asserted again that the Corporation which had existed until its unfair dissolution in May 1924 was doing a good job and had improved greatly from the period when 'the system of bigoted ascendancy' was rampant in the municipal council (10). The plea was made – 'We know the Dublin people well' – as an argument that the Corporation should be restored (11). The final pages focussed on the Catholic faith, leading to the following concluding paragraph (12):

> *It is true that the Dublin churches are the places where the city people are rich, because each day the thousands that throng them give evidence of it. Rich in their prayers to the Almighty God that He might send them better days and restore brotherhood and concord, and the ardent wish for the time when the bloody and unclean spirit of militarism amongst us will be cast out. Then in that day of the Lord, the Dublin people will come back into their own.*

The document was then dated 26 August 1924 and signed by eleven former members of Dublin Corporation.

It would be wrong to state that the press reacted negatively to the *Vindication* booklet – rather, they showed indifference and ignored it. There was some justification to this as it was a long-winded and poorly-written document with a bizarre closing chapter focussing on the Catholic Church and religious faith. The former councillors had gone to the trouble of publishing it themselves, but

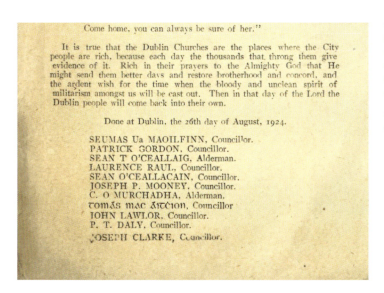

Eleven former members of the dissolved Dublin Corporation put their names to the *Vindication* document.

Old Dublin Society Library, RDS.

it was unlikely that they sold too many copies at a price of 3 pence. Richard Haslam's (2003) polite conclusion is that the document 'drew little notice' (13). The truth is that the citizens of Dublin quietly acquiesced to the dissolution of the Corporation and had moved on into the reign of the three Commissioners. The publication of *A Vindication of the Municipal Council of the City of Dublin* was seen as a desperate measure by former councillors trying to cling to relevancy.

In the meantime, the Commissioners were continuing their work to reform the activities of the Corporation and they had their sights set on the Stanley Street Workshops. Inspector O'Dwyer had recommended the immediate cessation of the workshops as a manufacturing concern but had favoured the continuation of the repair shop on a reduced basis. At the meeting of Thursday 11 September in City Hall, the future of the workshops was debated. Since the last meeting, Commissioner Patrick Hernon, accompanied by the Town Clerk, John J. Murphy, and by Henry Thunder, Chief Clerk of the Stanley Street Workshops, had visited municipalities in England where similar workshops existed. Following a discussion, the Commissioners decided that the workshops should remain in existence, but they agreed with Inspector O'Dwyer that the scope of operations should be reduced to the execution of such repairs as could with advantage be carried out by direct labour (14). The Commissioners vowed as well to end what they described as an 'absurd arrangement' whereby some labourers in the workshops were also attached to Corporation departments, for example fitters in the Electricity and Main Drainage Department, and were effectively benefiting from an element of double pay. At the meeting a fortnight later, a letter was read from the Department of Local Government sanctioning the reorganisation of the Stanley Street Workshops as recommended by the Commissioners. The workshops were to continue for repairs on a three-year experimental period. At the end of that period, their future would be considered. The Minister also sanctioned the appointment of Henry Thunder as Manager of the Stanley Street Workshops with a rank of staff officer and an annual salary on the scale of £500 to £750. At the same meeting, the Commissioners announced the retirement of City Accountant, Henry Mangan, who was to be appointed as a member of the Railway Tribunal.

As the Commissioners settled in and the administration of the city entered a more stable period, the future of the capital was being considered by Government. In January 1923, the Government had been angered when it learned that Dublin Corporation's Law Agent, Ignatius Rice, was drafting a bill to extend the city's boundaries to include all urban districts in the county from Howth to Killiney, as well as Bray in county Wicklow and a large swathe of the adjoining countryside (15). An agitated Minister for Local Government, Ernest Blythe TD, told the Executive Council that since Dublin was now the seat of Government, its boundaries were 'no longer merely a matter for the Corporation' (16). Charles O'Connor, a former Local Government Board inspector, was commissioned by Minister Blythe to examine the Corporation's proposals and prepare a memorandum for Government on future boundaries (17). The O'Connor memorandum favoured a more modest extension of the city boundaries than that envisaged by the Corporation. On foot of O'Connor's recommendations, the Government appointed a twelve-member Commission of Inquiry in July 1924, just two months after the dissolution of the Corporation. The inquiry, chaired by William Magennis TD, Professor of Metaphysics at University College Dublin, was given a broad brief (18):

> To examine the several laws and the practice affecting the administration of local and public utility services, including local representation and taxation throughout the capital city of Dublin, and the county of Dublin, and to recommend such changes as may be desirable.

The Greater Dublin Commission of Inquiry met for two years before reporting in 1926. David Dickson (2014) describes its membership as 'a strange assortment of business, labour and academic figures' (19). Perhaps the Government felt that it was best that the inquiry did its work in the absence of an elected municipal council.

As Professor Magennis and his colleagues met throughout 1925, the work of Dublin's three Commissioners continued with the support of the Government. From late 1924, the Commissioners had begun to hold meetings on Saturdays and, at the meeting on 17 January 1925, they announced that the Minister for Local Government and Public Health had allocated them £45,000 for the relief of unemployment. When the Commissioners met on Saturday 6 June, the main item on the agenda was the status of the Lord Mayor, Laurence O'Neill, who continued to live in the Mansion House. On 9 May, on the orders of the Commissioners, the Town Clerk, John J. Murphy, had written to E. P. McCarron in the Department of Local Government and Public Health about the Lord Mayor, as follows:

9 May 1925

Dear Sir,

Re: Position of Lord Mayor

Immediately after the appointment of the County Borough Commissioners, I consulted the Law Agent with regard to continuing to pay to the Lord Mayor the salary attaching to the office and received his opinion to the effect that the Commissioners should not take the risk of paying the salary beyond the date of the order of the Ministry dissolving the Municipal Council. I enclose a copy of the Law Agent's opinion from which you will see that he considers the question as to whether Mr. O'Neill still occupies the position of Lord Mayor is one upon which he does not find himself in a position to express a confident opinion, and, to the present, the Commissioners have not taken any steps to obtain further advice in the matter.

On the 22nd September 1924, Mr. O'Neill handed me, as representing the Commissioners, possession of the public rooms in the Mansion House as distinct from the portion occupied by him as the private residence of the Lord Mayor. He still continues to attend daily at the Mansion House, and it is fairly certain that he has some of his own property therein, though the Corporation own the furniture. The Commissioners think that the question as to whether Mr. O'Neill continues to be the Lord Mayor and is rightfully in occupation of the Mansion House by virtue of his office is one which should now be determined. I have been instructed by them to ask you if you will kindly obtain from the Minister, for their guidance, an authoritative declaration as to the effect of the order of 20th May 1924 (dissolving the Municipal Council) on the position of Lord Mayor.

Yours faithfully,
John J. Murphy
Town Clerk

The reply from E. P. McCarron, on behalf of the Minister, came on Friday 5 June and stated that Laurence O'Neill had not held the office of Lord Mayor since the dissolution of the Corporation. The Commissioners noted this at their meeting the following day. When the news broke, Laurence O'Neill, gave an interview to the press in which he stated (20):

> I feel not a little puzzled that such a letter should have been sent after thirteen months, since the order suspending the Corporation specifically provided that the Lord Mayor and his colleagues who are nominated by the council to act on other boards as members of the Corporation should be allowed to do so. During the last thirteen months, I have acted as Lord Mayor at the Port and Docks Board, at the National University, and on other bodies, and no exception has been taken. I am still in occupancy of the Mansion House and have not been interfered with by anyone.

Laurence O'Neill quietly left the Mansion House in the latter half of 1925 and moved back to the family home, Bridge House in Portmarnock county Dublin. It was a difficult period of time for the former Lord Mayor who had enjoyed such a prominent status in the city. As described by his biographer, Thomas Morrissey (20):

> O'Neill, who enjoyed the limelight, was to find that once out of public office, his name and achievements were soon forgotten. Public appreciation, he was to lament more than once, was fickle and short-lived. To some extent he found himself tarred with the ill-reputation ascribed to the Corporation; and business rivals, who kept their distance while he was Lord Mayor, now felt free to undermine his ailing firm, which had been neglected both by his absence through illness and by his various municipal activities and expenditures, and also by the decline in customers for corn products with the withdrawal of the British army and the decrease in the number of horses. Before long, he was to find himself in financial difficulties.

O'Neill would contest the 1927 general election as an Independent but, with few resources to support his campaign, he failed to win a seat. So difficult were his financial circumstances that he wrote to William T. Cosgrave, President of the Executive Council of the Dáil, on a number of occasions, for help. After one such letter in which he pleaded – 'I will be frank with you, you are the only one in this world I would approach, as the bank has turned me down' – it was arranged that he would meet with Cosgrave (21). Following the meeting on 24 May 1928, Cosgrave authorised his officials to 'pay out of the Dáil Special Fund to Mr. Laurence O'Neill, Bridge House, Portmarnock, the sum of £250, which is repayable' (22). The following month, a further payment of £250 to O'Neill was authorised by Cosgrave.

By the time Laurence O'Neill left the Mansion House in late 1925, the three Commissioners were well established. With a minimum of fuss, they reformed aspects of the city's municipal administration. The press reduced its coverage of meetings to a bare minimum; after the failure of the *Vindication* document, the former councillors accepted their fate; and no more questions were being asked in the Dáil about the dissolution of the Corporation and the publication of Nicholas O'Dwyer's report.

At this time, the Department of Local Government and Public Health published its first report, covering the period from 1 April 1922 to 31 March 1925. It justified the passing of the Local Government (Temporary Provisions) Act 1923 and the introduction of the power of dissolution as follows (23):

> *Early in the period of administration under review, it was evident that there was a demand for powers to enable the removal of such elected councils as, by reason of incompetence or neglect, had shown themselves unfitted to discharge their public duties.*

The report praised the Commissioners who had replaced local elected councils which had been dissolved, stating: 'The appointees have proved worthy of the trust placed in them' (24). Appendix A of the department's report contained a detailed twelve-page summary statement from Dublin's three Commissioners, for the ten months of activity from May 1924 to 31 March 1925. The Commissioners had certainly made a positive impact in a relatively short period of time, at a policy level and at a mundane administrative level. An example of the latter is a simple reform they introduced for stationery supplies. It had been the custom for each department in the Corporation to order its own stationery. Consequently, there was no coordination across the organisation. The Commissioners decided

The Irish Times, Saturday 6 June 1925

OFFICE IN ABEYANCE

The Dublin Borough Commissioners will have before them today a letter from the Secretary of the Ministry of Local Government, which states that:

'From the date of the Minister's order dissolving the Council of the Borough of Dublin, the office of Lord Mayor has not been held by Mr. Laurence O'Neill.' The Council was dissolved in May, 1924.

LORD MAYOR SURPRISED

In the course of an interview yesterday the Lord Mayor expressed surprise that any such communication should have been addressed to the Commissioners by the Ministry of Local Government. Although thirteen months had elapsed since the dissolution of the Corporation, he himself had heard nothing of the matter, and he felt not a little puzzled how to account for the present state of affairs. The order dissolving the Council contained a provision that he and those other members of that Council that had been appointed to serve on certain public bodies, like the Port and Docks Board, should continue to act on those bodies. By virtue of his position he had become an ex-officio member of the Port Board and of certain other bodies, and, of course, after the abolition of the Corporation, had continued still to attend their meetings. No exception had ever been taken to that, and for that reason he was quite at a loss now to understand the position created by the Ministry's letter.

The Lord mayor added that he still occupied the Mansion House, and that his occupancy was not being interfered with.

Laurence O'Neill spoke to the press on 5 June 1925, after a letter from E. P. McCarron, on behalf of the Minister for Local Government and Public Health, stated that he had not held the office of Lord Mayor since the dissolution of the Corporation.

that all stationery required by a department in the Corporation would have to be ordered through the Finance and General Purposes Section. They reported: 'In this way alone is a check kept of the supplies to the departments, but it has resulted in economies being affected in the prices paid for the various articles by reason of the standardisation of forms and books' (25). Under the section on street cleansing, the Commissioners stated that they had taken steps to avail of the Government offer of grants for the reconstruction of trunk roads and the relief of unemployment. They pointedly added: 'The work under these grants had been held up owing to the unwillingness of the dissolved Corporation to agree to the terms on which the grants were offered' (26). Regarding the Stanley Street Workshops, the Commissioners justified their strategy of closing most of the sections but retaining some repair and maintenance work: 'Various other alterations and new arrangements were effected for greater efficiency, whilst the cost of the managerial staff was reduced from £3,407 to £2,066 per annum' (27). The Commissioners also took credit for a variety of other reforms, for example, opening children's departments in the Charleville Mall and Pearse Street libraries, and installing a new system of ventilation in the wash-house at the Iveagh market. They noted that this measure had resulted in a significant improvement for the women who had previously worked there 'in an atmosphere continuously super-charged with steam, the effect of which was injurious to their health' (28). Perhaps most importantly of all for Dublin's citizens and business people, the Commissioners explained that after only ten months in office, they had completed their consideration of the estimates for 1925/1926 and were able to reduce the city rates by two shillings in the pound, to seventeen shillings and two pence.

The Dublin Commissioners benefitted from the fact that the Government was more forthcoming with funds for them than it had been for the old Corporation. At the meeting in City Hall on Saturday 30 January 1926, the Commissioners expressed satisfaction that the Department of Local Government and Public Health had sanctioned a loan of £120,000 for the purpose of improving water supply to the north side of the city. This followed a public inquiry on water supply in Dublin and a report by the chair of the inquiry, Nicholas O'Dwyer. At the same meeting, the Commissioners agreed to seek a loan for the reconstruction of the City Abattoir and the purchase of new machinery. They also ratified the arrangement by which the Dublin Tramway Company's wayleave lease was extended for a further forty-two years, on their taking over and operating the tram service from

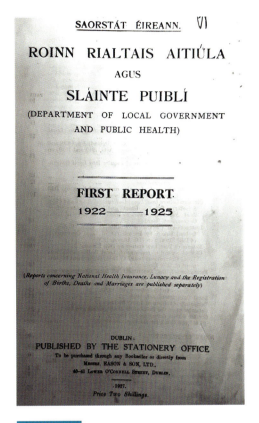

SAORSTÁT ÉIREANN. VI

ROINN RIALTAIS AITIÚLA

AGUS

SLÁINTE PUIBLÍ

(DEPARTMENT OF LOCAL GOVERNMENT
AND PUBLIC HEALTH)

FIRST REPORT

1922——1925

(Reports concerning National Health Insurance, Lunacy and the Registration of Births, Deaths and Marriages are published separately)

DUBLIN:
PUBLISHED BY THE STATIONERY OFFICE
To be purchased through any Bookseller or directly from
Messrs. EASON & SON, LTD.,
40-41 Lower O'Connell Street, Dublin.

1927.
Price Two Shillings.

The first annual report for the Department of Local Government and Public Health covered the period from 1 April 1922 to 31 March 1925. It justified the decision to dissolve local authorities who 'had shown themselves unfit to discharge their public duties' and it contained a detailed twelve-page report from the Dublin Commissioners for the ten months they had been in office.

Dublin to Lucan. The Commissioners were cracking down too on matters of staff discipline. They began to make salary deductions for non-punctual attendance, a measure which received the approval of E. P. McCarron and Minister Séamus Burke (29). The salary levels of the Commissioners themselves were rising. At the meeting of Saturday 31 July, the Commissioners read into the minutes the decision of the Government to increase their pay. Séamus Murphy and Patrick Hernon were now to receive an annual salary of £1,200, with Dr William Dwyer getting £700.

After two years of deliberation, the Greater Dublin Commission of Inquiry, chaired by Professor Magennis, reported in 1926. The commission's report 'was said to have been written by Magennis, working mainly on a submission put in by the Greater Dublin Movement' (30). The report was a radical one, described by Mary E. Daly as combining 'a disregard for existing institutions with a distrust of local democracy' (31). It recommended that Greater Dublin would absorb Rathmines, Pembroke and the adjoining rural areas, plus Dun Laoghaire, Blackrock, Dalkey and Killiney. Crucially, it called for an ending of the role of Lord Mayor, as well as other historic offices such as swordbearer, macebearer, and city marshal. The redundant Mansion House was to become an art gallery and the City Council would be restricted to matters of civic policy, budget, rating, adoptive legislation and general supervision (32). The most critical recommendation was that executive functions should be transferred from an elected council to a salaried city manager, appointed by the Minister for Local Government and Public Health: 'The scheme of city management under an elective council accords with the best experience of the United States, Germany, and the more progressive cantons of Switzerland. Civic administration is a business; accordingly, the Commission recommends the entrusting of the civic management of Greater Dublin to the business conduct of a body of Directors' (33).

Though the Government reaction to the report was unenthusiastic, Magennis and his colleagues on the Commission had 'provided a badly needed official boost for the introduction of town planning' (34). The Government ultimately dismissed many aspects of the report by passing it to a committee within the Department of Local Government and Public Health for further study. Opposition TD, Seán Lemass, stated that the Government was treating the report as 'a sort of joke' (35).

The headline recommendation though was the introduction of a city manager. Dáil deputy, Professor Ernest Henry Alton of Trinity College, described the proposal as 'hopelessly undemocratic' (36). He expressed concerns that the city manager would become all powerful within the proposed new system.

The Commission proposed that the city manager would be responsible for preparing the budget and for all appointments. Councillors could consider and approve the budget, but would have no role in the appointment, promotion or dismissal of officials. The manager could appeal to the minister against the council, but the only redress for the councillors was to hold a referendum – this first needed a two-thirds majority of the elected members (37). The initial response to the report was lukewarm but an important seed had been sown: 'The report marked the first quasi-official endorsement of the suggestion that a distinction in law should be made between the functions of elected politicians and of permanent officials in local government' (38).

Meanwhile, in Cork, John J. Horgan, the influential founding member of the Cork Progressive Association, wrote an article for the journal *Studies* in which he advocated for a new model of local democracy based on power-sharing between elected members and an appointed commissioner or city manager (39). He argued that the current Irish model was 'a somewhat confusing and an illogical mixture of both these tendencies' (40). Cork Corporation had been dissolved on 31 October 1924, with Commissioner Philip Monahan taking charge, after his spell in Kerry. The dissolution followed a nine-day public inquiry, chaired by the Government's most favoured inspector, Nicholas O'Dwyer. Horgan took it upon himself to draft the Cork City Management Bill 1926, based on the appointment of a manager (he recommended Philip Monahan) and a small council of twelve members. The Government did nothing with the proposal which greatly disappointed Horgan, who wrote to E. P. McCarron: 'I suppose it all means my poor legislative child is dead. Perhaps its ghost may arise in some other shape in the future' (41). McCarron replied: 'I have great hopes that the "legislative child" will not appear in Statistics of Infant Mortality' (42).

This proved to be the case. During a Dáil debate in November 1927, Minister for Local Government and Public Health, Richard Mulcahy TD (who had replaced Séamus Burke) said that even though the Commissioner system was working well in Dublin and Cork, he foresaw a time would come when both Corporations would be restored. Minister Mulcahy visited Cork in January 1928 and spoke of his desire to establish a reformed Cork Corporation with managerial control (43). He gave effect to this promise by introducing the Cork City Management Bill to the Dáil in June 1928. The bill took a long route through the Dáil and was keenly debated. Seán French TD – Lord Mayor of Cork when the Corporation was dissolved in 1924, and now a Fianna Fáil deputy – said during the second-stage debate that he wanted 'a City Manager appointed and not a city master' (44).

The Cork City Management Act, 1929, finally passed into law in February 1929. It contained many interesting provisions. After numerous re-writes, it had been agreed that Cork Corporation would contain twenty-one councillors. This group of twenty-one would be elected in 1929 – the first seven members elected would hold office until 1932, the next seven members elected would hold office until 1931 and the remaining seven members would hold office until 1930. Then, in 1930, and for every subsequent year, seven members would be elected for a three-year term (45). Under Section 10 of the legislation, Philip Monahan was named as the first city manager and it stated: 'the Manager shall hold office until he dies, resigns or is removed from office' (46). The elected members had the power to suspend the manager if they passed a resolution by not less than two-thirds of the council present and voting. Only the Minister, however, had the power to remove the manager. The Cork City Management Act, 1929, was

Members of the council after Cork Corporation was re-instated following local elections in 1929. Lord Mayor, Councillor Seán French, is third from the right on the front row, with City Manager, Philip Monahan, on his left. Monahan was Ireland's first City Manager.

Irish Examiner.

based on power-sharing; the councillors had responsibility for policy matters while Monahan was given full charge of the Corporation staff, the preparation of its budget and the control of expenditure.

The local government environment was changing significantly, with Cork as the guinea pig for the experimental city management system. What would the implications be for Dublin?

Chapter 17
Gerald Sherlock tries to turn the doubtful experiment into a success

Though very much aware of developments in Cork and the likelihood that the city management experiment would be extended to Dublin, the capital's Commissioners continued to work quietly and efficiently and with little fanfare. At their meeting in City Hall on Saturday 27 August 1927, the Commissioners sanctioned the retirement of Town Clerk, John J. Murphy, after thirty-six years in the service of the Corporation. This was to allow him to take up duties as the first chairman of the Electricity Supply Board (ESB). Ever mindful of money, the Commissioners agreed to release Murphy on the understanding that the Government would recoup to the Corporation the amount of pension payable to the Town Clerk during his period of service to the Government. Patrick Hernon paid a generous tribute to Murphy and proposed to his fellow Commissioners that the role of Town Clerk should be filled by Gerald J. Sherlock, who had been in the position of Assistant Town Clerk since June 1926. Sherlock had thirty years of Corporation service to his name, and the Commissioners approved his appointment at an annual salary of £1,200, rising to the maximum of £1,500 by annual increments of £50. The Commissioners further decided not to fill the role of Assistant Town Clerk at that time.

The Freedom of Dublin had not been conferred on anybody since the dissolution of the Corporation in 1924. That changed at the meeting of the Commissioners on Saturday 30 June 1928, when the following resolution was passed (1):

> *That the honorary Freedom of the city of Dublin be, and is hereby, conferred upon Baron Gunther von Hunefeld, Captain Hermann Koehl and Major James Fitzmaurice, and that they be elected honorary burgesses of this County Borough of Dublin, pursuant to the provisions of the Municipal Privilege Act (Ireland), 1876.*

The three recipients were known as the 'Atlantic Flyers' and they had completed the first trans-Atlantic aircraft flight from east to west in April, in a plane named the

'Bremen'. Major James Fitzmaurice was a Dubliner and he and his two colleagues departed Baldonnel at just after five-thirty on the morning of Thursday 12 April 1928, despite an unexpected obstruction in the form of a wandering sheep (2). After thirty-six and-a-half hours in the air, they landed on Greenly Island, situated between Labrador and Newfoundland in the Strait of Belle Isle in the Gulf of St. Lawrence, Canada: 'News of the successful East-West crossing of the Atlantic was greeted with jubilation throughout the world. It grabbed headlines in all the major newspapers both sides of the Atlantic. The event particularly captured the imagination of the American public' (3). On Tuesday 3 July, Dublin ground to a standstill as Fitzmaurice, von Hunefeld, and Koehl were conferred with the freedom of the city. At a special banquet in Clery's restaurant, Commissioner Séamus Murphy proposed the toast of 'Éire' and presented the three men with artistically illuminated scrolls before inviting them to sign the historic roll of Dublin freemen. During his speech, Major Fitzmaurice said that two Germans and one Irishman were a good combination: 'The Germans are good fellows to fight against, and they are also good fellows to fight with' (4).

The 'Atlantic Flyers' were conferred with the Freedom of Dublin in June 1928 and received an enthusiastic welcome during a parade through the city centre.

National Library of Ireland.

On Saturday 25 August 1928, the Commissioners agreed to add another person to the list of freemen of Dublin. They passed a resolution conferring the honour on Frank B. Kellogg, the American Secretary of State 'in recognition of his distinguished services to the cause of world peace' (5). Kellogg's conferring ceremony took place in the Mansion House on Thursday 30 August, in the presence of President of the Executive Council, William T. Cosgrave. As chairman of the Commissioners, Séamus Murphy delivered the opening remarks, saying to Kellogg: 'In you, the angels of peace have come to administer to men again. With your advent in Europe has come the birth of what may be termed the second era of peace' (6). In his acceptance speech, a grateful Kellogg noted (7):

I cannot tell you the deep emotion which I feel on visiting your city. As the scroll of the history of the centuries is unrolled, we see how many pages of that history have been written in Dublin, and how much of the world's panorama of history Dublin has been the scene of. It has seen the great victories of humanity, the romances and the tragedies. It has seen her sons go forth to the world and occupy great places.

Perhaps realising that their time was limited, the Commissioners became more noticeably public figures during this period and also increasingly outward focussed. 'Civic weeks' were organised in 1927 and 1929 involving military tattoos, historical pageants and firework displays: 'There was a strikingly non-partisan effort to stimulate public interest in the city's culture and commerce. Strategic planning, forgotten since 1916, came back into vogue, and there was a new determination to complete the reconstruction of the city centre' (8).

The three Commissioners were aware that the Government was preparing legislation relating to new local government arrangements in the city and were not surprised when the Local Government (Dublin) Bill was introduced in December 1929. Edward Sheehy (2003) notes that it was a long and complex bill which immediately ran into heavy weather: 'Its progress was not helped by a novel and unpopular proposal to modify the local government franchise in Dublin by instituting a "commercial register" giving special representation to business on the new city council' (9). Even though the Bill proposed by Minister Richard Mulcahy followed the principles of the Cork legislation, it proved contentious as it progressed slowly through the Dáil and the Seanad. Along the way, many amendments were made to the original bill. Speaking in the Dáil on Wednesday 26 February 1930, Seán T. O'Kelly criticised the fact that all but four of the ninety-five recommendations of the Greater Dublin Inquiry were ignored (10). He argued that the powers to be granted to the city manager were autocratic and he condemned the introduction of the commercial register. By the time the bill was discussed in the Seanad on Wednesday 28 May, Labour senator, and former member of Dublin Corporation, Thomas Farren broadly supported what was being proposed. Minister Richard Mulcahy had stated that the current Commissioners would be overlooked in favour of Town Clerk, Gerald Sherlock, to become Dublin's first city manager. Farren noted: 'The proposal with regard to the City Manager which is introduced is, to my mind, being done in the wrong way, but much of my objection to the City Managership has been removed by the fact that the City Manager to be appointed will be the Town Clerk. I always believed that the Town Clerk in the City of Dublin was in reality the City Manager, and for that reason I have no objection to the City Managership as outlined in the Bill, when the present executive officer of the municipality will be the City Manager' (11). Though far from satisfied with all of the content in the bill, Seán T. O'Kelly also expressed his support for Sherlock's appointment – he had feared that Dublin's first city manager would be one of the Government's 'pets' as he called them, i.e. the three Commissioners (12). The Bill was eventually passed in July 1930. The new regime would take effect after the holding of local elections; the council would comprise thirty-five members (compared to the previous eighty-four), with thirty 'ordinary' members and five commercial members.

Voting for the members of the new Dublin Corporation took place on Tuesday 30 September. One hundred and one candidates were nominated to contest for the thirty-five seats, five of which were to be filled by representatives of commerce in Dublin through a postal ballot. All of the main political parties were represented, including Fianna Fáil which had only been formed in March 1926, during the reign of the Commissioners. Some of the Independent candidates, including Senator Alfie Byrne, came together to run under the banner of the Greater Dublin Constitutional Group. Enthusiasm was low amongst the citizens of Dublin, with one newspaper report describing 30 September 1930 as 'the dullest and quietest election day in living memory' (13). On the day that the election results were published, 2 October, the editorial of *The Irish Times* remarked favourably on the new commercial register: 'We are very glad that the revived Corporation of Dublin will have a strong leaven of persons who are skilled in business and are pledged to keep their minds on business' (14).

Concern was expressed however about Fianna Fáil, who claimed five seats on the new Corporation: 'The Fianna Fáil Party may be satisfied with the success of some of its leading members. These persons have made no secret of their intention to carry politics, of the most full-blooded kind, into civic affairs, and here is a real danger' (15).

The editorial concluded as follows (16):

> *Will the city be administered by the new council so well, or half as well,*
> *as it has been administered during the last six years by the disbanded*

Local Government (Dublin) Act, 1930

Section 53

(1) Gerald Jarlath Sherlock, Town Clerk of the City of Dublin, shall be and is hereby appointed to be the City Manager as on and from the appointed day.

(2) Before the appointed day, the appointment of a person to be the Borough Manager or (in the case of the said Gerald Jarlath Sherlock being prevented by any event occurring before or after the passing of this Act from taking office as the City Manager) the City Manager shall be made by the Minister on the recommendation of the Local Appointments Commissioners, and those Commissioners are hereby required to make such recommendation on the request of the Minister.

(3) On or after the appointed day, the appointment of a person to be a manager shall be made by the council, and the office of manager shall be an office to which the Local Authorities (Officers and Employees) Act, 1926, applies.

(4) The manager shall hold office until he dies, resigns or is removed from office.

(5) The manager shall not be removed without the sanction of the Minister and shall not be either suspended or removed by the council save by a resolution passed by the council for the purpose of such suspension or such removal (as the case may be) and for the passing of which not less than two-thirds of the members of the council voted and which was so passed after not less than seven days, notice of the intention to propose such resolution had been given to every member of the council.

(6) There shall be paid by the Corporation to the manager such remuneration as the Minister shall from time to time determine.

(7) The manager may do all such matters and things, including the making of contracts for and on behalf of the Corporation and the affixing of the official seal of the Corporation to documents, as may be necessary for or incidental to the exercise or performance of any of the powers, functions and duties of the Corporation which are by this Act required to be exercised or performed by the manager.

(8) The manager shall not affix the official seal of the Corporation to any documents save in the presence of the Lord Mayor or Chairman (as the case may be).

Section 53 of the Local Government (Dublin) Act, 1930 stated that Gerald Jarlath Sherlock would be Dublin's first city manager and that he would hold office until he died, resigned, or was removed from office.

DUBLIN MUNICIPAL ELECTIONS, 1930.
Electoral Area No. 5.

Name_____   Your Number on Register is

Address_____   No._____

YOUR CANDIDATE IS

He stands for
Union Wages

Union
Conditions

Reduction of
Municipal
House Rents

Continuance
of Rent
Restriction
Act

Direct Labour
on all
Municipal
Undertakings

JOHN LUMSDEN, Plasterer
A Union Man who has fought unceasingly for his class
throughout a working life of forty years.

Plump Number ONE for
JOHN LUMSDEN
The Working Class Candidate
Irish Worker League

Election material for John Lumsden who sought a place on Dublin Corporation for Jim Larkin's Irish Workers' League. Lumsden received 611 votes and failed to win a seat in City Hall.

Irish Election Literature.

Commissioners? That is the main question, and, if we may judge the citizens' views by their apathy at the elections, they have no high hopes in the matter. Their attitude seems to reflect the favourite remark of an English Prime Minister – 'Why can't you leave it alone?' Nevertheless, we know that the business members of the new City Council will do their best; and, if public opinion supports them, they may be able to turn a doubtful experiment into an unqualified success.

It is fair to say that an eclectic mix of public representatives were elected to fill the Corporation's thirty-five seats.

Greater Dublin Constitutional Group	11
Independents	7
Fianna Fáil	5
Labour	3
Chamber of Commerce	3
Irish Workers' League	1
National Progressives	1
Revolutionary Workers	1
Licensed Trade	1
National Business Association	1
Labour – Municipal Workers	1
TOTAL	**35**

To a large extent, the electorate did not vote for political parties. Though Fianna Fáil claimed five seats, none of the party's representatives topped the poll in an electoral ward. The party had nominated nineteen candidates, fourteen of whom were unsuccessful. The Constitutional Group took eleven seats but they were a loose affiliation. Not all of the members of the Constitutional Group were Independents – indeed, some were members of the ruling Government party, Cumann na nGaedheal. What bound the members of the Constitutional Group together was that they had each taken a pre-election pledge to eschew politics and dedicate themselves to the administration of affairs based on business-like efficiency.

An intriguing element of the new Corporation was the election of Jim Larkin Snr. for the Irish Workers' League and Jim Larkin Jr. for the Revolutionary Workers.

Liverpool-born, 'Big Jim' Larkin was associated with the Great Lock-Out of 1913 and he was elected to Dáil Éireann in September 1927, representing Independent Labour. However, he was disqualified from the national parliament on the grounds of bankruptcy having refused to pay a libel award against him in a case taken by William O'Brien. He contested the Dublin Corporation election of 1930 in the same ward as one of his long-time rivals, Senator Alfie Byrne. During the campaign, Byrne took out an advertisement in the *Evening Herald* warning voters that Larkin claimed to be a direct representative of Soviet Russia and that he retained the Soviet flag (17). On election day, Byrne was assaulted by supporters of Larkin outside a polling station but did not sustain serious injuries. Both men were elected on the first count having passed the quota of two thousand, two hundred and twenty-three votes in their ward. Byrne received a massive total of six thousand, four hundred and thirty-four votes with Larkin elected second with two thousand, six hundred and thirty-seven votes. With 'Young Jim' Larkin also elected, the *Roscommon Herald* noted: 'The old Corporation was abolished for fear one Jim Larkin would get into it, and now, when it has been revived after a long period of incubation, it produces not one Jim Larkin but two. Dublin's Corporation has something in common with Dublin Stout. The longer it was kept bottled up, the more gas it produced' (18).

'Big Jim' Larkin, famous for the Dublin Lock-Out of 1913, was elected to the new Dublin Corporation in 1930, representing the Irish Workers' League.

National Library of Ireland.

The one hundred and fifty-ninth, and final, meeting of the Dublin Commissioners took place in City Hall on Saturday 11 October. As well as the three Commissioners, Town Clerk, Gerald Sherlock, and Law Adviser, Ignatius Rice, were present. It was a low-key meeting in which the regular business of the Corporation was conducted. According to *The Irish Times*, the meeting ended, as did the reign of the Commissioners, 'without ceremony of any kind' (19). The three

Commissioners, Séamus Murphy, Dr William C. Dwyer, and Patrick J. Hernon, undoubtedly served Dublin well and fulfilled their roles with great dedication. Even though Murphy was ill during the summer of 1924, the minutes of the Corporation show that all three Commissioners attended every meeting from May 1924 to October 1930. During their time in charge, rates were substantially reduced, water supply to the north side of the city was greatly improved, the number of Corporation tenants more than doubled and social services, especially in the area of child welfare, were expanded (20).

Following the quiet departure of the three Commissioners, the first meeting of the new Dublin Corporation was held in City Hall on Tuesday 14 October. Though the election of 30 September had failed to generate much excitement, the first meeting of the Corporation was a different matter: 'The public gallery was filled during the meeting, while the precincts of the City Hall were crowded with people who cheered the members of the new body as they arrived' (21). This was a big occasion for Gerald Sherlock, Dublin's first city manager. Three days previously, he had been present at the final meeting of the Commissioners and attended to their needs in his capacity as Town Clerk. Sherlock was first to speak and explained to the elected members that he was required to chair the meeting until a Lord Mayor was elected. He referred to 'the great experiment now about to be tried in Dublin municipal government' and spoke of his desire to work productively with the members. Addressing the councillors directly, he concluded his remarks by wishing them well: 'I believe that, inspired by a sincere desire for the welfare and advancement of the city, your labours for it will be fruitful and good' (22). He then called for nominations for Lord Mayor for the year ahead.

Former Lord Mayor, Laurence O'Neill, stood and proposed Senator Alfie Byrne for the office. Before O'Neill was able to continue with his nomination speech, 'Big Jim' Larkin interrupted and asked if the Corporation was in conformity with the Constitution in conferring the title of Lord Mayor on an Irish citizen.

Gerald Sherlock was Dublin's first city manager and he served from 1930-1936'.

Author's sketch of Gerald Sherlock, based on his picture in the Irish Press, 10 February 1932.

He moved that the word 'Lord' should be removed from the title. The first duty of Gerald Sherlock, as city manager and chair of the meeting until the election of a Lord Mayor, was to rule Larkin's proposal out of order. Laurence O'Neill resumed his speech and, as well as singing the praises of Alfie Byrne, he took the opportunity to congratulate Sherlock on his historic appointment as Dublin's first city manager. Byrne's nomination was seconded by Patrick Belton of the National Progressives.

Councillor Tom Kelly, previously a Sinn Féin member of the Corporation, but now representing Fianna Fáil, nominated his party colleague and TD, Seán T. O'Kelly. Tom Kelly, himself elected as Lord Mayor in 1920 but unable to take up the office due to ill-health, heavily criticised the Greater Dublin Constitutional Group, of which Alfie Byrne was a key member. He said that councillors standing under the banner of the Constitutional Group had contested the elections on the basis of being above politics but their first act was to select a political candidate for the Mayoralty. The Constitutional Group was also criticised by Councillor Mary Sheehy Kettle who stated that she would vote for Seán T. O'Kelly as a protest against the 'camouflage and hypocrisy' of Alfie Byrne and his group members. At this point, 'Big Jim' Larkin took centre stage again. He complained that politics had been introduced since the start of the meeting and he said that he would only refer to Laurence O'Neill as 'Mr.' and not as 'Alderman'. This led to a heated, if amusing, exchange between the pair.

O'Neill: I'm am Alderman and a Senator too.

Larkin: Alderman by accident.

O'Neill: No, by the votes of the people.

Larkin: I challenge you to resign and go forward on a political ticket. Then you will not have a seat in the Council any more.

O'Neill: Really .....

Larkin: You got in as an Independent, not as a politician. I cannot stand any jellyfish politician, a man without backbone. Someday, I will probably read in the newspaper about your first speech in the House of Commons.

O'Neill: For twenty years, you have been telling lies.

After more exchanges between the protagonists, the city manager managed to restore order and called for a vote on the Mayoralty. This resulted in Senator Alfie Byrne defeating Seán T. O'Kelly TD by twenty votes to thirteen. Byrne was accordingly declared Lord Mayor of Dublin, which led to a woman in the public gallery shouting, 'God save the King! Ireland for England!' and directing some insulting remarks to the new Lord Mayor (23). The commotion caused by this outburst enabled a photographer in the gallery to take a flashlight picture of the proceedings, an incident described by Tom Kelly as an 'outrage'. Councillor Caffrey, Independent, remarked that the odour from the flashlight resembled a stink bomb, a fitting tribute to the proceedings (24).

Senator Alfie Byrne was elected Lord Mayor of Dublin after the Corporation was re-instated in 1930. The man known as the 'Shaking Hand of Dublin' held the role continuously until 1939 and later served another term as Lord Mayor from June 1954.

Dublin City Library and Archive.

After an absence of six and-a-half years the first meeting of the new Corporation was in danger of descending into a farce but the new Lord Mayor, Senator Alfie Byrne, took the chair and delivered a measured and positive speech. He stated that they were starting the epoch of Greater Dublin and there was a responsibility on the elected members to work with the city manager to make the new system of municipal government work. For his own part, he promised to be absolutely impartial and stressed that he would not be the Lord Mayor for any one section of the citizens – he would represent them all fairly.

The *London Evening Standard* saluted Byrne's election as Lord Mayor and highlighted his rags-to-riches tale: 'He has risen from a seven shillings a week job in a bicycle shop at the foot of Dawson Street to the Mansion House at the top of the same street' (25). Alfie Byrne's biographer, Trevor White (2017), highlights this remarkable journey of three hundred metres over thirty-six years, noting that on 14 October 1930, Byrne became the first person to serve as a Councillor, Alderman, Member of Parliament, TD, Senator, and Lord Mayor of Dublin (26).

While Alfie Byrne entered the record books on this night, of more significance was the fact that Dublin Corporation was back in business, having been dramatically dissolved in May 1924. Local democracy, for all of its flaws, was restored and the era of the Commissioners was over.

Chapter 18
Vindicating Dublin – Conclusion

The title of this book refers to the document produced by Seán T. O'Kelly and ten of his former councillor colleagues in August 1924 following the dissolution of Dublin Corporation. They offered a strident vindication of Ireland's oldest public body, arguing that the decision to remove the council's elected members from office was unjust and unwise. Seán T. O'Kelly (who later became Tánaiste, Minister for Local Government and Public Health, and President of Ireland) was one of the most prominent voices to dissent against the inquiry, which led to the dissolution. He argued: 'The inquiry is nothing more than a sham … a mere excuse for the purpose of later doing the same with the Dublin Corporation as they had succeeded in doing with the Dublin Union' (1). O'Kelly and his colleagues were not alone in thinking this. Indeed, the former Chief Secretary for Ireland, Augustine Birrell, wrote the following in his 1937 memoirs: 'Mr. Cosgrave has abolished the Corporation of Dublin by a stroke of his pen. Any English Chief Secretary who had attempted to do the same piece of good work would have been compelled to resign by a combination of Unionists and Nationalists in the House of Commons. I had to be content with the abolition of the Corporation of Sligo' (2).

Seán T. O'Kelly was a major political figure in Ireland. First elected to Dublin Corporation in 1906, he took part in the Easter Rising a decade later. He was elected to the underground Dáil in December 1918 and he took an anti-Treaty stance in the Civil War. He joined Éamon de Valera's newly founded Fianna Fáil party and was appointed Minister for Local Government. He went on to serve two terms as President of Ireland.

Dublin City Library and Archive.

The power to dissolve local councils in Ireland first appeared in the Poor Relief Act, 1838 but had been used sparingly by the Local Government Board and certainly never against an institution as powerful as Dublin Corporation. After the Free State Government introduced the 1923 legislation, seven local public bodies were dissolved between May 1923 and March 1924. Of these, only two were county councils. The other five can be classified as minor local authorities. In all cases, the problems experienced by these bodies most certainly predated the revolutionary period (3).

Kerry County Council	9 May 1923
Leitrim County Council	29 May 1923
Kerry County Board of Health	8 June 1923
Mohill Rural District Council	31 August 1923
Dublin Board of Guardians	21 November 1923
Roscommon Town Commissioners	26 February 1924
New Ross Urban District Council	11 March 1924

The stakes were raised considerably in March 1924 with the establishment of a public inquiry to examine the affairs of Dublin Corporation. It was generally understood that the calling of an inquiry into the workings of a local authority led to its dissolution. At least Dublin Corporation was afforded the respect of a comprehensive inquiry over fourteen days of testimony. The inquiry into Mayo County Council in December 1930 lasted a mere twenty minutes (4).

The dissolution of Dublin Corporation in 1924, followed later in the year by Cork Corporation, was part of a bigger plan by W. T. Cosgrave and E. P. McCarron to create a technocratic and depoliticised local government system (5). During a subsequent speech to the Cumann na nGaedheal Annual Convention in May 1925, Cosgrave stated (6):

> *The meeting of the local authority is not the place for discussions of political issues. In the past, these questions were indeed obtruded – to the disadvantages of local administration, but there was an excuse in the absence of a national assembly where they could properly be dealt with. The Oireachtas, the sovereign assembly of the nation, is now available to settle such matters.*

In the politically sensitive post-Civil War years, the determination to divorce local government from national issues could be regarded as appropriate but also idealistic, if not naive (7).

As demonstrated in the early chapters of this book, Dublin Corporation was a highly political institution from the period of the Easter Rising in 1916, through to the War of Independence and the Civil War. In the words of Basil Chubb (1982), the Corporation was a thriving centre of nationalism. Even though the council played no formal role in the Easter Rising, City Hall was the centre of the insurrection (see chapter 2). The decision by Alderman Tom Kelly to read aloud the Castle Document during a Corporation meeting was a significant moment in the build-up to the Rising. City Hall became a garrison for the Irish Citizen Army during the rebellion; Councillor Richard O'Carroll was shot dead by Captain John Bowen-Colthurst; Corporation employee, Éamonn Ceannt, was one of those who signed the Proclamation of the Irish Republic and was executed; many of the councillors were arrested in the aftermath of the Rising, including Patrick T. Daly, Laurence O'Neill, Tom Kelly, Seán T. O'Kelly, William Partridge and William T. Cosgrave. The structural damage caused to City Hall and to the centre of the city created an enormous financial burden for the Corporation, described as a 'catastrophe' by Lord Mayor, Councillor James Gallagher, who immediately announced a recruitment embargo. The minutes of Corporation meetings after the Easter Rising show that there was a growing bitterness by the elected members towards the British authorities. The Corporation was outspoken in calling for the release of those who has been interned without trial and an amnesty for those who had been sentenced to prison. Given that the Easter Rising was largely a Dublin-based affair, it would have been impossible for the Corporation to be apolitical during 1916.

Inevitably, national politics were increasingly to the fore in the years which followed. In the early months of 1917, some of the Corporation's elected members remained in prison and the new Lord Mayor, Councillor Laurence O'Neill, emerged as prominent figure locally and nationally. He hosted political meetings in the Mansion House and was invited to be a member of the Irish Convention, which was formed to present proposals to the British Government for the future governing of Ireland within the Empire. The conscription crisis and the 'German Plot' hardened political opinion and anti-British sentiment and the vibrant and populist Sinn Féin party took full advantage to claim a spectacular success in the General Election of December 1918. This election heralded a major political realignment and, in giving effect to its pre-election promise, Sinn Féin members boycotted the Westminster parliament and established its own assembly. In Dublin, it was now impossible to separate local and national politics – the historic first meeting of the Dáil was held in the Lord Mayor's Mansion House and some leading members of the Corporation were also members of the Dáil. The War of Independence visited more death and destruction on Dublin. For the second time in six years, O'Connell Street was reduced to rubble and, in December 1920, British troops took over City Hall. A couple of weeks earlier, a meeting of the Corporation was interrupted by British troops who arrested six councillors. By 1920, Dublin Corporation was also effectively bankrupt. A breakdown in the relationship with the Local Government Board (LGB) meant reduced funding and many parts of the city lay in ruins.

When the Dáil ratified the Treaty on 7 January 1922, it unfortunately did not signify a period of peace as the Civil War unfolded. Dublin Corporation remained largely neutral during the conflict but it incurred the wrath of the Free State Government by consistently raising concerns about the treatment of prisoners. The elected members in City Hall also attempted to broker a ceasefire during the Civil War but their efforts were described as 'Ill-considered' by the Government. After the Civil War ended, Dublin Corporation continued to irritate the Government and William T. Cosgrave. Resolutions were frequently passed in relation to the ill-treatment of prisoners and the relationship between the Corporation and the

Government hit an all-time low in December 1923 when the elected members appeared to reject a grant for road improvements.

At this point, the Government had passed the Temporary Provisions Act of 1923 and had dissolved five local bodies, including the County Councils in Kerry and Leitrim. By May 1923, Dublin Corporation was in the firing line. It was the target of an extremely hostile press campaign led by *The Irish Times*, the *Irish Independent* and the *Evening Herald*, while the Dublin Citizens' Association publicly called for the dissolution of the council. The Corporation was on the back foot and tensions were high, as exemplified by the hostile meeting in the Mansion House with a delegation of the city's business interests (see chapter 6). As the summer progressed, there was an increasing estrangement between the Corporation and the Government, which was not helped by the discovery of the body of Noel Lemass or by the allegation from Councillor Hanna Sheehy-Skeffington that a prisoner had died due to ill-treatment by authorities. Once more, the council sought permission for a delegation of its members to visit Dublin prisons; once more, the Government, through General Richard Mulcahy, refused the request. By the end of the year, the relationship between the local authority and the Government was strained to breaking point. The council continued to agitate on the issue of prisoner treatment, while also criticising the reduction of the old age pension, rejecting the grant for the repair of trunk roads, and likening the Government to the Black and Tans.

Cosgrave and his cabinet colleagues felt that the members of Dublin Corporation were being disrespectful and effectively treating them like a foreign government. There was only ever going to be one outcome and there was no surprise when a letter by E. P. McCarron on 20 February 1924 announced the holding of a public inquiry, to be chaired by Nicholas O'Dwyer. As cited previously (see chapter 5), the Free State Government had very quickly developed an 'utter contempt' for local democracy and the elected members of Dublin Corporation felt that the holding of an inquiry was a charade – the decision had already been made to dissolve the council. The irony is that Cosgrave and his colleagues in central Government were well versed in how the local councils across the country had successfully undermined British rule. They now felt that local autonomy had to be curtailed so that the local authorities could not defy the Free State Government in the same manner that they had defied the British. For their part, councils such as Dublin Corporation transferred their resentment from the British Government to the Irish Government. Though the Corporation had a clear pro-Treaty majority, attendance at meetings was poor which allowed the more vocal anti-Treaty members to dictate the proceedings. The Corporation was also somewhat stale and the Government's decision to postpone the scheduled local elections of 1923 meant that there was no renewal of membership.

The inquiry, which started on 11 March, was shambolic. Eunan O'Halpin (1991) describes it as 'perfunctory' (8) and the confused start to the proceedings brought no credit to the Government. McCarron's letter in February had referred to 'serious complaints' regarding maladministration by the Corporation. Not unreasonably – based on the principle of being innocent until proven guilty – the members of Dublin Corporation sought details of the specific charges which were being brought to bear against them. It turned out that there were none. Embarrassingly, when the inquiry started in earnest on 19 March, Norman Keough – representing the Citizens' Association – was unprepared and he did not seem to grasp that the onus was on him to make a case against the Corporation. Keough's efforts over the fourteen days of the proceedings were lamentable and he was not helped by the ill-disciplined W. J. Larkin who quit in the middle of the inquiry. The legal representatives for the Corporation – Patrick Lynch and James Lardner – were cogent, professional and well-prepared. They comfortably out-manoeuvred their opponents and had every reason to be satisfied with their performance as they dismantled many of the criticisms made against the Corporation.

For his part, Nicholas O'Dwyer dutifully went through the motions of running a comprehensive inquiry but the outcome had already been decided by the Government. The anticipated news that Dublin Corporation was to be dissolved broke on 20 May but the details surrounding Nicholas O'Dwyer's report and the his recommendations remain a mystery to this day. In spite of numerous calls in the Dáil, it appears that the Inspector's report was never officially published. Instead, a select group of journalists in Dublin were given sight of a sixty-six page document and they gleefully reported on criticisms made by O'Dwyer in relation to excessive rates, the Stanley Street Workshops, the housing problem and high wages. Overall, however, O'Dwyer referred to the fact that administration in Dublin Corporation had been maintained to a very high standard and it seems that he made no specific recommendation in relation to dissolution. The National Archives of Ireland has, in its catalogue, a file listed as 'D/E Dublin files, Box 167 – Dissolution of Dublin Corporation'; this file, presumably containing a copy of

Nicholas O'Dwyer's report, is missing and is not available. Equally, there is no copy of the report or official documentation relating to the dissolution of Dublin Corporation in the Custom House, head-quarters of what is now called the Department of Housing, Local Government and Heritage. The mystery remains.

Interestingly, Nicholas O'Dwyer was also the Government-appointed Inspector into the workings of Cork Corporation later in 1924. On that occasion his inquiry report was published: 'The report, comprised of twenty-two pages, was surprisingly disjointed and poorly written. In no way did it do justice to the comprehensive evidence which had been presented to the inquiry over nine long days of testimony. Contrary to expectations, it did not even conclude with a firm recommendation for the minister' (9).

In relation to Dublin Corporation, Mary E. Daly (1997) states that the decision to dissolve the council was not clear-cut and 'seems to give some credence to the belief that the Cosgrave Government was determined to reduce the autonomy of local authorities' (10). She further notes that the Corporation's record would not have justified its suspension in the era of the Local Government Board and British rule. Politically, Dublin Corporation was a difficult council, with a dominance of Sinn Féin councillors elected in 1920. Predictably they subsequently spilt into pro-Treaty and anti-Treaty sides and *The Irish Times* regularly questioned if the council adequately reflected and represented the citizens of Dublin. The pity, therefore, is that the Government did not afford the citizens the opportunity to

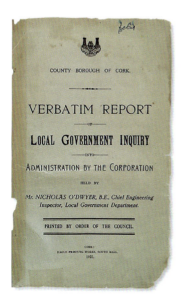

Cork Corporation produced and published a verbatim report from its public inquiry which began in August 1924. Dublin Corporation did not do so. Also, the report by Nicholas O'Dwyer into the performance of Cork Corporation is available in the National Archives. His report into the performance of Dublin Corporation is missing and a mystery remains about what it contains.

From Dissolved (2017) by Aodh Quinlivan

express their feelings. The decision by the Government to postpone the 1923 local elections deprived the people of Dublin the opportunity to pass judgement on the performance of the Corporation and its members through the ballot box. Judging by the large attendance in the public galleries during the inquiry, it can be asserted that the people would have gladly availed of the opportunity to elect a new council which, perhaps, would have driven much-needed administrative reforms. In the absence of local elections, the same, divided Dublin Corporation lumbered along, under the continual Mayoralty of Laurence O'Neill. Many of the councillors had been there for a sustained period of time, even before the Easter Rising of 1916. Quite a few of them had been imprisoned in the aftermath of the Rising and/or during the War of Independence. They were deeply political and a long way removed from the technocratic and depoliticised local government system envisioned by W. T. Cosgrave and E. P. McCarron.

The period from 1916-1924 was an extraordinary one for Dublin Corporation and the city of Dublin. The council straddled a frenzied period of transition from British control to the Free State. City Hall was seized, office accommodation for the Corporation was inadequate, some councillors spent significant periods of time in prison, the city suffered devastating damage, meetings were frequently interrupted by armed forces and records destroyed. After the formation of the Free State Government, John J. Murphy, Town Clerk, wrote repeatedly to the Department of Finance seeking financial assistance due to damage in the city, including the Stanley Street Workshops. One such letter, covering the second half of 1922, included the following (11):

- Electric meters destroyed at various premises in Dublin City due to armed conflict in June 1922;

- Lamps damaged at various places in Dublin City due to armed conflict in July 1922;

- Stanley Street, Dublin workshops destroyed due to fire and occupation by Irregular forces on 5 July 1922;

- Corporation Fruit and Fish Market, Dublin damaged due to armed conflict in June 1922;

- Property destroyed by fire at Rotunda Rink Post Office, Dublin on 5 November 1922;

- Damage to electricity station at Fleet Street, Dublin due to armed conflict in June 1922;

- Service cables damaged at various premises in Dublin City due to armed conflict in June or July 1922;

- Damage to technical schools at Bolton Street, Dublin and Kevin Street, Dublin due to armed conflict between June and September 1922;

- Damage to the municipal buildings at Castle Street, Dublin by National Army recruits in July 1922;

- Damage to sewer at Chancery Place, Dublin by Irregular forces tunneling in 1922;

- Electrics damaged at Tara Street, Dublin and the Kildare Street Club, Dublin due to armed occupation in 1922;

- Two bicycles taken at Aungier Street, Dublin and Dartry Road, Dublin on 5 and 18 August 1922.

Administration was far-from-perfect but, had Dublin Corporation performed effectively during this period, it would have been extraordinary. The funding situation was dire which exacerbated an ongoing housing crisis. As previously cited (see chapter 3), in August 1918, P. C. Cowan, Chief Engineering Officer with the Local Government Board, presented a damning report on the housing situation in Dublin. However, it is noteworthy that he concluded that little or no blame could be laid at the door of the Corporation due to its lack of resources and powers.

The Free State Government, under William T. Cosgrave, a former member of Dublin Corporation, regarded local government as a nuisance. As stated by Mark Callanan (2018): 'It seems that both sides of the Civil War divide that had fought together for Irish independence viewed self-government as something that applied only to national government exercised from Dublin – self-government was not a principle to be extended to the local level' (12). Tom Garvin (2001) notes that 'the virtuous felt themselves obliged to take away from the local councils powers that might be wielded by unsuitable people … consequently, they created the most centralised democratic state in Europe' (13).

Dublin Corporation was dissolved in 1924 as part of this zeal for centralisation: 'Successful revolutionaries like to keep the reins of power in their own hands.

Democracy was all right as long as the voters could be trusted to vote the right way' (14). The dissolution decision was a blatantly political one and, once a public inquiry was called, the fate of Dublin Corporation was sealed. During a debate in December 1924 in the Dáil on proposed local government legislation, James Everett TD of the Labour Party stated:

> *Some [local authorities] have been dissolved because they appointed*
> *Republican Lord Mayors, others because they passed resolutions*
> *protesting against certain actions of the Irish Government. For that*
> *reason, and no other, I think many of them have been dissolved by*
> *the Government. They thought it better to dissolve these bodies and*
> *appoint Commissioners instead, that would carry out the orders of the*
> *Government (15).*

Behind the scenes, the Secretary of the Department of Local Government and Public Health, E. P. McCarron[3], played a vital role. Due to his background in the Local Government Board, he was greatly distrusted by those in local government circles and was known as 'the great little council smasher of the decade' (16). The *Mayo News* wrote a particularly venomous piece about him in 1930, following the shambolic local inquiry in that county:

> *After the 1916 War of Independence, any council that dared to employ*
> *Irish rebels was smashed – signed E. P. McCarron.*

> *During the aftermath of the war, any public body that did not hunt out*

---

3 Edward (E. P.) McCarron was appointed by the Free State Government in September 1922 as the Secretary in the Department of Local Government and Public Health. He held that position until he was dismissed in November 1936 under a cloud of controversy. McCarron had a strained relationship with Seán T. O'Kelly who had taken over as Minister in March 1932. O'Kelly and McCarron crossed swords in 1936 about the appointment of Dr Blake as the resident medical superintendent in Ballinasloe Mental Hospital. McCarron allegedly had made a number of changes to a letter being sent by the minister. O'Kelly told the Executive Council that an incident had occurred which led him to believe that he could no longer have complete confidence in McCarron. McCarron refused to be moved to the position of Commissioner for Public Works at his existing salary and the cabinet made an order to remove him from office, effective from 1 December 1936. McCarron did not go quietly and he released copies of correspondence to the press, including letters exchanged with the President of the Executive Council, Éamon de Valera (for a full account of McCarron's dismissal, see Mary E. Daly, *The Buffer State: The Historical Roots of the Department of the Environment*, Dublin: Institute of Public Administration, pp. 163-167).

those with Irish leanings got their quietus – signed E. P. McCarron.

During the Black and Tan terror, the councils that were not pro-British and Tan had to go into hiding per orders – signed E. P. McCarron.

After the Treaty, councils that worked to bury the hatchet of Civil War had their pro-Irish officials hunted – signed E. P. McCarron.

What is the secret behind all this? That E. P. McCarron will serve anyone who pays his salary? (17).

On the evidence presented at the 1924 inquiry, Dublin Corporation did not deserve to be dissolved, but this is what happened with Séamus Murphy, Patrick J. Hernon and Dr William C. Dwyer starting their term as Commissioners in late May.

There can be no disputing that the Commissioners performed well in fulfilling their roles. They were diligent and thorough and provided much needed stability and calm after a decade of turmoil. The Commissioners offered political impartiality and administrative professionalism – qualities which were highly valued by the Government. In dealing with the dissolved local authorities, the Department of Local Government and Public Health found the Commissioners to be 'more respectful of the law, and probably more amendable to central direction, than the councils they replaced' (18). Another important consideration for the Government was that the Commissioners were popular with the electorate and with the newspapers: 'Far from engendering hostility in the local electorate, furthermore, Commissioners became the objects of local praise for their efficiency and frugality' (19).

A major advantage of the Commissionership years in Dublin between 1924 and 1930 was that it gave the Government breathing space to formulate and introduce proposals for the reform of governance arrangements in the capital. Perhaps this was the real reason that Dublin Corporation was dissolved. Edward Sheehy (2003) argues: '… the inquiry, such as it was, discovered little evidence to support the indictment and the suspicion has persisted that the Government welcomed the opportunity of denying a platform to their political opponents and critics' (20). Apart from the displaced members of Dublin Corporation, there was no outcry against the decision to dissolve the Corporation: 'This unprecedented display of force by Government against the most ancient form of local self-rule in Ireland was received with equanimity by the citizens, who seemed to share the accepted view of the Corporation as a combination of corruption and inefficiency' (21). With an unwieldly and troublesome council of eighty members on the side-lines, and with the public and business community satisfied with the Commissioners, the Government wasted no time in moving ahead with plans for the reorganisation of Dublin. Two months after the Corporation was dissolved, the Greater Dublin Commission was established, under the Chairmanship of William Magennis TD, Professor of Metaphysics at University College Dublin (see Chapter 16). The Magennis Commission followed on from the memorandum on Dublin's future boundaries, produced by Charles O'Connor, the former Local Government Board inspector. By the time Greater Dublin Commission submitted its report in 1926 – 'Magennis had dominated his committee by monopolising discussion and badgering witnesses to such an extent that attendance by the other members gradually diminished' (22) – there was a general consensus that change was needed to allow the capital to develop. During a Dáil debate in 1926, some months before the Magennis report was published, the Junior Minister responsible forecast that neither Dublin nor Cork Corporations would be revived in their former state (23). The legislation extended the tenure of the Cork and Dublin Commissioners to 31 March 1929 to allow time for the consideration of proposed reforms. Ultimately, as described in Chapter 16, Cork crossed the line first with the appointment of Philip Monahan as the country's first City Manager, under the Cork City Management Act, 1929. Dublin followed suit and the Local Government (Dublin) Act 1930 installed Gerald Sherlock as Manager and created the need for the city's first local elections in a decade.

While the councillors elected in September 1930 were sceptical about the new power-sharing arrangements between the City Manager and the council, their fears were eased somewhat by the appointment of Gerald Sherlock. He was seen as a safe pair of hands and he was well known to the members given that he had succeeded John J. Murphy as Town Clerk in August 1927. Remarkably, he had served as Assistant Town Clerk for the previous thirty-three years, from 1894. While stories circulated about discord and conflict in Cork Corporation, where members struggled with the autocratic approach of Philip Monahan who had graduated from Commissioner to City Manager, there were no such problems for Sherlock who was well-respected. David Dickson (2014) observes, 'Sherlock interpreted his new powers quite conservatively, handing back decision-making where possible to the Council and its committees, and in so doing he stood in contrast to his assertive opposite number in Cork' (24).

The fact that the appointments of Monahan and Sherlock, by virtue of being named in legislation, contradicted the Local Authorities (Officers and Employees) Act 1926 seems to have been swept under the carpet. According to the legislation, higher executive, professional and technical officers should have been appointed through the Local Appointments Commission, following the advertising of a vacancy, application, and interview. The first City Managers in Cork and Dublin were immune to this process.

There's an amusing story about what happened on Gerald Sherlock's retirement as Dublin City Manager in 1936. Initially, his post was filled on an acting basis by the Corporation's Financial Officer, John Keane. When the position was advertised in early 1937, Philip Monahan applied and subsequently attended for interview in May. Job interviews were a new experience for Monahan as he had been directly appointed to his current and previous positions. From the beginning of the process, the Cork City Manager was not impressed that the Mayo County Secretary, Michael Egan, had been selected to be on the interview panel. As a higher ranking local government officer, Monahan thought it was inappropriate that he should be interviewed by a County Secretary. Early on in the interview, Egan asked Monahan the age at which a person qualified for a driving licence. Monahan paused for a moment and then asked Egan to repeat the question. On hearing the question for a second time, the Cork City Manager answered: 'Excuse me, gentlemen. If the kind of person you want for the job needs to be a specialist in that subject, then I am not the right person.' He then stood up, put on his coat and left the room. Monahan clearly felt that the question was beneath him. He duly returned to Cork and never again applied for another job (25).

Though Gerald Sherlock in 1930 was a comforting link for the members to the old Corporation regime, the environment had changed dramatically since 1924. The reorganisation which had taken place meant that the Dublin city area had more than doubled with the inclusion of places like Rathmines and Pembroke. The Corporation itself was streamlined with a significant reduction in elected members from eighty to thirty-five. This number included five seats which were filled by representatives of the Dublin business community. As explained in the previous chapter, the Dublin Corporation elections of 1930 produced a varied mix of public representatives. With the Greater Dublin Constitutional Group to the fore, there would be an increased focus on business but politics was always going to be significant as well, in no small part due to the presence of Jim Larkin Snr. and Jim Larkin Jr. in City Hall. On the administrative side, the Commissioners had instilled a higher level of professionalism and more efficient processes and procedures were in place, with a constant eye on value for money. The smooth transition in 1930 from the reign of the Commissioners to the new managerial system was also facilitated by the election of a familiar figure as Lord Mayor, Alfie Byrne. Byrne was a very popular figure in Dublin, although the former Commissioners – Séamus Murphy, Dr William C. Dwyer, and Patrick J. Hernon – would have frowned upon some of his extravagance. Byrne's annual salary as Lord was £2,500, a significant rise from the previous figure of £1,600. This made the Lord Mayor of Dublin the highest-paid politician in the country (26). While the Corporation supplied Byrne with a secretary and a steward, he hired an additional secretary, a chauffeur and a maid. It has to be pointed out however that he paid for these extra posts from his private pocket (27).

With Alfie Byrne as Lord Mayor and Gerald Sherlock as City Manager, Dublin Corporation was back in business after a dissolution which lasted six and-a-half years. The dramatic inquiry from 11 March to 4 April 1924 proved to be a critical juncture in the development of local government in Ireland which led to the eventual emergence of the management model which underpins the entire system to this day.

The burning question remains: Why was Dublin Corporation dissolved? No specific charges were laid against the council, the 'prosecution' case was poorly argued by Norman Keough and W. J. Larkin; there was no proof of corruption; and, as far as we can tell in the continuing absence of the official report, Nicholas O'Dwyer did not make a specific recommendation for dissolution. This book asserts that there were two motivations behind the dissolution decision. First, there was a jostling for political position with Dublin not only the home of the ancient Corporation but also the seat of national power as the new Government, in the aftermath of the Civil War, sought to assert control. Cosgrave and his central Government cabinet colleagues were agitated by the Corporation, which continued to engage itself in issues such as the treatment of prisoners. Better than anybody else, Cosgrave knew how the councils had been used to subvert British rule. He did not want them to subvert Irish rule in the same manner:

'The more leeway such bodies had, the more these could embarrass and defy central Government' (28). The Government wanted to control the councils. As explained by Desmond Roche (1982), the Government's attitude towards local government arose due to the combined effect of Nationalist ideology, the general disorder of the Civil War period, and the tradition of corruption and favouritism that characterised the approach local authorities took to recruiting staff (29). The decision to dissolve Dublin Corporation was one undoubtedly driven by politics. Secondly, the Government wanted to proceed with the reorganisation of governance structures in Dublin. Attempting to do this while an awkward, politically-driven Corporation with eighty members was in place, would have been very difficult: 'Direct rule provided a unique opportunity for the restructuring of local government without short-term local political considerations dominating the debate' (30). The Government took the calculated decision to push the local elected members to the side-line while it proceeded with reorganisation – safe in the knowledge that the three Commissioners were reliable, professional, politically neutral and, critically, popular with the citizens. The dissolution of Dublin Corporation was a means to an end – the introduction of a management system where, in the inimitable words of Eunan O'Halpin (1991), the City Managers in Cork and Dublin 'were seen as skilled technicians, applying the antiseptic standards of scientific administration to matters previously dealt with in the unsavoury gutter of local politics' (31).

Addendum –
Dublin Corporation dissolved in 1969

Dublin Corporation was again dissolved and the councillors removed from office in April 1969. On that occasion, the Fine Gael and Labour-dominated council was deemed by Fianna Fáil Minister for Local Government, Kevin Boland TD, not to have struck an adequate rate for the year ahead. Minister Boland dissolved the Corporation after holding a statutory inquiry and appointed a Commissioner, John Garvin, to work with the City Manager, Matthew Macken. In the process, local elections were postponed until 1974. The Corporation was, in effect, restored by the Labour Minister for Local Government, James Tully TD, in 1973. He appointed forty-five Commissioners – all members of the Corporation in 1969, plus enough additional nominees to make up for casual vacancies.

See Neil Collins (1987), *Local Government Managers at Work*, Dublin: Institute of Public Administration, p. 33.

Chapter References

Chapter 1 – Dublin and the Corporation in 1914 and 1915

1. Basil Chubb (1982), *The Government and Politics of Ireland*, London: Longman Publishing, p. 293; Chubb quotes L. Paul-Dubois who wrote, *L'Irlande contemporaine at la question irlansdaise* (Paris, 1907)

2. Marie O'Neill (1994), 'Dublin Corporation in the Troubled Times 1914-1924', *Dublin Historical Record*, vol. 47, no. 1, Diamond Jubilee Issue, Spring 1994, pp. 56-70

3. Joseph V. O'Brien (1982), *Dear, Dirty Dublin – A City in Distress, 1899-1916*, Berkeley and Los Angeles, University of California Press, p. 99

4. Editorial in *The Irish Times*, 24 January 1913

5. *Ibid*.

6. Joseph V. O'Brien, as per 3 above, p. 96

7. 'History of the Irish Volunteer' at http://irishvolunteers.org/

8. Gerry White (2017), 'They have rights who dare maintain them': The Irish Volunteers, 1913-15', *Atlas of the Irish Revolution*, Cork: Cork University Press, p. 165

9. Minutes of Dublin Corporation (1914), No. 604, p. 369

10. Pádraig Yeates (2011), *A City in Wartime: Dublin 1914-18*, Dublin: Gill and Macmillan, pp. 6-7

11. *Ibid*, p. 7. For a definitive account of the Great LockOut, see Pádraig Yeates (2000), *Lockout: Dublin, 1913*, Dublin: Gill and Macmillan

12. *The Irish Times*, Monday 25 January 1915

13. *The Irish Times*, Saturday 30 January 1915

14. *The Irish Times*, Tuesday 2 February 1915

15. See Aodh Quinlivan (2013), *The Freedom of Cork: A Chronicle of Honour*, Cork: The Collins Press, pp. 59-62

16. Letter to *The Irish Times*, 'Dublin Corporation and Dr Kuno Meyer', Tuesday 16 February 1915

17. *The Irish Times*, Wednesday 23 February 1915

18. Joseph V. O'Brien, as per 3 above, p. 255

19. Minutes of Dublin Corporation 1-15 March 1915

20. *Ibid.*

21. Marie O'Neill, as per 2 above, p. 60

22. As cited by Thomas J. Morrissey (2014), *Patriot and Man of Peace*, Dublin: Dublin City Council, p. 43

23. Pádraig Yeates (2011), as per 7 above, pp. 30-31

24. Ibid. Yeates (2011), as quoted on p. 31

25. Marie O'Neill, as per 2 above, p. 60

26. Thomas J. Morrissey, as per 22 above, quoted on pp. 48-49

Chapter 2 – The Easter Rising

1. *The Irish Times*, Tuesday 25 January 1916; see also, minutes of Dublin Corporation 1916, pp. 82-84

2. *The Irish Times*, Friday 11 February 1916, as reproduced by Ronan McGreevy in *The Irish Times* of 11 February 2016

3. John Dorney (2017), *The Civil War in Dublin: The fight for the Irish capital 1922-1924*, Kildare: Merrion Press, p. 9

4. Pádraig Yeates (2016), 'The politics of Dublin City Council and the 1916 Rising' in John Gibney (ed.), *Dublin City Council and the 1916 Rising*, pp. 13-34, Dublin: Dublin City Council, p. 23

5. *Ibid.* p. 20

6. Sheila Carden (2016), 'Alderman Tom Kelly', in John Gibney (ed.), *Dublin City Council and the 1916 Rising*, pp. 52-65, Dublin: Dublin City Council, p. 54

7. Michael T. Foy (2014), *Tom Clarke – The True Leader of the Easter Rising*, Dublin: The History Press Ireland, p. 197

8. James Stephens (1965), *The Insurrection in Dublin* (3rd edition), Dublin: Scepter Publications, p. 73

9. Eoin Neeson (1998), *Birth of a Republic*, Dublin: Prestige Books, p. 125

10. Dublin Corporation minutes 19 April 1916, as reported in the *Irish Independent* of 20 April 1916 – also Yeates (as per 5 above), p. 22

11. Michael T. Foy (2014), as per 7 above, p. 197

12. Sheila Carden (2007), *The Alderman: Alderman Tom Kelly and Dublin Corporation*, Dublin: Dublin City Council, p. 100. See also Capuchin Annual 1942, p. 600

13. Sheila Carden, as per 7 above, p. 55

14. Pádraig Yeates, as per 4 above, p. 13

15. *Ibid*.

16. Laurence W. White (2016), 'Councillor Richard O'Carroll, Councillor William Partridge, the Labour Party and the 1916 Rising', in John Gibney (ed.), *Dublin City Council and the 1916 Rising*, pp. 35-51, Dublin: Dublin City Council, p. 48

17. Conor McNamara (2016), 'Under the starry plough: The City Hall garrison' in John Gibney (ed.), *Dublin City Council and the 1916 Rising*, pp. 120-136, Dublin: Dublin City Council, p. 120

18. *Ibid*. p. 120-121

19. *Ibid*. p. 129

20. Brian Barton (2017), 'Courts Martial and Executions' in *Atlas of the Irish Revolution*, edited by John Crowley, Donal Ó Drisceoil and Mike Murphy, Cork: Cork University Press, p. 277

21. John A Murphy (2017), The Proclamation of the Irish Republic, 1916, in *Atlas of the Irish Revolution*, edited by John Crowley, Donal Ó Drisceoil and Mike Murphy, Cork: Cork University Press, p. 267

22. Shay Cody (2016), 'Éamonn Ceannt: Dublin Corporation employee, trade unionist, and the 1916 Rising', in John Gibney (ed.), *Dublin City Council and the 1916 Rising*, pp. 137-147, Dublin: Dublin City Council, p. 143

23. *Ibid*. Cody, p. 145

24. Brian Barton (2002), *From Behind a Closed Door: Secret Court Martial Records of the Easter Rising*, Belfast: Blackstaff Press, pp. 188-189; as quoted by Cody (2016), as per 22 above

25. Shay Cody (2016), as per 22 above, p. 146

26. Piaras F. Mac Loughlainn (1996), *Last Words: Letters and statements of the leaders executed after the Rising at Easter 1916*, Dublin: The Stationery Office, p. 136

27. Donal Fallon (2016), 'John MacBride: The making of the major' in John Gibney (ed.), *Dublin City Council and the 1916 Rising*, Dublin: Dublin City Council, pp. 148-163

28. Pádraig Yeates, as per 5 above, p. 23

29. Thomas J. Morrissey (2014), *Laurence O'Neill – Patriot and Man of Peace*, Dublin: Dublin City Council, p. 53

30. *Ibid*. p. 54

31. *Ibid*. p. 54

32. Michael Laffan (2014), *Judging W. T. Cosgrave*, Dublin: Royal Irish Academy, p. 55

33. *Ibid*. p. 55

34. *Ibid*. p. 56

35. Marie O'Neill (1994), 'Dublin Corporation in the Troubled Times 1914-1924', *Dublin Historical Record*, Vol. 47, No. 1, Diamond Jubilee Issue (Spring, 1994), p. 60

36. *The Irish Times*, Thursday 11 May 1916

37. Marie O'Neill, as per 35 above, p. 60

38. Pádraig Yeates (2011), *A City in Wartime, Dublin 1914-18*, Dublin: Gill and Macmillan, p. 127

39. *Ibid*. p. 127-128

40. *Ibid*. p. 128 and from minutes of Dublin Corporation

41. *The Irish Times*, Tuesday 6 June 1916

42. *Ibid*.

43. Pádraig Yeates (2011), as per 38 above, p. 130

44. Minutes of Dublin Corporation, 3 July 1916, no. 478, pp. 300-301

45. *Ibid*. Minutes of Dublin Corporation 3 July 1916

46. *The Irish Times*, Tuesday 4 July 1916

47. Thomas J. Morrissey (2014), as per 29 above, p. 54

48. *The Irish Times*, Tuesday 3 October 1916

49. *Ibid*. Editorial Tuesday 3 October 1916, entitled 'The Dublin Corporation'.

50. *Ibid*.

Chapter 3 – Municipal problems, the Irish Convention and the conscription crisis

1. Thomas J. Morrissey (2014), *Laurence O'Neill – Patriot and Man of Peace*, Dublin: Dublin City Council, p. 63; also, *Evening Herald*, 23 January 2017

2. *Ibid*. p. 65

3. Pádraig Yeates (2011), *A City in Wartime, Dublin 1914-18*, Dublin: Gill and Macmillan, p. 157

4. *Ibid*. p. 177

5. Marie O'Neill (1994), 'Dublin Corporation in the Troubled Times 1914-1924', *Dublin Historical Record*, Vol. 47, No. 1, Diamond Jubilee Issue (Spring, 1994), p. 62

6. Minutes of Dublin Corporation, special meeting, No. 280, pp. 172-173; as cited by Morrissey, as per 1 above, p. 77

7. *The Irish Times*, Tuesday 3 April 1917

8. *Ibid.*

9. *Ibid.*

10. *The Weekly Irish Times*, Saturday 26 May 1917

11. Thomas J. Morrissey, as per above, p. 77

12. *The Irish Times*, Tuesday 22 May 1917

13. *Ibid.*

14. Pádraig Yeates (2011), as per 3 above, p. 196

15. *Ibid.*

16. Thomas J. Morrissey (2014), as per 1 above, p. 79

17. *Ibid.* p. 80

18. Ronan Fanning (2017), 'Britain's Irish Question' pp. 297-301 in *Atlas of the Irish Revolution*, edited by John Crowley, Donal Ó Drisceoil and Mike Murphy, Cork: Cork University Press, p. 301

19. Aodh Quinlivan (2006), *Philip Monahan – A Man Apart: The Life and Times of Ireland's First Local Authority Manager*, Dublin: Institute of Public Administration, p. 21

20. *Daily Express*, 2 October 1917

21. *Irish Independent*, 1 October 1917, as cited by Pádraig Yeates, as per 3 above, p. 206

22. Thomas J. Morrissey (2014), as per 1 above, p. 89

23. *Ibid.* p. 93

24. Minutes of Dublin Corporation, 3 December 1917, no. 731, p. 484; as reported in *The Irish Times*, Tuesday 4 December 1917

25. *Ibid.*

26. *The Irish Times*, Tuesday 24 January 1918

27. *Ibid.* and Minutes of Dublin Corporation, 23 January 1918, No. 76, p. 62

28. Thomas J. Morrissey (2014), as per 1 above, p. 102

29. *Ibid.* p. 104

30. *The Irish Times*, Tuesday 12 March 1918

31. *Freeman's Journal*, 26 March 1918

32. See Pauric Travers (2017), 'The Conscription Crisis and the General Election of 1918' in John Crowley, Donal Ó Drisceoil and Mike Murphy (eds), *Atlas of the Irish Revolution*, Cork: Cork University Press, pp. 323-329

33. Thomas J. Morrissey (2014), as per 1 above, p. 106

34. Eoin Neeson (1998), *Birth of a Republic*, Dublin: Prestige Books, p. 195

35. Dorothy Macardle (1968), *The Irish Republic*, London: Corgi Publishers; as quoted by Neeson (1998), as per 34 above, p. 195

36. Pauric Travers (2017), as per 32 above, p. 325

37. *Irish Independent*, 19 April 1918

38. Thomas J. Morrissey (2014), as per 1 above, p. 110

39. *Ibid.* p. 110

40. Extracts from the official reports of the anti-conscription conference, as quoted by Thomas J. Morrissey (2014), as per 1 above, p. 112

41. *Daily Express*, Saturday 4 May 1918

42. Marie O'Neill (1994), as per 5 above, p. 63

43. See article by Mary McAuliffe, 'Lá na mBan: a day of mass civil disobedience', *Irish Independent*, 10 June 2018

44. Pauric Travers (2017), as per 32 above, p. 323

45. See Aodh Quinlivan (2006), *Philip Monahan, A Man Apart: The Life and Times of Ireland's First Local Authority Manager*, Dublin: Institute of Public Administration, p. 22

46. Pádraig Yeates (2011), as per 3 above, p. 237

47. See John McGuffin (1973), *Internment*, Dublin: Anvil Books

48. For an interesting insight into Captain John Bowen-Colthurst, see the eBook by Bryan Bacon (2015), *A Terrible Duty – The Madness of Captain Bowen-Colthurst*, Thena Press

49. Thomas J. Morrissey (2014), as per 1 above, p. 120

50. *Ibid.* p. 122

51. *The Irish Times*, Tuesday 24 September 1918

52. *The Dublin Saturday Post*, August 1918, as quoted by Thomas Morrissey (2014), as per 1 above, p. 120

53. See 'Ambitious plan for Dublin housing announced', Century Ireland - https://www.rte.ie/centuryireland/index.php/articles/ambitious-plan-for-dublin-housing-announced

54. Pauric Travers (2017), as per 32 above, p. 329

55. Eoin Neeson (1998), as per 34 above, p. 197

56. *Ibid.* p. 198

57. John Dorney (2017), *The Civil War in Dublin*, Kildare: Merrion Press, p. 11

58. Pádraig Yeates (2011), as per 3 above, p. 300

59. Pauric Travers (2017), as per 32 above, p. 329

60. Dorothy Macardle (1968), as per 35 above, p. 267

Chapter 4 – The War of Independence

1. *The Irish Times*, Wednesday 22 January 1919

2. *Ibid.*

3. Mary Daly (2017), 'The First Dáil', pp. 334-339 in John Crowley, Donal Ó Drisceoil and Mike Murphy (eds), *Atlas of the Irish Revolution*, Cork: Cork University Press, p. 334

4. As quoted by Thomas J. Morrissey (2014), *Laurence O'Neill – Patriot and Man of Peace*, Dublin: Dublin City Council, p. 141

5. John Dorney (2017), *The Civil War in Dublin*, Kildare: Merrion Press, p. 11

6. *The Irish Times*, Friday 24 January 1919

7. *Freeman's Journal*, Wednesday 5 March 1919

8. Thomas J. Morrissey (2014), *Laurence O'Neill – Patriot and Man of Peace*, Dublin: Dublin City Council, pp. 146-147; also, *Irish Independent* and *The Irish Times*, Tuesday 25 March 1919

9. *Ibid.* p. 147

10. *Ibid.* p. 149

11. As quoted by Eoin Neeson (1998), *Birth of a Republic*, Dublin: Prestige Books, p. 203

12. Eoin Neeson (1998), *Birth of a Republic*, Dublin: Prestige Books, p. 207

13. *The Irish Times*, Wednesday 2 April 1919

14. John Dorney (2017), as per 5 above, p. 11

15. *Freeman's Journal* (1919), Tuesday 10 June 1919

16. *The Irish Times*, Tuesday 12 August 1919

17. Eoin Neeson (1998), as per 12 above, p. 211

18. *The Irish Times*, Tuesday 28 October 1919

19. Thomas J. Morrissey (2016), 'Patriot and Man of Peace: Laurence O'Neill, 1864-1943', pp. 66-88 in John Gibney (ed.), *Dublin City Council and the*

1916 Rising, p. 81

20. Thomas J. Morrissey (2014), as per 8 above, p. 156

21. *Ibid*. p. 157

22. Sheila Carden (2016), 'Alderman Tom Kelly', pp. 52-65 in John Gibney (ed.), *Dublin City Council and the 1916 Rising*, Dublin: Dublin City Council, p. 60

23. *The Irish Times*, Tuesday 16 December 1919

24. *Ibid*.

25. *Ibid*.

26. Pádraig Yeates (2012), *A City in Turmoil, Dublin 1919-21*, Dublin: Gill and Macmillan, p. 81

27. Thomas J. Morrissey (2014), as per 8 above, p. 162

28. Pádraig Yeates (2012), as per 26 above, p. 83

29. Thomas J. Morrissey (2014), as per 8 above, p. 163

30. Marie O'Neill (1994), 'Dublin Corporation in the Troubled Times 1914-1924', *Dublin Historical Record*, Vol. 47, No. 1, Diamond Jubilee Issue (Spring, 1994), p. 64

31. Eoin Neeson (1998), as per 12 above, p. 210

32. Aodh Quinlivan (2006), *Philip Monahan, A Man Apart: The Life and Times of Ireland's First Local Authority Manager*, Dublin: Institute of Public Administration, p. 29; see also John McColgan (1983), *British Policy and the Irish Administration 1920-1922*, London: HarperCollins

33. See Kieran McCarthy and John O'Mahony (2010), *Witness to Murder: The Tomás MacCurtain Inquest*, Cork: Irish Examiner

34. *Weekly Irish Times*, Saturday 27 March 1920

35. Micheál Martin (2009), *Freedom to Choose: Cork and Cork Politics. 1918-1932*, Cork: The Collins Press

36. F. S. L. Lyons (2010), 'The War of Independence, 1919-1921' pp. 240-259,

in W. E. Vaughan (ed.), *A New History of Ireland: Ireland Under the Union 1870-1921*, Oxford: Oxford University Press, p. 247

37. Thomas J. Morrissey (2014), as per 8 above, p. 165

38. *Ibid*. p. 166

39. Minutes of Dublin Corporation for 3 May 1920; see *The Irish Times*, Tuesday 4 May 1920

40. *Ibid*.

41. Tom Garvin (2001), 'The Dáil Government and Irish Local Democracy', pp. 24-34 in Mary E. Daly (ed.), *County & Town – One Hundred Years of Local Government in Ireland*, Dublin: Institute of Public Administration, p. 26

42. Marie O'Neill (1994), as per 30 above, p. 66

43. Aodh Quinlivan (2006), as per 32 above, p. 33

44. City and County Managers' Association (1991), *City and County Management 1929-1990*, Dublin: Institute of Public Administration, p. 129

45. Mary E. Daly (1997), *The Buffer State – The Historical Roots of the Department of the Environment*, p. 60

46. *Ibid*. p. 60; see also Michael Laffan (2014), *Judging W. T. Cosgrave*, Dublin: Royal Irish Academy, p. 69

47. Aodh Quinlivan (2006), as per 32 above, p. 34

48. Dave Hannigan (2010), *Terence MacSwiney – The Hunger Strike That Rocked an Empire*, Dublin: O'Brien Press, p. 251

49. *The Irish Times*, Thursday 28 October 1920

50. Dorothy Macardle (1968), *The Irish Republic*, London: Corgi Publishers, p. 360

51. Thomas J. Morrissey (2014), as per 8 above, p. 179

52. See Eunan O'Halpin (2020), *Kevin Barry: An Irish Rebel in Life and Death*, Kildare: Irish Academic Press

53. Eoin Neeson (1998), as per 12 above, p. 234

54. Michael Foy (2017), 'Michael Collins and the Intelligence War' pp. 420-427 in John Crowley, Donal Ó Drisceoil and Mike Murphy (eds), *Atlas of the Irish Revolution*, Cork: Cork University Press, p. 425

55. See Michael Foley (2020), *The Bloodied Field*, Dublin: The O'Brien Press

56. Diarmaid Ferriter (2020), 'Bloody Sunday 1920 Changed British Attitudes to Ireland', *The Irish Times*, 21 November 2020

57. Pádraig Yeates (2012), as per 26 above, p. 82

58. *The Irish Times*, Tuesday 7 December 1920

59. Thomas J. Morrissey (2007), *William O'Brien, 1881-1968: Socialist, Republican, Dáil Deputy, Trade Union Leader and Editor*, Dublin: Four Courts Press, p. 184

60. Thomas J. Morrissey (2014), as per 8 above, p. 184

61. *Ibid*. p. 188

62. *Ibid*. p. 189

63. Pádraig Yeates (2012), as per 26 above, p. 246

64. Minutes of Dublin Corporation, 7 March 1921, no. 166, p. 139-140

65. *Ibid*. See also *The Irish Times*, Tuesday 8 March 1921

66. *The Irish Times*, Tuesday 15 March 1921

67. *Ibid*.

68. Minutes of Dublin Corporation, Wednesday 9 February 1921, no. 126, p. 102

69. See Aodh Quinlivan (2017), *Dissolved – The remarkable story of how Cork lost its Corporation in 1924*, Cork: Cork City Libraries, p. 5

70. *The Irish Times*, Tuesday 4 July 1921

71. Thomas J. Morrissey (2016), as per 19 above, p. 84

Chapter 5 – The Treaty, the Civil War and the power of dissolution

1. Thomas J. Morrissey (2014), *Laurence O'Neill – Patriot and Man of Peace*, Dublin: Dublin City Council, p. 199

2. Aodh Quinlivan (2020), *Forgotten Lord Mayor: Donal Óg O'Callaghan, 1920-1924*, Cork: Cork City Libraries

3. David McCullagh (2017), *De Valera, Rise 1882-1932*, Dublin: Gill Books

4. Michael Laffan (2014), *Judging W. T. Cosgrave*, Dublin: Royal Irish Academy, p. 76

5. *Ibid*. p. 103

6. *The Irish Times*, Wednesday 7 December 1921

7. Thomas J. Morrissey (2014), as per 1 above, p. 205

8. *Ibid*. p. 205

9. Richard Aldous (2009), *Great Irish Speeches*, London: Quercus

10. *Ibid*. Text of speech delivered by Michael Collins to Dáil Éireann, 19 December 1921, pp. 70-74

11. *The Irish Times*, Monday 9 January 1922

12. Richard Aldous (2009), as per 7 above. Text of speech delivered by Mary MacSwiney to Dáil Éireann, 7 January 1922, pp. 75-77

13. *The Irish Times*, Monday 9 January 1922

14. *The Irish Times*, Tuesday 31 January 1922

15. Anne Matthews (2010), *Renegades: Irish Republican Women 1900-1922*, Cork: Mercier Press, pp. 311-315

16. Bill Kissane (2017), 'The Politics of the Treaty Split and the Civil War', pp. 649-660 in John Crowley, Donal Ó Drisceoil and Mike Murphy (eds), *Atlas of the Irish Revolution*, Cork: Cork University Press, p. 657

17. Archbishop Byrne papers, Opening Address at Peace Conference 1922, as quoted by Thomas J. Morrissey (2014), as per 1 above, p. 213

18. *The Irish Times*, Monday 1 May 1922

19. *The Irish Times*, Tuesday 2 May 1922

20. Minutes of Dublin Corporation 9 May 1922, No. 345, p. 258

21. *The Irish Times*, Wednesday 10 May 1922

22. John Dorney (2017), *The Civil War in Dublin: The fight for the Irish capital 1922-1924*, Kildare: Merrion Press, p. 43

23. Eoin Neeson (1998), *Birth of a Republic*, Dublin: Prestige Books, p. 282

24. For a definitive account of this election, see Michael Gallagher (1979), 'The Pact General Election of 1922', *Irish Historical Studies*, Vol. 21, Issue 84, pp. 404-421

25. *Irish Independent*, Monday 19 June 1922

26. Thomas J. Morrissey (2014), as per 1 above, p. 215

27. John Dorney (2017), as per 20 above, p. 70; Original source: Mulcahy papers, UCD, P7/B/192

28. *Ibid*. John Dorney (2017), p. 70

29. Eoin Neeson (1998), as per 21 above, p. 288

30. Thomas J. Morrissey (2014), as per 1 above, p. 215

31. *The Irish Times*, Tuesday 18 July 1922

32. John Dorney (2017), as per 20 above, p. 106

33. Minutes of Dublin Corporation Saturday 26 August 1922

34. *The Irish Times*, Monday 28 August 1922

35. Thomas J. Morrissey (2014), as per 1 above, p. 21

36. *The Irish Times*, Tuesday 10 October 1922

37. Thomas J. Morrissey (2014), as per 1 above, p, 218

38. *The Irish Times*, Tuesday 24 October 1922

39. John Dorney (2017), as per 30 above, p. 135

40. Cabinet minutes 18 November 1922, Mulcahy Papers UCD P7/B/245, as quoted by John Dorney (2017), as per 30 above, p. 135

41. IRA intelligence report, 19 November 1922, Twomey Papers UCD P69/11

42. *The Weekly Irish Times*, Saturday 11 November 1922

43. *The Irish Times*, Tuesday 14 November 1922

44. *The Weekly Irish Times*, Saturday 25 November 1922

45. *Ibid.*

46. See John Dorney (2017), as per 30 above, pp. 196-198

47. *Ibid*. Original source: Dublin Corporation Sworn Inquiry into Prisoners, October and November 1922, National Archives, TAOIS/S/1369 Box 3

48. John Dorney (2017), as per 30 above, p. 198

49. Thomas J. Morrissey (2014), as per 1 above, p. 218

50. Marie O'Neill (1994), 'Dublin Corporation in the Troubled Times 1914-1924', *Dublin Historical Record*, vol. 47, no. 1, Diamond Jubilee Issue, Spring 1994, p. 68

51. John Dorney (2017), as per 30 above, p. 211

52. *The Irish Times*, Saturday 25 November 1922

53. *The Irish Times*, Tuesday 12 December 1922

54. *Ibid.*

55. *The Irish Times*, Tuesday 16 January 1923

56. Diarmaid Ferriter (2004), *The Transformation of Ireland: 1900-2000*, London: Profile Books, p. 256

57. See Aodh Quinlivan (2017), *Dissolved – The remarkable story of how Cork lost its Corporation in 1924*, Cork: Cork City Libraries, pp. 7-11

58. Neil Collins (1987), *Local Government Managers at Work*, Dublin: Institute of Public Administration, p. 16

59. Pat Walsh (2009), *The Curious Case of the Mayo Librarian*, Cork: Mercier Press, p. 45

60. Neil Collins (1987), as per 51 above, p. 16

61. Resumed committee-stage debate on the Local Government (Temporary Provisions) Bill, Dáil Éireann, Volume 2, 28 February 1923

62. *Ibid.*

63. *The Irish Times*, Tuesday 23 January 1923

64. Marie O'Neill (1994), as per 48 above, p. 68

65. *Ibid.* pp. 69-69

66. *The Irish Times*, Tuesday 29 May 1923

67. *Ibid.*

68. Eunan O'Halpin (1991), 'The origins of city and county management' pp. 1-20 in J. Boland, R. Haslam, B. Johnston, B. Kiernan, J. O'Donnell and G. Ward (eds)., *City and County Management 1929-1990: A Retrospective*, Dublin: Institute of Public Administration, p. 4-5

69. Mark Callanan (2018), *Local Government in the Republic of Ireland*, Dublin: Institute of Public Administration, p. 19

Chapter 6 – Preparing the pitch

1. *The Irish Times*, Tuesday 24 April 1923

2. *Ibid.*

3. *Ibid.*

4. *The Irish Times*, Tuesday 1 May 1923

5. *Ibid.*

6. John Dorney (2017), *The Civil War in Dublin: The fight for the Irish capital 1922-1924*, Kildare: Merrion Press, p. 265

7. Minutes of Dublin Corporation meeting Monday 24 September 1923

8. *Ibid.* See also *The Irish Times*, Tuesday 25 September 1923

9. See Thomas J. Morrissey (2014), *Patriot and Man of Peace*, Dublin: Dublin City Council, p. 220

10. John Dorney (2017), as per 6 above, p. 259

11. Minutes of Dublin Corporation meeting Monday 15 October 1923

12. *Ibid.*

13. *The Irish Times*, Tuesday 30 October 1923

14. *The Irish Times*, Tuesday 6 November 1923

15. Minutes of Dublin Corporation meeting Monday 5 November 1923

16. Minutes of Dublin Corporation meeting Monday 3 December 1923

17. *The Irish Times*, Tuesday 18 December 1923

18. Thomas J. Morrissey (2014), as per 9 above, p. 220

19. *The Irish Times*, Saturday 19 January 1924

20. *Irish Independent*, Friday 22 February 1924

21. *Evening Herald*, Friday 22 February 1924

22. *Irish Independent*, Tuesday 26 February 1924

23. Thomas J. Morrissey (2014), as per 9 above, p. 228

24. Minutes of Dublin Corporation meeting Monday 3 March 1924; see also *The Irish Times*, Tuesday 4 March 1924

25. *The Irish Times*, Tuesday 4 March 1924

26. *Ibid.*

27. *Ibid.*

28. *The Irish Times*, Tuesday 11 March 1924

29. *Freeman's Journal*, Tuesday 11 March 1924

Chapter 7 – A false start

1. Information on Nicholas O'Dwyer from the *Dictionary of Irish Architects 1729-1940* (Irish Architectural Archive) and from his appreciation in the Engineers' Journal (No. 10, 1957)

2. *The Irish Times*, Wednesday 12 March 1924

3. See David McCullagh (2017), *De Valera, Rise 1882-1932*, Dublin: Gill Books, p. 123; McCullagh refers to election handbills produced by Sinn Féin and Éamon de Valera which sought to discredit Patrick Lynch at the 1917 East Clare by-election.

4. *Ibid.*

5. *Ibid.*

6. *Ibid.*

7. *Ibid.*

8. *The Irish Times*, Wednesday 19 March 1924

9. *Ibid.*

10. *Ibid.*

11. *Ibid.*

12. *Ibid.*

13. *Ibid.*

14. *Freeman's Journal*, Wednesday 19 March 1924

15. *Freeman's Journal*, Thursday 20 March 1924 – Letter by Alderman Seán T. O'Kelly

16. *Ibid.*

Chapter 8 – No blows struck to damage the Corporation

1. From the proceedings of the inquiry, as reported in *The Irish Times*, Thursday 20 March 1924

2. *Ibid.*

3. *Ibid.*

4. *Ibid.*

5. *Ibid.*

6. *Ibid.*

7. *Ibid.*

8. *Ibid.*

9. *Ibid.*

10. *Ibid.*

11. From the proceedings of the inquiry, as reported in *The Irish Times*, Friday 21 March 1924

12. *Ibid.*

13. *Ibid.*

14. From the proceedings of the inquiry, as reported in *The Irish Times*, Saturday 22 March 1924

15. *Ibid.*

Chapter 9 – An ignominious end for W. J. Larkin

1. See Robert Lynch (2008), 'The People's Protectors? The Irish Republican Army and the "Belfast Pogrom", 1920-1922', *Journal of British Studies*, Vol. 47, pp. 375-391

2. From the proceedings of the inquiry, as reported in *The Irish Times*, Tuesday 25 March 1924

3. See John Jefferies (2017), *Death on the Pier: The Cobh Pier Head Shooting and the Story of the Moon Car*, Cork: self-published

4. *The Irish Times*. Tuesday 25 March 1924

5. *Ibid.*

6. *Ibid.*

7. *Ibid.*

8. *Ibid.*

9. From the proceedings of the inquiry, as reported in *The Irish Times*, Wednesday 26 March 1924

10. *Ibid.*

11. *Ibid.*

12. *Ibid.*

13. *Ibid.*

14. *Ibid.*

15. *Ibid.*

16. From the proceedings of the inquiry, as reported in *The Irish Times*, Thursday 27 March 1924

17. *Ibid.*

18. *Ibid.*

19. *Ibid.*

20. *Ibid.*

21. *Ibid.*

Chapter 10 – The business capacity of the elected members is challenged

1. *The Irish Times*, Thursday 27 March, under heading 'Proposed Re-Grading of Officials'.

2. *The Irish Times*, Thursday 27 March, under heading 'Dublin City Rates – Statement by Town Clerk'.

3.   From the proceedings of the inquiry, as reported in *The Irish Times*, Friday 28 March 1924

4.   *Ibid.*

5.   *Ibid.*

6.   Pauric J. Dempsey (2009), 'Eason, John Charles Malcolm', *Dictionary of Irish Biography, James McGuire and James Quinn (eds)*, Cambridge: Cambridge University Press (https://dib.cambridge.org/viewReadPage. do?articleId=a2872#)

7.   *The Irish Times*, as per 3 above

Chapter 11 – Bribery allegations, senile decay and salary increases

1.   From the proceedings of the inquiry, as reported in *The Irish Times*, Tuesday 1 April 1924

2.   *Ibid.*

3.   *Ibid.*

4.   *Ibid.*

5.   *Ibid.*

6.   *Ibid.*

7.   *The Irish Times*, Tuesday 1 April, under heading 'Dublin Municipal Affairs: Re-Grading Scheme Adopted'

8.   From the proceedings of the inquiry, as reported in *The Irish Times*, Wednesday 2 April 1924

9.   *Ibid.*

10.   In relation to John J. Myers, see Las Fallon (2013), *Dublin Fire Brigade and the Irish Revolution, Dublin: South Dublin Libraries; also the review of the book in History Ireland* by Kevin Myers - https://www.historyireland. com/20th-century-contemporary-history/dublin-fire-brigade-and-the-irish-revolution/

Chapter 12 – The Inquiry tamely ends

1. From the proceedings of the inquiry, as reported in *The Irish Times*, Thursday 3 April 1924

2. *Ibid.*

3. *Ibid.*

4. See Peter Clarke (2005), 'The Story of Bernard F. Shields: the first Professor of Accountancy in the UK', *Accounting History (Australia)*, Vol. 10, No. 2, pp. 103-123

5. *The Irish Times*, Friday 16 January 1920

6. From the proceedings of the inquiry, as reported in *The Irish Times*, Friday 4 April 1924

7. *Ibid.*

8. *Ibid.*

9. From the proceedings of the inquiry, as reported in *The Irish Times*, Saturday 5 April 1924

10. *Ibid.*

Chapter 13 – The axe falls on a dying body

1. From reports of the Dublin Corporation meeting of Monday 7 April 1924, in *The Irish Times* and the *Freeman's Journal*, Tuesday 8 April 1924

2. *Ibid.*

3. *Ibid.*

4. *Ibid.*

5. From report of the Dublin Corporation meeting of Thursday 24 April 1924, in *The Irish Times*, Friday 25 April 1924

6. *Ibid.*

7. From report of the Dublin Corporation meeting of Friday 25 April 1924, in *The Irish Times*, Saturday 26 April 1924

8. *Ibid.*

9. From report of the Dublin Corporation meeting of Monday 28 April 1924, in *The Irish Times*, Tuesday 29 April 1924

10. *Ibid.*

11. From report of the Dublin Corporation meeting of Monday 12 May 1924, in *The Irish Times*, Tuesday 13 May 1924

12. *Ibid.*

13. *Ibid.*

14. Letter to the Editor of *The Irish Times* by Thomas Picton Bradshaw, published Saturday 17 May 1924

15. From report of the Dublin Corporation meeting of Monday 19 May 1924, in *The Irish Times*, Tuesday 20 May 1924

16. David Dickson (2014), Dublin: The Making of a Capital City, Cambridge, Massachusetts: The Belknap Press of Harvard University Press, p. 474

17. Ministerial order issued by Séamus Burke TD, dated 20 May 1924

18. Editorial in *The Irish Times*, Wednesday 21 May 1924

19. *Ibid.*

20. *Ibid.*

21. *Irish Independent*, Wednesday 21 May 1924

22. *Belfast Newsletter*, Wednesday 21 May 1924

Chapter 14 – A king without a kingdom

1. Interview with the Lord Mayor, *The Irish Times*, Wednesday 21 May 1924

2. NLI. O'Neill papers, correspondence between O'Neill and Cosgrave, 16 May 1924; Ms. 15, 294/15; as quoted by Thomas J. Morrissey (2014), *Patriot and Man of Peace*, Dublin: Dublin City Council, p. 230

3. *The Irish Times*, as per 1 above, Wednesday 21 May 1924

4. *Evening Herald*, Wednesday 21 May 1924

5. *The Irish Times*, Thursday 22 May 1924

6. Thomas Johnson TD, as quoted by Thomas J. Morrissey (2014), *Patriot and Man of Peace*, Dublin: Dublin City Council, p. 229

7. *The Irish Times*, Thursday 22 May 1924 – Interview with Mr. Howard Hely

8. See Thomas J. Morrissey (2014), *Patriot and Man of Peace*, Dublin: Dublin City Council, p. 230

9. Report of meeting in *The Irish Times*, Tuesday 27 May 1924

10. *Ibid.*

11. *Ibid.*

12. *Ibid.*

13. *Ibid.*

14. Public Inquiry Report by Nicholas O'Dwyer; *The Irish Times*, Wednesday 28 May 1924

15. *Ibid.*

16. *Ibid.*

17. *Irish Independent* editorial, Wednesday 28 May 1924

18. *Evening Herald*, Wednesday 28 May 1924

Chapter 15 – Municipal strike disrupts the start of the Tailteann Games

1. *The Irish Times*, Friday 30 May 1924, report of the first meeting of the Dublin Commissioners

2. *Freeman's Journal*, Saturday 7 June 1924

3. *Ibid.*

4. *Ibid.*

5. *Ibid.*

6.   *Ibid.*

7.   *Ibid.*

8.   Minutes of the Municipal Council of the City of Dublin for the meeting of the Commissioners on Thursday 12 June 1924.

9.   *The Irish Times*, Thursday 19 June 1924, 'Dublin Commissioner's Illness'.

10. Minutes of the Municipal Council of the City of Dublin for the meeting of the Commissioners on Thursday 3 July 1924.

11. *The Irish Times*, Thursday 24 July 1924, 'Strike Threat in Dublin'.

12. *The Irish Times Weekly*, Saturday 2 August 1924, 'Municipal Strike in Dublin'.

13. *The Irish Times*, Tuesday 29 July 1924, 'President Cosgrave's Firm Speech'.

14. *Ibid.*

15. *Ibid.*

16. Programme of the 1924 Aonach Tailteann, NAI D/T S 1592; see also 'The Tailteann Games 1924-1936' by Cathal Brennan, *The Irish Story*, http://www.theirishstory.com/2011/02/23/the-tailteann-games-1924 1936/#.XJjgiLp2uUm

17. See Mike Cronin (2003), 'Projecting the nation through sport and culture', *Journal of Contemporary History*, Vol. 38, No. 3

18. See J.J. Walsh (1944), *Recollections of a Rebel*, Tralee: The Kerryman Ltd.

19. *The Irish Times*, Monday 4 August 1924, 'Settlement of Strike'.

20. *The Irish Times*, Friday 8 August 1924, 'The Municipal Strike'.

21. *The Irish Times*, Monday 4 August, as per 19 above.

Chapter 16 – The Dublin Commissioners make their mark as Cork is used as a guinea pig

1. *A Vindication of the Municipal Council of the City of Dublin* (1924), by eleven former members of Dublin Corporation – see Old Dublin Society Collection, RDS Library and Archives.

2. *Ibid.* p. 3

3. *Ibid.* p. 3

4. *Ibid.* p. 18

5. *Ibid.* p. 25

6. *Ibid.* p. 27

7. *Ibid.* p. 27

8. *Ibid.* p. 27

9. *Ibid.* p. 27

10. *Ibid.* p. 30

11. *Ibid.* p. 31

12. *Ibid.* p. 31

13. Richard Haslam (2003), 'The Origins of Irish Local Government', p. 32 in Mark Callanan and Justin F. Keogan (eds.), *Local Government in Ireland: Inside Out* Dublin: Institute of Public Administration, pp. 14-40,

14. *The Irish Times*, Friday 12 September 1924, 'Stanley Street Workshops'.

15. Mary E. Daly (1997), *The Buffer State – The Historical Roots of the Department of the Environment*, p. 122

16. *Ibid.* p. 122

17. *Ibid.* p. 122; see also D/E Dublin files, Box 239.

18. *Ibid.* p. 123

19. David Dickson (2014), Dublin: *The Making of a Capital City*, Cambridge, Massachusetts: The Belknap Press of Harvard University Press, p. 475

20. Thomas J. Morrissey (2014), *Patriot and Man of Peace*, Dublin: Dublin City Council, p. 232

21. *Ibid*. p. 238; see also National Archives of Ireland, Taoiseach's Department correspondence, Taois/S 7474.

22. Thomas J. Morrissey, as per 20 above, p. 238

23. Department of Local Government and Public Health, First Report 1922-1925, Dublin; The Stationery Office, p. 22

24. *Ibid*. p. 24

25. *Ibid*. Appendix A, Summary Statement by the Commissioners, p. 155

26. *Ibid*. p. 155

27. *Ibid*. p. 160

28. *Ibid*. p. 162

29. A letter dated 15 April 1926 from E. P. McCarron stated that the Minister desired to express approval of the Commissioners' policy to make salary deductions for non-punctual attendance at work. The letter was read into the minutes of the meeting in City Hall on 1 May 1926.

30. Edward Sheehy (2003), 'City and County Management', p. 126 in Mark Callanan and Justin F. Keogan (eds.), *Local Government in Ireland: Inside Out*, Dublin: Institute of Public Administration, pp. 123-142

31. Mary E. Daly, as per 15 above, p. 123

32. Edward Sheehy, as per 30 above, p. 126

33. Greater Dublin Commission of Inquiry (1926), *Report of the Greater Dublin Commission of Inquiry*, Dublin: Government Publications.

34. Ruth McManus (2002), Dublin 1910-1940: *Shaping the City and Suburbs*, Dublin: Four Courts Press, p. 89

35. As quoted by Edward Sheehy, as per 30 above, p. 126.

36. *Ibid*. p. 126

37. See Mary E. Daly, as per 15 above, p. 124.

38. Eunan O'Halpin, 'The origins of city and county management', in *City and County Management, 1929-1991: A Retrospective*, Dublin: Institute of Public Administration, p. 9

39. John J. Horgan (1926), Local Government Developments at Home and Abroad', *Studies*, Vol. XV, pp. 529-541.

40. *Ibid*. p. 539.

41. Mary E. Daly, as per 15 above, p. 126

42. *Ibid*. p. 126

43. Aodh Quinlivan (2006), *Philip Monahan – A Man Apart: The Life and Times of Ireland's First Local Authority Manager*, Dublin: Institute of Public Administration, p. 88.

44. Resumed second-stage debate, Dáil Éireann, Thursday 12 July 1928.

45. Aodh Quinlivan, as per 43 above, p. 100

46. *Ibid*. p. 100

Chapter 17 – Gerald Sherlock tries to turn the doubtful experiment into a success

1. Minutes of the Municipal Council of the City of Dublin, Saturday 30 June 1928

2. See 'Ask About Ireland' article at http://www.askaboutireland.ie/reading-room/environment-geography/transport/the-flight-of-the-bremen/fitzmaurices-first-attemp/

3. *Ibid*.

4. *The Irish Times*, Wednesday 4 July 1928 – 'Freedom of Dublin for Bremen Airmen'.

5. Minutes of the Municipal Council of the City of Dublin, Saturday 25 August 1928.

6. *The Irish Times*, Friday 31 August 1928 – 'A Freeman of Dublin'.

7. *Ibid*.

8.   As quoted by David Dickson (2014), *Dublin: The Making of a Capital City*, Cambridge, Massachusetts: The Belknap Press of Harvard University Press, p. 474

9.   Edward Sheehy (2003), 'City and County Management', p. 128 in Mark Callanan and Justin F. Keogan (eds.), *Local Government in Ireland: Inside Out*, pp. 123-142, Dublin: Institute of Public Administration.

10. Dáil Éireann debate, Wednesday 26 February 1930, as quoted by Mary E. Daly (1997), *The Buffer State – The Historical Roots of the Department of the Environment*, p. 128.

11. Seanad Éireann debate, Wednesday 28 May 1930.

12. Mary E. Daly (1997), *The Buffer State – The Historical Roots of the Department of the Environment*, Dublin: Institute of Public Administration, p. 128.

13. *Weekly Irish Times*, Saturday 4 October 1930.

14. Editorial in *The Irish Times*, Thursday 2 October 1930.

15. *Ibid.*

16. *Ibid.*

17. Trevor White (2017), *Alfie – The Life and Times of Alfie Byrne*, Dublin: Penguin Ireland, p. 43.

18. *Roscommon Herald*, Saturday 18 October 1930.

19. *The Irish Times*, Monday 13 October 1930.

20. David Dickson (2014), *Dublin: The Making of a Capital City*, Cambridge, Massachusetts: The Belknap Press of Harvard University Press, p. 474.

21. *Weekly Irish Times*, Saturday 18 October 1930.

22. Minutes of the Municipal Council of the City of Dublin, meeting of Tuesday 14 October 1930, p. 220.

23. *Weekly Irish Times*, as per 21 above.

24. *Ibid.*

25. As quoted by Trevor White (2017), *Alfie – The Life and Times of Alfie Byrne*, Dublin: Penguin Ireland, p. 44-45.

26. *Ibid*. Trevor White, p. 45.

Chapter 18 – Vindicating Dublin – Conclusion

1.   *The Irish Times*, Wednesday 19 March 1924

2.   Augustine Birrell (1937), *Things Past Redress*, London: Faber and Faber, p. 219

3.   Mary E. Daly (1997), *The Buffer State – The Historical Roots of the Department of the Environment*, Dublin: Institute of Public Administration, p. 121

4.   *Western People*, 20 December 1930, p. 3

5.   Aodh Quinlivan (2006), *Philip Monahan – A Man Apart: The Life and Times of Ireland's First Local Authority Manager*, Dublin: Institute of Public Administration, p.67

6.   UCDA P24/616, Cumann na nGaedheal Annual Convention, 13 May 1925, as cited in Patricia Duffin (1992), 'An Examination of Local Government under the Cumann na nGaedheal Administration', MA thesis, University College Dublin. Also cited in Mary E. Daly (1997), *The Buffer State – The Historical Roots of the Department of the Environment*, Dublin: Institute of Public Administration, p. 118

7.   See Mary E. Daly (1997), *The Buffer State – The Historical Roots of the Department of the Environment*, Dublin: Institute of Public Administration, p. 118

8.   Eunan O'Halpin (1991), 'The origins of city and county management' pp. 1-20 in J. Boland, R. Haslam, B. Johnston, B. Kiernan, J. O'Donnell and G. Ward (eds)., *City and County Management 1929-1990: A Retrospective*, Dublin: Institute of Public Administration, p. 8

9.   Aodh Quinlivan (2017), *Dissolved – The remarkable story of how Cork lost its Corporation in 1924*, Cork: Cork City Libraries, p. 111

10. Mary E. Daly, *The Buffer State*, as per 3 above, p. 121

11. Correspondence from John J. Murphy, Town Clerk, Dublin Corporation, to the Department of Finance seeking financial compensation – National Archives of Ireland, FIN/COMP/2/28/1352

12. Mark Callanan (2018), *Local Government in the Republic of Ireland*, Dublin: Institute of Public Administration, p. 21

13. Tom Garvin (2001), 'The Dáil Government and Irish Local Democracy', pp. 24-34 in Mary E. Daly (ed.), *County & Town – One Hundred Years of Local Government in Ireland*, Dublin: Institute of Public Administration, pp. 33-34

14. *Ibid.*

15. Dáil Éireann committees stage debate on the Local Government Bill, 3 December 1924

16. *Mayo News*, 20 December 1930, p. 5

17. *Ibid.*

18. Eunan O'Halpin, as per 8 above, p. 8

19. Department of Local Government and Public Health (1930), *Fourth Report 1928-1929*. pp. 13-14

20. Edward Sheehy (2003), 'City and County Management', p. 126 in Mark Callanan and Justin F. Keogan (eds.), *Local Government in Ireland: Inside Out,* pp. 123-142, Dublin: Institute of Public Administration, p. 125

21. *Ibid.*

22. Neil Collins (1987), *Local Government Managers at Work*, Dublin: Institute of Public Administration, p. 24

23. *Ibid.*

24. David Dickson (2014), *Dublin: The Making of a Capital City*, Cambridge, Massachusetts: The Belknap Press of Harvard University Press, p. 475

25. Aodh Quinlivan (2006), *Philip Monahan – A Man Apart: The Life and Times of Ireland's First Local Authority Manager,* Dublin: Institute of Public Administration, p. 169

26. Trevor White (2017), *Alfie – The Life and Times of Alfie Byrne*, Dublin: Penguin Ireland, p. 47

27. *Ibid*.

28. Eunan O'Halpin, as per 8 above, pp. 4-5

29. See Desmond Roche (1982), *Local Government in Ireland*, Dublin: Institute of Public Administration – as quoted by Mark Callanan (2018), *Local Government in the Republic of Ireland*, Dublin: Institute of Public Administration, p. 19

30. David Dickson (2014), as per 24 above, p. 474

31. Eunan O'Halpin, as per 8 above, p. 17

Bibliography

Richard **Aldous** (2009), *Great Irish Speeches*, London: Quercus

Bryan **Bacon** (1915), *A Terrible Duty – The Madness of Captain Bowen-Colthurst*, Thena Press

Brian **Barton** (2002), *From Behind a Closed Door: Secret Court Martial Records of the Easter Rising*, Belfast: Blackstaff Press

Brian **Barton** (2017), 'Courts Martial and Executions' in *Atlas of the Irish Revolution*, edited by John Crowley, Donal Ó Drisceoil and Mike Murphy, Cork: Cork University Press

Augustine **Birrell** (1937), *Things Past Redress*, London: Faber and Faber

Mark **Callanan** (2018), *Local Government in the Republic of Ireland*, Dublin: Institute of Public Administration

Sheila **Carden** (2007), *The Alderman: Alderman Tom Kelly and Dublin Corporation*, Dublin: Dublin City Council

Sheila **Carden** (2016), 'Alderman Tom Kelly', in John Gibney (ed.), *Dublin City Council and the 1916 Rising*, pp. 52-65, Dublin: Dublin City Council

Basil **Chubb** (1982), *The Government and Politics of Ireland*, London: Longman Publishing

Peter **Clarke** (2005), 'The Story of Bernard F. Shields: the first Professor of Accountancy in the UK', *Accounting History (Australia)*, Vol. 10, No. 2, pp. 103-123

Shay **Cody** (2016), 'Éamonn Ceannt: Dublin Corporation employee, trade unionist, and the 1916 Rising', in John Gibney (ed.), *Dublin City Council and the 1916 Rising*, Dublin: Dublin City Council, pp. 137-147

Neil **Collins** (1987), *Local Government Managers at Work*, Dublin: Institute of Public Administration

City and County Managers' Association (1991), *City and County Management 1929-1990*, Dublin: Institute of Public Administration

Mike **Cronin** (2003), 'Projecting the nation through sport and culture', *Journal of Contemporary History*, Vol. 38, No. 3

John **Crowley**, Donal **Ó Drisceoil**, and Mike **Murphy** (2017) (eds.), *Atlas of the Irish Revolution*, Cork: Cork University Press

Mary E. **Daly** (1997), *The Buffer State – The Historical Roots of the Department of the Environment*, Dublin: Institute of Public Administration

Mary E. **Daly** (2017), 'The First Dáil', pp. 334-339 in John Crowley, Donal Ó Drisceoil and Mike Murphy (eds), *Atlas of the Irish Revolution*, Cork: Cork University Press

Department of Local Government and Public Health (1930), *Fourth Report, 1928-1929*, Dublin: Government Publications

Pauric J. **Dempsey** (2009), 'Eason, John Charles Malcolm', *Dictionary of Irish Biography*, James McGuire and James Quinn (eds), Cambridge: Cambridge University Press

David **Dickson** (2014), *Dublin: The Making of a Capital City*, Cambridge, Massachusetts: The Belknap Press of Harvard University Press

John **Dorney** (2017), *The Civil War in Dublin: The fight for the Irish capital 1922-1924*, Kildare: Merrion Press

Patricia **Duffin** (1992), 'An Examination of Local Government under the Cumann na nGaedheal Administration', MA thesis, University College Dublin

Donal **Fallon** (2016), 'John MacBride: The making of the major' in John Gibney (ed.), *Dublin City Council and the 1916 Rising*, Dublin: Dublin City Council, pp. 148-163

Las **Fallon** (2013), *Dublin Fire Brigade and the Irish Revolution*, Dublin: South Dublin Libraries

Ronan **Fanning** (2017), 'Britain's Irish Question' in *Atlas of the Irish Revolution*, edited by John Crowley, Donal Ó Drisceoil and Mike Murphy, Cork: Cork University Press, pp. 297-301

Diarmaid **Ferriter** (2004), *The Transformation of Ireland: 1900-2000*, London: Profile Books

Michael **Foley** (2020), *The Bloodied Field*, Dublin: The O'Brien Press

Michael T. **Foy** (2014), *Tom Clarke – The True Leader of the Easter Rising*, Dublin: The History Press Ireland

Michael **Foy** (2017), 'Michael Collins and the Intelligence War' in John Crowley, Donal Ó Drisceoil and Mike Murphy (eds), *Atlas of the Irish Revolution*, Cork: Cork University Press, pp. 420-427

Tom **Garvin** (2001), 'The Dáil Government and Irish Local Democracy' in Mary E. Daly (ed.), *County & Town – One Hundred Years of Local Government in Ireland*, Dublin: Institute of Public Administration, pp. 24-34

John **Gibney** (2016) (ed.), *Dublin City Council and the 1916 Rising*, Dublin: Dublin City Council

Greater Dublin Commission of Inquiry (1926), *Report of the Greater Dublin Commission of Inquiry*, Dublin: Government Publications

Dave **Hannigan** (2010), *Terence MacSwiney – The Hunger Strike That Rocked an Empire*, Dublin: O'Brien Press

Richard **Haslam** (2003), 'The Origins of Irish Local Government', p. 32 in Mark Callanan and Justin F. Keogan (eds.), *Local Government in Ireland: Inside Out*, pp. 14-40, Dublin: Institute of Public Administration

John J. **Horgan** (1926), Local Government Developments at Home and Abroad', *Studies*, Vol. XV, pp. 529-541

John **Jefferies** (2017), *Death on the Pier: The Cobh Pier Head Shooting and the Story of the Moon Car*, Cork: self-published

Bill **Kissane** (2017), 'The Politics of the Treaty Split and the Civil War' in John Crowley, Donal Ó Drisceoil and Mike Murphy (eds), *Atlas of the Irish Revolution*, Cork: Cork University Press, pp. 649-660

Michael **Laffan** (2014), *Judging W. T. Cosgrave*, Dublin: Royal Irish Academy

Robert **Lynch** (2008), 'The People's Protectors? The Irish Republican Army and the "Belfast Pogrom", 1920-1922', *Journal of British Studies*, Vol. 47, pp. 375-391

F. S. L. **Lyons** (2010), 'The War of Independence, 1919-1921', in W. E. Vaughan (ed.), *A New History of Ireland: Ireland Under the Union 1870-1921*, Oxford: Oxford University Press, pp. 240-259

Dorothy **Macardle** (1968), *The Irish Republic*, London: Corgi Publishers

Pádraig **Mac Consaidí**n (2013), 'Seán T. O'Kelly', in Aodh Quinlivan (2013), *The Freedom of Cork: A Chronicle of Honour*, Cork: The Collins Press, pp. 78-82

Piaras F. **Mac Loughlainn** (1996), *Last Words: Letters and statements of the leaders executed after the Rising at Easter 1916*, Dublin: The Stationery Office

Micheál **Martin** (2009), *Freedom to Choose: Cork and Cork Politics. 1918-1932*, Cork: The Collins Press

Anne **Matthews** (2010), *Renegades: Irish Republican Women 1900-1922*, Cork: Mercier Press, pp. 311-315

Mary **McAuliffe** (2018), 'Lá na mBan: a day of mass civil disobedience', *Irish Independent*, 10 June

Kieran **McCarthy** and John **O'Mahony** (2020), *Witness To Murder: The Tomás MacCurtain Inquest*, Cork: Irish Examiner

John **McColgan** (1983), *British Policy and the Irish Administration 1920-1922*, London: HarperCollins

David **McCullagh** (2017), *De Valera, Rise 1882-1932*, Dublin: Gill Books

John **McGuffin** (1973), *Internment*, Dublin: Anvil Books

Ruth **McManus** (2002), *Dublin 1910-1940: Shaping the City and Suburbs*, Dublin: Four Courts Press

Conor **McNamara** (2016), 'Under the starry plough: The City Hall garrison' in John Gibney (ed.), *Dublin City Council and the 1916 Rising*, pp. 120-136, Dublin: Dublin City Council

Thomas J. **Morrissey** (2007), William **O'Brien**, *1881-1968: Socialist, Republican, Dáil Deputy, Trade Union Leader and Editor*, Dublin: Four Courts Press

Thomas J. **Morrissey** (2014), *Patriot and Man of Peace*, Dublin: Dublin City Council

John A. **Murphy** (2017), *The Proclamation of the Irish Republic, 1916, in Atlas of the Irish Revolution*, edited by John Crowley, Donal Ó Drisceoil and Mike Murphy, Cork: Cork University Press

Eoin **Neeson** (1998), *Birth of a Republic*, Dublin: Prestige Books

Joseph V. **O'Brien** (1982), *Dear, Dirty Dublin – A City in Distress, 1899-1916*, Berkeley and Los Angeles, University of California Press

Eunan **O'Halpin** (1991), 'The origins of city and county management' pp. 1-20 in J. Boland, R. Haslam, B. Johnston, B. Kiernan, J. O'Donnell and G. Ward (eds)., *City and County Management 1929-1990: A Retrospective*, Dublin: Institute of Public Administration

Eunan **O'Halpin** (2020), K*evin Barry: An Irish Rebel in Life and Death*, Kildare: Irish Academic Press

Seán T. **O'Kelly** (1924) with Seamus Ó'Maoilfhinn, Patrick Gordon, Laurence Raul, John O'Callaghan, Joseph Mooney, Charles Murphy, Thomas Atkins, John Lawlor, Patrick T. Daly and Joseph Clarke), *A Vindication of the Municipal Council of the City of Dublin* - published privately, see Old Dublin Society Collection, RDS Library and Archives

Marie **O'Neill** (1994), 'Dublin Corporation in the Troubled Times 1914-1924', *Dublin Historical Record*, vol. 47, no. 1, Diamond Jubilee Issue, Spring 1994, pp. 56-70

Aodh **Quinlivan** (2006), *Philip Monahan – A Man Apart: The Life and Times of Ireland's First Local Authority Manager*, Dublin: Institute of Public Administration

Aodh **Quinlivan** (2013), *The Freedom of Cork: A Chronicle of Honour*, Cork: The Collins Press

Aodh **Quinlivan** (2017), *Dissolved – The remarkable story of how Cork lost its Corporation in 1924*, Cork: Cork City Libraries

Aodh **Quinlivan** (2020), *Forgotten Lord Mayor: Donal Óg O'Callaghan, 1920-1924*, Cork: Cork City Libraries

Desmond **Roche** (1982), *Local Government in Ireland*, Dublin: Institute of Public Administration

Edward **Sheehy** (2003), 'City and County Management', p. 126 in Mark Callanan and Justin F. Keogan (eds.), *Local Government in Ireland: Inside Out*, pp. 123-142, Dublin: Institute of Public Administration

James **Stephens** (1965), *The Insurrection in Dublin* (3rd edition), Dublin: Scepter Publications

Pauric **Travers** (2017), 'The Conscription Crisis and the General Election of 1918' in John Crowley, Donal Ó Drisceoil and Mike Murphy (eds), *Atlas of the Irish Revolution*, Cork: Cork University Press, pp. 323-329

W. E. **Vaughan** (2010) (ed.), *A New History of Ireland: Ireland Under the Union 1870-1921*, Oxford: Oxford University Press

J. J. **Walsh** (1944), *Recollections of a Rebel*, Tralee: The Kerryman Ltd.

Pat **Walsh** (2009), *The Curious Case of the Mayo Librarian*, Cork: Mercier Press

Gerry **White** (2017), 'They have rights who dare maintain them': The Irish Volunteers, 1913-15', *Atlas of the Irish Revolution*, Cork: Cork University Press

Laurence W. **White** (2016), 'Councillor Richard O'Carroll, Councillor William Partridge, the Labour Party and the 1916 Rising', in John Gibney (ed.), *Dublin City Council and the 1916 Rising*, Dublin: Dublin City Council, pp. 35-51

Trevor **White** (2017), *Alfie – The Life and Times of Alfie Byrne*, Dublin: Penguin Ireland

Pádraig **Yeates** (2000), *Lockout: Dublin, 1913*, Dublin: Gill and Macmillan

Pádraig **Yeates** (2011), *A City in Wartime: Dublin 1914-18*, Dublin: Gill and Macmillan

Pádraig **Yeates** (2012), *A City in Turmoil, Dublin 1919-21*, Dublin: Gill and Macmillan

Pádraig **Yeates** (2016), 'The politics of Dublin City Council and the 1916 Rising' in John Gibney (ed.), *Dublin City Council and the 1916 Rising*, Dublin: Dublin City Council, pp. 13-34

Index

EVENING H[ERALD]

Vol. 33. No. 120. Telegrams "Herald, Dublin." DUBLIN, TUESDAY, M[...]
Editorial Phone 6081 (4 lines).

Dublin Corpora[tion]

[CORP]ORATION GONE

[Gov]ernment Order Now in Force

TO-DAY

[Commissioners...]

Dublin has no [...] to-day from [...] local Governm [...] Dublin Corpora [...] dissolved and the [...]

[...] govern and [...]

In the other [...] to last after this [...]

[PROCLA]MATIONS

[...]ion of National [...]

To report upon the statutory fun[c]-tions of the Council have largely ex-[...]ded, and at the present time the ef-[...] administration of the city, as the Capital of the Free State, are become a [...]tion of national interest. It is pro-[...] to have the problem of the city [...] treated adequately and [...] complete delay in the light of [...] results achieved elsewhere in mod-[...] [...]ments in city management.

—E. P. McCARRON,
(Sanction.)

"The Town Clerk, City Hall, Dublin."

(COPY.)

Minister of Local Government "The La[...] [...] Government Temporary (Insurance) [...]"

[illegible body text continues]

SEAMUS O'MURCHADHA,
DR. W. DWYER, and
P. J. [H]EGARTY.

THE BRAY TRAGEDY

Inquest Story of Deceaseds' Affection

MOTHER'S WISH

Seemed Broken-Hearted At Thought of Separation

The inquest on William Whelan (23), and John Finn (27), the victims of the appalling tragedy at Bray yesterday, was opened at Bray to-day.

Throughout the morning crowds of people assembled at the wayside inn at the rear of which the tragedy was enacted.

Relatives of both the victims were pre-sent at the inquest, and showed signs of intense grief.

A sad scene was witnessed when Mrs. Whelan went to view the body of her dead son.

which lay with that of his companion in an outhouse of the licensed premises where the inquest was held. She broke down, and had to be assisted from the [room].

Miss Bridget Finn, Clonmore terrace, North Strand, Dublin, identified the body as that of her brother, John Finn. Wit-[ness] said he appeared to be a little de-[pressed] [...] express since Friday last.

Witness further stated that her brother left home about 2.45 p.m. yesterday, say-ing that he was going to Bray. So far as she knew he was always on friendly terms with Whelan.

They had both been in the National Army [...] brother of [...] First Lieutenant Whelan, she said, had been living with them until he [...] when visit-ing she [...]

WANTED HER SON HOME

[...] he was [...] working. Witness's mother [...] Whelan to go home.

DUBLIN [...]

Murdered In[fant] Par[...]

GRUESOM[E]

Body in Advan[ced] [D]ecomp[...]

An inquest was hel[d] to-day by Dr. Oswald [...] City Coroner, on the [...] fant, aged about 2 [...] found on a piece of [...] Rotunda Market, Co[...] a paper parcel.

Mr. Roche, 10 Rot[...] to finding the body [...] police.

Sergt. P. McMaho[n] that the pape of the [...] One inscription [...] 134, Cork," and ano[ther] contains Tel. Rolls[...]

The place where [...] was [...]

AN OPE[...]

Dr. Imeler, who [...] tion examination, [...] was marked and dis[...] was in an advanced [...]

Round the neck [...] was found materia[l...] The end of this ma[terial...] bedded in the child[...]

Death was due to [...] of these wrappings [...] Coroner—Is that [...]

MUR[...]

Witness—Yes.
The jury returne[d] [...] murder against [...] known.

ALIBI TH[...]

Farmer's Expe[...] Arm[...]

WESTME[...]